THE EVERLASTING
MAN

G. K.
CHESTERTON

* * *

THE EVERLASTING
MAN

* * *

Edited and introduced by
STEPHEN REUEL

MANSION
VOICE

Mansion Voice was founded in 2018 by Stephen Reuel, who wished to do more than write and promote fiction of his own, but also to facilitate and promote the works of authors he was inspired by, learned from and admired.

To this end, Mansion Voice specialises in producing high quality editions of classic works that advance conservative Christian and libertarian views. Yet new heroes, too, are always sought, as forgotten heroes are continually found; for true eloquence does not whither with age, and truth outlasts all lifetimes.

* * *

'Let nothing be done through strife or vainglory,
but in lowliness of mind let each esteem others
better than themselves.'
– PHILIPPIANS 2:3

* * *

First published in 1925

Cover design by Mansion In House
Cover images © shutterstock.com: Resurrection of Jesus
Christ / Thoom, 482667661

ISBN: 9781791947514

CONTENTS

EDITOR'S PREFACE

THIS AUTHOR IS a libertarian who holds individual liberty above governmental liberty, private property above public property, and the economic welfare of the many to be safer when left in their own hands than in the hands of a political few.

Libertarianism, in active subscribers, may be likened to the 'science' of liberty, in that proponents, pursuing more liberty, seek first to understand what liberty *is*, and to know what it means to be *free*; and a *science* because the path to liberty is not always obvious and the value of liberty is so often discovered through, and appreciated best after, trials and errors.

This author is also a Christian who holds that all mankind is beloved by the almighty creator God; that, however fallen, all of us are meant to enjoy and to respect liberty; howbeit, only through redemptive faith in Jesus Christ can full liberty ever be attained.

Holding these truths, the purpose of this edition of *The Everlasting Man* is not to glorify its author irrespective of whatever his human failings, nor to condone, less to promote, every belief he held, but simply to celebrate, remember and share the insights of one Christian hero as lessons deserving by their own merits to be learned still today. For these truths nurture each other.

Stephen Reuel
December 2018

Introduction to
G. K. Chesterton

GILBERT KEITH CHESTERTON was born on the 29th of May, 1874, in Campden Hill in Kensington, London, to Marie Louise, née Grosjean, and Edward Chesterton.

He was educated at St. Paul's School. After this, he attended the Slade School of Art, University College London, thinking to become an illustrator, and while there also took classes in literature, though he did not graduate in either subject.

Although they themselves were irregularly practising Unitarians, his parents had him baptised at the age of one month into the Church of England. It was his wife, Frances Blogg, whom he married in 1901 and remained faithful to until his death, whom he credited with leading him back to Anglicanism. He later converted to Catholicism in 1922.

His literary career began in September, 1895, with the London publisher Redway, before moving to the publishing house T. Fisher Unwin in October, 1896, where he remained until 1902. In this year he was given him a weekly opinion column with the *Daily News*, followed by another weekly column with *The Illustrated London News*, for which he wrote for the next 30 years. It is said that he went on to write around 80 books, several hundred poems, some 200 short stories, 4000 essays, and several plays.

As well as his literature and journalism, in 1931 the BBC invited him to give a series of radio talks, an invitation he accepted tentatively at first; yet allowed to improvise on the scripts, from 1932 until his death, he delivered over 40, very popular, talks per year.

His influence was great during his lifetime and remains notable to this day, with his unique and recognisable style, and distinctive, 'paradoxical' wit. He loved to debate, and often debated his famous friends George Bernard Shaw and H. G. Wells, with whom he had many disagreements in religion and politics.

His major works include his novels *The Napoleon of Notting Hill* (1905), *The Man Who Was Thursday* (1908), the famous *Father Brown* detective series (beginning in 1911), and *Manalive* (1912); and his non-fiction works *Heretics* (1905), *Orthodoxy* (1908), *What's Wrong With the World* (1910), and his biographies on St Francis of Assisi and on St. Thomas Aquinas.

Chesterton died of congestive heart failure on the morning of the 14th of June, 1936, at his home in Beaconsfield, Buckinghamshire, and is buried in the Catholic Cemetery in Beaconsfield.

PREFATORY NOTE

THIS BOOK NEEDS a preliminary note that its scope be not misunderstood. The view suggested is historical rather than theological, and does not deal directly with a religious change which has been the chief event of my own life; and about which I am already writing a more purely controversial volume. It is impossible, I hope, for any Catholic to write any book on any subject, above all this subject, without showing that he is a Catholic; but this study is not specially concerned with the differences between a Catholic and a Protestant. Much of it is devoted to many sorts of Pagans rather than any sort of Christians; and its thesis is that those who say that Christ stands side by side with similar myths, and his religion side by side with similar religions, are only repeating a very stale formula contradicted by a very striking fact. To suggest this I have not needed to go much beyond matters known to us all; I make no claim to learning; and have to depend for some things, as has rather become the fashion, on those who are more learned. As I have more than once differed from Mr. H. G. Wells in his view of history, it is the more right that I should here congratulate him on the courage and constructive imagination which carried through his vast and varied and intensely interesting work; but still more on having asserted the reasonable right of the amateur to do what he can with the facts which the specialists provide.

G. K. Chesterton
1925

INTRODUCTION:
THE PLAN OF THIS BOOK

THERE ARE TWO ways of getting home; and one of them is to stay there. The other is to walk round the whole world till we come back to the same place; and I tried to trace such a journey in a story I once wrote. It is, however, a relief to turn from that topic to another story that I never wrote. Like every book I never wrote, it is by far the best book I have ever written. It is only too probable that I shall never write it, so I will use it symbolically here; for it was a symbol of the same truth. I conceived it as a romance of those vast valleys with sloping sides, like those along which the ancient White Horses of Wessex are scrawled along the flanks of the hills. It concerned some boy whose farm or cottage stood on such a slope, and who went on his travels to find something, such as the effigy and grave of some giant; and when he was far enough from home he looked back and saw that his own farm and kitchen-garden, shining flat on the hill-side like the colours and quarterings of a shield, were but parts of some such gigantic figure, on which he had always lived, but which was too large and too close to be seen. That, I think, is a true picture of the progress of any really independent intelligence today; and that is the point of this book.

The point of this book, in other words, is that the next best thing to being really inside Christendom is to be really outside it. And a particular point of it is that the popular critics of Christianity are not really outside it. They are on a debatable ground, in every sense of the term. They are doubtful in their very doubts. Their criticism has taken on a curious tone; as of a random and illiterate heckling. Thus they make current and anti-clerical cant as a sort of small-talk. They will complain of parsons dressing like parsons; as if we should be any more free if all the police who

shadowed or collared us were plain clothes detectives. Or
they will complain that a sermon cannot be interrupted,
and call a pulpit a coward's castle; though they do not call
an editor's office a coward's castle. It would be unjust both
to journalists and priests; but it would be much truer of a
journalist. The clergyman appears in person and could easily be kicked as he came out of church; the journalist con-
ceals even his name so that nobody can kick him. They
write wild and pointless articles and letters in the press
about why the churches are empty, without even going
there to find out if they are empty, or which of them are
empty. Their suggestions are more vapid and vacant than
the most insipid curate in a three-act farce, and move us to
comfort him after the manner of the curate in the Bab Bal-
lads: 'Your mind is not so blank as that of Hopley Porter.'
So we may truly say to the very feeblest cleric: 'Your mind
is not so blank as that of Indignant Layman or Plain Man
or Man in the Street, or any of your critics in the newspapers; for they have not the most shadowy notion of what
they want themselves. Let alone of what you ought to give
them.' They will suddenly turn round and revile the
Church for not having prevented the War, which they
themselves did not want to prevent; and which nobody
had ever professed to be able to prevent, except some of
that very school of progressive and cosmopolitan sceptics
who are the chief enemies of the Church. It was the anti-
clerical and agnostic world that was always prophesying the
advent of universal peace; it is that world that was, or
should have been, abashed and confounded by the advent
of universal war. As for the general view that the Church
was discredited by the War – they might as well say that
the Ark was discredited by the Flood. When the world
goes wrong, it proves rather that the Church is right. The
Church is justified, not because her children do not sin,
but because they do. But that marks their mood about the
whole religious tradition they are in a state of reaction
against it. It is well with the boy when he lives on his father's land; and well with him again when he is far enough

from it to look back on it and see it as a whole. But these people have got into an intermediate state, have fallen into an intervening valley from which they can see neither the heights beyond them nor the heights behind. They cannot get out of the penumbra of Christian controversy. They cannot be Christians and they cannot leave off being Anti-Christians. Their whole atmosphere is the atmosphere of a reaction: sulks, perversity, petty criticism. They still live in the shadow of the faith and have lost the light of the faith.

Now the best relation to our spiritual home is to be near enough to love it. But the next best is to be far enough away not to hate it. It is the contention of these pages that while the best judge of Christianity is a Christian, the next best judge would be something more like a Confucian. The worst judge of all is the man now most ready with his judgements; the ill-educated Christian turning gradually into the ill-tempered agnostic, entangled in the end of a feud of which he never understood the beginning, blighted with a sort of hereditary boredom with he knows not what, and already weary of hearing what he has never heard. He does not judge Christianity calmly as a Confucian would; he does not judge it as he would judge Confucianism. He cannot by an effort of fancy set the Catholic Church thousands of miles away in strange skies of morning and judge it as impartially as a Chinese pagoda. It is said that the great St. Francis Xavier, who very nearly succeeded in setting up the Church there as a tower over-topping all pagodas, failed partly because his followers were accused by their fellow missionaries of representing the Twelve Apostles with the garb or attributes of Chinamen. But it would be far better to see them as Chinamen, and judge them fairly as Chinamen, than to see them as featureless idols merely made to be battered by iconoclasts; or rather as cockshies to be pelted by empty-handed cockneys. It would be better to see the whole thing as a remote Asiatic cult; the mitres of its bishops as the towering head dresses of mysterious bonzes; its pastoral staffs as the sticks twisted like serpents carried in some Asiatic procession; to see the prayer book as fantastic as the prayer-wheel and the Cross as crooked as the Swastika. Then at least we should not lose our temper as some of the sceptical critics seem to lose their temper, not to mention their wits. Their anti-clericalism has become an atmosphere, an atmosphere of negation and hostility from which they cannot escape. Compared with that, it would be better to see the whole thing as something belonging to another continent, or to another planet. It would be more philosophical to stare indifferently at bonzes than to be perpetually and pointlessly grumbling at bishops. It would be better to walk past a church as if it were a pagoda than to stand permanently in the porch, impotent either to go inside and help or to go outside and forget. For those in whom a mere reaction has thus become an obsession, I do seriously recommend the imaginative effort of conceiving the Twelve Apostles as Chinamen. In other words, I recommend these critics to try to do as much justice to Christian saints as if they were Pagan sages.

But with this we come to the final and vital point I shall try to show in these pages that when we *do* make this imaginative effort to see the whole thing from the outside, we find that it really looks like what is traditionally said about it inside. It is exactly when the boy gets far enough off to see the giant that he sees that he really is a giant. It is exactly when we do at last see the Christian Church afar under those clear and level eastern skies that we see that it is really the Church of Christ. To put it shortly, the moment we are really impartial about it, we know why people are partial to it. But this second proposition requires more serious discussion; and I shall here set myself to discuss it.

As soon as I had clearly in my mind this conception of something solid in the solitary and unique character of the divine story, it struck me that there was exactly the same strange and yet solid character in the human story that had led up to it; because that human story also had a root that was divine. I mean that just as the Church seems to grow more remarkable when it is fairly compared with the common religious life of mankind, so mankind itself seems to grow more remarkable when we compare it with the common life of nature. And I have noticed that most modern history is driven to something like sophistry, first to soften the sharp transition from animals to men, and then to soften the sharp transition from heathens to Christians. Now the more we really read in a realistic spirit of those two transitions the sharper we shall find them to be. It is because the critics are *not* detached that they do not see this detachment; it is because they are not looking at things in a dry light that they cannot see the difference between black and white. It is because they are in a particular mood of reaction and revolt that they have a motive for making out that all the white is dirty grey and the black not so black as it is painted. I do not say there are not human excuses for their revolt; I do not say it is not in some ways sympathetic; what I say is that it is not in any way scientific. An iconoclast may be indignant; an iconoclast may be justly indignant; but an iconoclast is not impartial. And it is stark hypocrisy to pretend that nine-tenths of the higher critics and scientific evolutionists and professors of comparative religion are in the least impartial. Why should they be impartial, what is being impartial, when the whole world is at war about whether one thing is a devouring superstition or a divine hope? I do not pretend to be impartial in the sense that the final act of faith fixes a man's mind because it satisfies his mind. But I do profess to be a great deal more impartial than they are; in the sense that I can tell the story fairly, with some sort of imaginative justice to all sides; and they cannot. I do profess to be impartial in the sense that I should be ashamed to talk such nonsense about the Lama of Thibet as they do about the Pope of Rome, or to have as little sympathy with Julian the Apostate as they have with the Society of Jesus. They are not impartial; they never by any chance hold the historical scales even; and above all they are never impartial upon this point of evolution and transition. They suggest everywhere the grey gradations of twilight, because they believe it is the twilight of the gods. I propose to maintain that whether or no it is the twilight of gods, it is not the daylight of men.

I maintain that when brought out into the daylight these two things look altogether strange and unique; and that it is only in the false twilight of an imaginary period of transition that they can be made to look in the least like anything else. The first of these is the creature called man and the second is the man called Christ. I have therefore divided this book into two parts: the former being a sketch of the main adventure of the human race in so far as it remained heathen; and the second a summary of the real difference that was made by it becoming Christian. Both motives necessitate a certain method, a method which is not very easy to manage, and perhaps even less easy to define or defend.

In order to strike, in the only sane or possible sense, the note of impartiality, it is necessary to touch the nerve of novelty. I mean that in one sense we see things fairly when we see them first. That, I may remark in passing, is why children generally have very little difficulty about the dogmas of the Church. But the Church, being a highly practical thing for working and fighting, is necessarily a thing for men and not merely for children. There must be in it for working purposes a great deal of tradition, of familiarity, and even of routine. So long as its fundamentals are sincerely felt, this may even be the saner condition. But when its fundamentals are doubted, as at present, we must try to recover the candour and wonder of the child; the unspoilt realism and objectivity of innocence. Or if we cannot do that, we must try at least to shake off the cloud of mere custom and see the thing as new, if only by seeing it as unnatural. Things that may well be familiar so long as familiarity breeds affection had much better become unfamiliar when familiarity breeds contempt. For in connection with things so great as are here considered, whatever our view of them, contempt must be a mistake. Indeed contempt must be an illusion. We must invoke the most wild and soaring sort of imagination; the imagination that can see what is there.

The only way to suggest the point is by an example of something, indeed of almost anything, that has been considered beautiful or wonderful. George Wyndham once told me that he had seen one of the first aeroplanes rise for the first time and it was very wonderful but not so wonderful as a horse allowing a man to ride on him. Somebody else has said that a fine man on a fine horse is the noblest bodily object in the world. Now, so long as people feel this in the right way, all is well. The first and best way of appreciating it is to come of people with a tradition of treating animals properly; of men in the right relation to horses. A boy who remembers his father who rode a horse, who rode it well and treated it well, will know that the relation can be satisfactory and will be satisfied. He will be all the more indignant at the ill-treatment of horses because he knows how they ought to be treated; but he will see nothing but what is normal in a man riding on a horse. He will not listen to the great modern philosopher who explains to him that the horse ought to be riding on the man. He will not pursue the pessimist fancy of Swift and say that men must be despised as monkeys and horses worshipped as gods. And horse and man together making an image that is to him human and civilised, it will be easy, as it were, to lift horse and man together into something heroic or symbolical; like a vision of St. George in the clouds. The fable of the winged horse will not be wholly unnatural to him: and he will know why Ariosto set many a Christian hero in such an airy saddle, and made him the rider of the sky. For the horse has really been lifted up along with the man in the wildest fashion in the very word we use when we speak 'chivalry.' The very name of the horse has been given to the highest mood and moment of the man; so that we might almost say that the handsomest compliment to a man is to call him a horse.

But if a man has got into a mood in which he is *not* able to feel this sort of wonder, then his cure must begin right at the other end. We must now suppose that he has drifted into a dull mood, in which somebody sitting on a horse means no more than somebody sitting on a chair. The wonder of which Wyndham spoke, the beauty that made the thing seem an equestrian statue, the meaning of the more chivalric horseman, may have become to him merely a convention and a bore. Perhaps they have been merely a fashion; perhaps they have gone out of fashion; perhaps they have been talked about too much or talked about in the wrong way; perhaps it was then difficult to care for horses without the horrible risk of being horsy. Anyhow, he has got into a condition when he cares no more for a horse than for a towel-horse. His grandfather's charge at Balaclava seems to him as dull and dusty as the album containing such family portraits. Such a person has not really become enlightened about the album; on the contrary, he has only become blind with the dust. But when he has reached *that* degree of blindness, he will not be able to look at a horse or a horseman at all until he has seen the whole thing as a thing entirely unfamiliar and almost unearthly.

Out of some dark forest under some ancient dawn there must come towards us, with lumbering yet dancing motions, one of the very queerest of the prehistoric creatures. We must see for the first time the strangely small head set on a neck not only longer but thicker than itself, as the face of a gargoyle is thrust out upon a gutter-spout, the one disproportionate crest of hair running along the ridge of that heavy neck like a beard in the wrong place; the feet, each like a solid club of horn, alone amid the feet of so many cattle; so that the true fear is to be found in showing, not the cloven, but the uncloven hoof. Nor is it mere verbal fancy to see him thus as a unique monster; for in a sense a monster means what is unique, and he is really unique. But the point is that when we thus see him as the first man saw him, we begin once more to have some imaginative sense of what it meant when the first man rode him. In such a dream he may seem ugly, but he does not seem unimpressive; and certainly that two-legged dwarf who could get on top of him will not seem unimpressive. By a longer and more erratic road we shall come back to the same marvel of the man and the horse; and the marvel will be, if possible, even more marvellous. We shall have again a glimpse of St. George; the more glorious because St. George is not riding on the horse, but rather riding on the dragon.

In this example, which I have taken merely because it is an example, it will be noted that I do not say that the nightmare seen by the first man of the forest is either more true or more wonderful than the normal mare of the stable seen by the civilised person who can appreciate what is normal. Of the two extremes, I think on the whole that the traditional grasp of truth is the better. But I say that the truth is found at one or other of these two extremes, and is lost in the intermediate condition of mere fatigue and for-getfulness of tradition. In other words, I say it is better to see a horse as a monster than to see it only as a slow sub-stitute for a motor-car. If we have got into that state of mind about a horse as something stale, it is far better to be frightened of a horse because it is a good deal too fresh.

Now, as it is with the monster that is called a horse, so it is with the monster that is called a man. Of course the best condition of all, in my opinion, is always to have re-garded man as he is regarded in my philosophy. He who holds the Christian and Catholic view of human nature will feel certain that it is a universal and therefore a sane view, and will be satisfied. But if he has lost the sane vision, he can only get it back by something very like a mad vision; that is, by seeing man as a strange animal and realising how strange an animal he is. But just as seeing the horse as a prehistoric prodigy ultimately led back to, and not away from, an admiration for the mastery of man, so the really detached consideration of the curious career of man will lead back to, and not away from, the ancient faith in the dark designs of God. In other words, it is exactly when we do see how queer the quadruped is that we praise the man who mounts him; and exactly when we do see how queer the biped is that we praise the Providence that made him.

In short, it is the purpose of this introduction to maintain this thesis: that it is exactly when we do regard man as an animal that we know he is not an animal. It is precisely when we do try to picture him as a sort of horse on its hind legs, that we suddenly realise that he must be something as miraculous as the winged horse that towered up into the clouds of heaven. All roads lead to Rome, all ways lead round again to the central and civilised philosophy, including this road through elf-land and topsy-turvydom. But it may be that it is better never to have left the land of the reasonable tradition, where men ride lightly upon horses and are mighty hunters before the Lord.

So also in the specially Christian case we have to react against the heavy bias of fatigue. It is almost impossible to make the facts vivid, because the facts are familiar; and for fallen men it is often true that familiarity is fatigue. I am convinced that if we could tell the supernatural story of Christ word for word as of a Chinese hero, call him the Son of Heaven instead of the Son of God, and trace his rayed nimbus in the gold tread of Chinese embroideries or the gold lacquer of Chinese pottery, instead of in the gold leaf of our own old Catholic paintings, there would be a unanimous testimony to the spiritual purity of the story. We should hear nothing then of the injustice of substitution or the illogicality of atonement, of the superstitious exaggeration of the burden of sin or the impossible insolence of an invasion of the laws of nature. We should admire the chivalry of the Chinese conception of a god who fell from the sky to fight the dragons and save the wicked from being devoured by their own fault and folly. We should admire the subtlety of the Chinese view of life, which perceives that all human imperfection is in very truth a crying imperfection. We should admire the Chinese esoteric and superior wisdom, which said there are higher cosmic laws than the laws we know; we believe every common Indian conjurer who chooses to come to us and talk in the same style. If Christianity were only a new ori-

ental fashion, it would never be reproached with being an
old and oriental faith. I do not propose in this book to
follow the alleged example of St. Francis Xavier with the
opposite imaginative intention, and turn the Twelve Apostles into Mandarins; not so much to make them look like
natives as to make them look like foreigners. I do not propose to work what I believe would be a completely successful practical joke; that of telling the whole story of the
Gospel and the whole history of the church in a setting of
pagodas and pigtails; and noting with malignant humour
how much it was admired as a heathen story, in the very
quarters where it is condemned as a Christian story. But I
do propose to strike wherever possible this note of what is
new and strange, and for that reason the style even on so
serious a subject may sometimes be deliberately grotesque
and fanciful. I do desire to help the reader to see Christendom from the outside in the sense of seeing it as a whole,
against the background of other historic things; just as I
desire him to see humanity as a whole against the background of natural things. And I say that in both cases,
when seen thus, they stand out from their background like
supernatural things. They do *not* fade into the rest with the
colours of impressionism; they stand out from the rest
with the colours of heraldry; as vivid as a red cross on a
white shield or a black lion on a ground of gold. So stands
the Red Clay against the green field of nature, or the White
Christ against the red clay of his race.

But in order to see them clearly we have to see them as
a whole. We have to see how they developed as well as
how they began; for the most incredible part of the story is
that things which began thus should have developed thus.
Anyone who chooses to indulge in mere imagination can
imagine that other things might have happened or other
entities evolved. Anyone thinking of what might have happened may conceive a sort of evolutionary equality; but
anyone facing what did happen must face an exception and
a prodigy. If there was ever a moment when man was only
an animal, we can if we choose make a fancy picture of his

career transferred to some other animal. An entertaining fantasia might be made in which elephants built in elephantine architecture, with towers and turrets like tusks and trunks, cities beyond the scale of any colossus. A pleasant fable might be conceived in which a cow had developed a costume, and put on four boots and two pairs of trousers. We could imagine a Super-monkey more marvellous than any Superman, a quadrumanous creature carving and painting with his hands and cooking and carpentering with his feet. But if we are considering what did happen, we shall certainly decide that man has distanced everything else with a distance like that of the astronomical spaces and a speed like that of the still thunderbolt of the light. And in the same fashion, while we can if we choose see the Church amid a mob of Mithraic or Manichean superstitions squabbling and killing each other at the end of the Empire, while we can if we choose imagine the Church killed in the struggle and some other chance cult taking its place, we shall be the more surprised (and possibly puzzled) if we meet it two thousand years afterwards rushing through the ages as the winged thunderbolt of thought and everlasting enthusiasm; a thing without rival or resemblance; and still as new as it is old.

PART I

ON THE CREATURE CALLED MAN

1
THE MAN IN THE CAVE

FAR AWAY IN some strange constellation in skies infinitely remote, there is a small star, which astronomers may some day discover. At least I could never observe in the faces or demeanour of most astronomers or men of science any evidence that they had discovered it; though as a matter of fact they were walking about on it all the time. It is a star that brings forth out of itself very strange plants and very strange animals; and none stranger than the men of science. That at least is the way in which I should begin a history of the world if I had to follow the scientific custom of beginning with an account of the astronomical universe. I should try to see even this earth from the outside, not by the hackneyed insistence of its relative position to the sun, but by some imaginative effort to conceive its remote position for the dehumanised spectator. Only I do not believe in being dehumanised in order to study humanity. I do not believe in dwelling upon the distances that are supposed to dwarf the world; I think there is even something a trifle vulgar about this idea of trying to rebuke spirit by size. And as the first idea is not feasible, that of making the earth a strange planet so as to make it significant, I will not stoop to the other trick of making it a small planet in order to make it insignificant. I would rather insist that we do not even know that it is a planet at all, in the sense in which we know that it is a place; and a very extraordinary place too. That is the note which I wish to strike from the first, if not in the astronomical, then in some more familiar fashion.

One of my first journalistic adventures, or misadventures, concerned a comment on Grant Allen, who had

written a book about the Evolution of the Idea of God. I
happened to remark that it would be much more interesting if God wrote a book about the evolution of the idea of
Grant Allen. And I remember that the editor objected to
my remark on the ground that it was blasphemous; which
naturally amused me not a little. For the joke of it was, of
course, that it never occurred to him to notice the title of
the book itself, which really was blasphemous; for it was,
when translated into English, 'I will show you how this
nonsensical notion that there is a God grew up among
men.' My remark was strictly pious and proper; confessing
the divine purpose even in its most seemingly dark or
meaningless manifestations. In that hour I learned many
things, including the fact that there is something purely
acoustic in much of that agnostic sort of reverence. The
editor had not seen the point, because in the title of the
book the long word came at the beginning and the short
word at the end; whereas in my comment the short word
came at the beginning and gave him a sort of shock. I have
noticed that if you put a word like God into the same sentence with a word like dog, these abrupt and angular words
affect people like pistol-shots. Whether you say that God
made the dog or the dog made God does not seem to matter; that is only one of the sterile disputations of the too
subtle theologians. But so long as you begin with a long
word like evolution the rest will roll harmlessly past; very
probably the editor had not read the whole of the title, for
it is rather a long title and he was rather a busy man.

But this little incident has always lingered in my mind
as a sort of parable. Most modern histories of mankind
begin with the word evolution, and with a rather wordy
exposition of evolution, for much the same reason that
operated in this case. There is something slow and soothing and gradual about the word and even about the idea.
As a matter of fact it is not, touching these primary things,
a very practical word or a very profitable idea. Nobody can
imagine how nothing could turn into something. Nobody
can get an inch nearer to it by explaining how something

could turn into something else. It is really far more logical to start by saying 'In the beginning God created heaven and earth' even if you only mean 'In the beginning some unthinkable power began some unthinkable process.' For God is by its nature a name of mystery, and nobody ever supposed that man could imagine how a world was created any more than he could create one. But evolution really is mistaken for explanation. It has the fatal quality of leaving on many minds the impression that they do understand it and everything else; just as many of them live under a sort of illusion that they have read the *Origin of Species*.

But this notion of something smooth and slow like the ascent of a slope, is a great part of the illusion. It is an illogicality as well as an illusion; for slowness has really nothing to do with the question. An event is not any more intrinsically intelligible or unintelligible because of the pace at which it moves. For a man who does not believe in a miracle, a slow miracle would be just as incredible as a swift one. The Greek witch may have turned sailors to swine with a stroke of the wand. But to see a naval gentleman of our acquaintance looking a little more like a pig every day, till he ended with four trotters and a curly tail would not be any more soothing. It might be rather more creepy and uncanny. The medieval wizard may have flown through the air from the top of a tower; but to see an old gentleman walking through the air in a leisurely and lounging manner, would still seem to call for some explanation. Yet there runs through all the rationalistic treatment of history this curious and confused idea that difficulty is avoided or even mystery eliminated, by dwelling on mere delay or on something dilatory in the processes of things. There will be something to be said upon particular examples elsewhere; the question here is the false atmosphere of facility and ease given by the mere suggestion of going slow; the sort of comfort that might be given to a nervous old woman travelling for the first time in a motor-car.

Mr. H. G. Wells has confessed to being a prophet; and in this matter he was a prophet at his own expense. It is curious that his first fairy-tale was a complete answer to his last book of history. The Time Machine destroyed in advance all comfortable conclusions founded on the mere relativity of time. In that sublime nightmare the hero saw trees shoot up like green rockets, and vegetation spread visibly like a green conflagration, or the sun shoot across the sky from east to west with the swiftness of a meteor. Yet in his sense these things were quite as natural when they went swiftly; and in our sense they are quite as supernatural when they go slowly. The ultimate question is why they go at all; and anybody who really understands that question will know that it always has been and always will be a religious question; or at any rate a philosophical or metaphysical question. And most certainly he will not think the question answered by some substitution of gradual for abrupt change; or in other words by a merely relative question of the same story being spun out or rattled rapidly through, as can be done with any story at a cinema by turning a handle.

Now what is needed for these problems of primitive existence is something more like a primitive spirit. In calling up this vision of the first things, I would ask the reader to make with me a sort of experiment in simplicity. And by simplicity I do not mean stupidity, but rather the sort of clarity that sees things like life rather than words like evolution. For this purpose it would really be better to turn the handle of the Time Machine a little more quickly and see the grass growing and the trees springing up into the sky, if that experiment could contract and concentrate and make vivid the upshot of the whole affair. What we know, in a sense in which we know nothing else, is that the trees and the grass did grow and that a number of other extraordinary things do in fact happen; that queer creatures support themselves in the empty air by beating it with fans of various fantastic shapes; that other queer creatures steer themselves about alive under a load of mighty waters; that other queer creatures walk about on four legs and that the queerest creature of all walks about on two. These are things and not theories; and compared with them evolution and the atom and even the solar system are merely theories. The matter here is one of history and not of philosophy; so that it need only be noted that no philosopher denies that a mystery still attaches to the two great transitions: the origin of the universes itself and the origin of the principal of life itself. Most philosophers have the enlightenment to add that a third mystery attaches to the origin of man himself. In other words, a third bridge was built across a third abyss of the unthinkable when there came into the world what we call reason and what we call will. Man is not merely an evolution but rather a revolution. That he has a backbone or other parts upon a similar pattern to birds and fishes is an obvious fact, whatever be the meaning of the fact. But if we attempt to regard him, as it were, as a quadruped standing on his hind legs, we shall find what follows more fantastic and subversive than if he were standing on his head.

I will take one example to serve for an introduction to the story of man. It illustrates what I mean by saying that a certain childish directness is needed to see the truth about the childhood of the world. It illustrates what I mean by saying a mixture of popular science and journalistic jargon have confused the facts about the first things so that we cannot see which of them really comes first. It illustrates, though only in one convenient illustration, all that I mean by the necessity of seeing the sharp differences that give its shape to history, instead of being submerged in all these generalisations about slowness and sameness. For we do indeed require, in Mr. Wells's phrase, an outline of history. But we may venture to say, in Mr. Mantalini's phrase, that this evolutionary history has no outline or is a deemed outline. But above all it illustrates what I mean by saying that the more we really look at man as an animal, the less he will look like one.

Today all our novels and newspapers will be found swarming with numberless allusions to a popular character called a Cave-Man. He seems to be quite familiar to us, not

only as a public character but as a private character. His
psychology is seriously taken into account in psychological
fiction and psychological medicine. So far as I can understand, his chief occupation in life was knocking his wife
about, or treating women in general with what is, I believe,
known in the world of the film as 'rough stuff'. I have
never happened to come upon the evidence for this idea;
and I do not know on what primitive diaries or prehistoric
divorce-reports it is founded. Nor, as I have explained
elsewhere, have I ever been able to see the probability of it,
even considered a priori. We are always told without any
explanation or authority that primitive man waved a club
and knocked the woman down before he carried her off.
But on every animal analogy, it would seem an almost
morbid modesty and reluctance on the part of the lady,
always to insist on being knocked down before consenting
to be carried off. And I repeat that I can never comprehend why, when the male was so very rude, the female
should have been so very refined. The cave-man may have
been a brute, but there is no reason why he should have
been more brutal than the brutes. And the loves of the
giraffes and the river romances of the hippopotami are
effected without any of this preliminary fracas or shindy.
The cave-man may have been no better than the cave-bear;
but the child she-bear, so famous in hymnology, is not
trained with any such bias for spinsterhood. In short these
details of the domestic life of the cave puzzle me upon
either the revolutionary or the static hypothesis; and in any
case I should like to look into the evidence for them; but
unfortunately I have never been able to find it. But the
curious thing is this: that while ten thousand tongues of
more or less scientific or literary gossip seemed to be talking at once about this unfortunate fellow, under the title of
the cave-man, the one connection in which it is really relevant and sensible to talk about him as the cave-man has
been comparatively neglected. People have used this loose
term in twenty loose ways; but they have never even
looked at their own term for what could really be learned

from it.

In fact, people have been interested in everything about the cave-man except what he did in the cave. Now there does happen to be some real evidence of what he did in the cave. It is little enough, like all the prehistoric evidence, but it is concerned with the real cave-man and his cave and not the literary cave-man and his club. And it will be valuable to our sense of reality to consider quite simply what that real evidence is, and not to go beyond it. What was found in the cave was not the club, the horrible gory club notched with the number of women it had knocked on the head. The cave was not a Bluebeard's Chamber filled with the skeletons of slaughtered wives; it was not filled with female skulls all arranged in rows and all cracked like eggs. It was something quite unconnected, one way or the other, with all the modern phrases and philosophical implications and literary rumours which confuse the whole question for us. And if we wish to see as it really is this authentic glimpse of the morning of the world, it will be far better to conceive even the story of its discovery as some such legend of the land of morning. It would be far better to tell the tale of what was really found as simply as the tale of heroes finding the Golden Fleece or the Gardens of the Hesperides, if we could so escape from a fog of controversial theories into the clear colours and clean cut outlines of such a dawn. The old epic poets at least knew how to tell a story, possibly a tall story but never a twisted story, never a story tortured out of its own shape to fit theories and philosophies invented centuries afterwards. It would be well if modern investigators could describe their discoveries in the bald narrative style of the earliest travellers, and without any of these long allusive words that are full of irrelevant implication and suggestion. Then we might realise exactly what we do know about the cave-man, or at any rate about the cave.

A priest and a boy entered sometime ago a hollow in the hills and passed into a sort of subterranean tunnel that led into a labyrinth of such sealed and secret corridors of rock. They crawled through cracks that seemed almost impassable, they crept through tunnels that might have been made for moles, they dropped into holes as hopeless as wells, they seemed to be burying themselves alive seven times over beyond the hope of resurrection. This is but the commonplace of all such courageous exploration; but what is needed here is someone who shall put such stories in the primary light, in which they are not commonplace There is, for instance, something strangely symbolic in the accident that the first intruders into that sunken world were a priest and a boy, the types of the antiquity and of the youth of the world. But here I am even more concerned with the symbolism of the boy than with that of the priest. Nobody who remembers boyhood needs to be told what it might be to a boy to enter like Peter Pan under a roof of the roots of all the trees and go deeper and deeper, till he reach what William Morris called the very roots of the mountains. Suppose somebody, with that simple and unspoiled realism that is a part of innocence, to pursue that journey to its end, not for the sake of what he could deduce or demonstrate in some dusty magazine controversy, but simply for the sake of what he could see. What he did see at last was a cavern so far from the light of day that it might have been the legendary Domdaniel cavern that was under the floor of the sea. This secret chamber of rock, when illuminated after its long night of unnumbered ages, revealed on its walls large and sprawling outlines diversified with coloured earths; and when they followed the lines of them they recognised, across that vast void of ages, the movement and the gesture of a man's band. They were drawings or paintings of animals; and they were drawn or painted not only by a man but by an artist. Under whatever archaic limitations, they showed that love of the long sweeping or the long wavering line which any man who has ever drawn or tried to draw will recognise; and about which no artist will allow himself to be contradicted by any scientist. They showed the experimental and adventurous spirit of the artist, the spirit that does not avoid but attempts difficult things; as where the draughtsman had represented the action of the stag when he swings his head clean round and noses towards his tail, an action familiar enough in the horse. But there are many modern animal-painters who would set themselves something of a task in rendering it truly. In this and twenty other details it is clear that the artist had watched animals with a certain interest and presumably a certain pleasure. In that sense it would seem that he was not only an artist but a naturalist; the sort of naturalist who is really natural.

Now it is needless to note, except in passing, that there is nothing whatever in the atmosphere of that cave to suggest the bleak and pessimistic atmosphere of that journalistic cave of the winds, that blows and bellows about us with countless echoes concerning the Cave-Man. So far as any human character can be hinted at by such traces of the past, that human character is quite human and even humane. It is certainly not the ideal of an inhuman character, like the abstraction invoked in popular science. When novelists and educationists and psychologists of all sorts talk about the cave-man, they never conceive him in connection with anything that is really in the cave. When the realist of the sex novel writes, 'Red sparks danced in Double-dick's brain; he felt the spirit of the cave-man rising within him,' the novelist's readers would be very much disappointed if Dagmar only went off and drew large pictures of cows on the drawing-room wall. When the psychoanalyst writes to a patient, 'The submerged instincts of the cave-man are doubtless prompting you to gratify a violent impulse,' he does not refer to the impulse to paint in water-colours; or to make conscientious studies of how cattle swing their heads when they graze. Yet we do know for a fact that the cave-man did these mild and innocent things and we have not the most minute speck of evidence that he did any of the violent and ferocious things. In other words the cave-man as commonly presented to us is simply a myth or rather a muddle; for a myth has at least an imaginative outline of truth. The whole of the current way of talking is simply a confusion and a misunderstanding, founded on no sort of scientific evidence and valued only as an excuse for a very modern mood of anarchy. If any gentleman wants to knock a woman about, he can surely be a cad without taking away the character of the cave-man, about whom we know next to nothing except what we can gather from a few harmless and pleasing pictures on a wall.

But this is not the point about the pictures or the particular moral here to be drawn from them. That moral is something much larger and simpler, so large and simple that when it is first stated it will sound childish. And indeed it is in the highest sense childish; and that is why I have in this apologue in some sense seen it through the eyes of a child. It is the biggest of all the facts really facing the boy in the cavern; and is perhaps too big to be seen. If the boy was one of the flock of the priest, it may be presumed that be had been trained in a certain quality of common sense; that common sense that often comes to us in the form of tradition. In that case he would simply recognise the primitive man's work as the work of a man, interesting but in no way incredible in being primitive. He would see what was there to see; and he would not be tempted into seeing what was not there, by any evolutionary excitement of fashionable speculation. If he had heard of such things he would admit, of course, that the speculations might be true and were not incompatible with the facts that were true. The artist may have had another side to his character besides that which he has alone left on record in his works of art. The primitive man may have taken a pleasure in beating women as well as in drawing animals; all we can say is that the drawings record the one but not the other. It may be true that when the cave-man's finished jumping on his mother, or his wife as the case may be, he loves to hear the little brook a-gurgling, and also to watch the deer as they come down to drink at the brook. These things are not impossible, but they are irrelevant. The common sense of the child could confine itself to learning from the facts what the facts have to teach; and the pictures in the cave are very nearly all the facts there are. So far as that evidence goes, the child would be justified in assuming that a man had represented animals with rock and red ochre for the same reason as he himself was in the habit of trying to represent animals with charcoal and red chalk. The man had drawn a stag just as the child had drawn a horse; because it was fun. The man had drawn a stag with his head turned as the child had drawn a pig with his eyes shut; because it was difficult. The child and the man, being both human, would be united by the brotherhood of men; and the brotherhood of men is even nobler when it bridges the abyss of ages than when it bridges only the chasm of class. But anyhow he would see no evidence of the Cave-Man of crude evolutionism; because there is none to be seen. If somebody told him that the pictures had all been drawn by St. Francis of Assisi out of pure and saintly love of animals, there would be nothing in the cave to contradict it.

Indeed I once knew a lady who half-humorously suggested that the cave was a crèche, in which the babies were put to be specially safe, and that coloured animals were drawn on the walls to amuse them; very much as diagrams of elephants and giraffes adorn a modern infant school. And though this was but a jest, it does draw attention to some of the other assumptions that we make only too readily. The pictures do not prove even that the cave-men lived in caves, any more than the discovery of a wine-cellar in Balham (long after that suburb had been destroyed by human or divine wrath) would prove that the Victorian middle classes lived entirely underground. The cave might have had a special purpose like the cellar; it might have been a religious shrine or a refuge in war or the meeting-place of a secret society or all sorts of things. But it is quite true that its artistic decoration has much more of the atmosphere of a nursery than of any of these nightmares of anarchical fury and fear. I have conceived a child as standing in the cave; and it is easy to conceive any child, modern or immeasurably remote, as making a living gesture as to pat the painted beasts upon the wall. In that gesture there is a foreshadowing, as we shall see, later, of another cavern and another child.

But suppose the boy had not been taught by a priest but by a professor, by one of the professors who simplify the relation of men and beasts to a mere evolutionary variation. Suppose the boy saw himself, with the same simplicity and sincerity, as a mere Mowgli running with the pack of nature and roughly indistinguishable from the rest save by a relative and recent variation. What would be for him the simplest lesson of that strange stone picture-book? After all, it would come back to this; that he had dug very deep and found the place where a man had drawn the picture of a reindeer. But he would dig a good deal deeper before he found a place where a reindeer had drawn a picture of a man. That sounds like a truism but in this connection it is really a very tremendous truth. He might descend to depths unthinkable, he might sink into sunken continents as strange as remote stars, he might find himself in the inside of the world as far from men as the other side of the moon; he might see in those cold chasms or colossal terraces of stone, traced in the faint hieroglyphic of the fossil, the ruins of lost dynasties of biological life, rather like the ruins of successive creations and separate universes than the stages in the story of one. He would find the trail of monsters blindly developing in directions outside all our common imagery of fish and bird; groping and grasping and touching life with every extravagant elongation of horn and tongue and tentacle; growing a forest of fantastic caricatures of the claw and the fin and the finger. But nowhere would he find one finger that had traced one significant line upon the sand; nowhere one claw that had even begun to scratch the faint suggestion of a form. To all appearance, the thing would be as unthinkable in all those countless cosmic variations of forgotten eons as it would be in the beasts and birds before our eyes. The child would no more expect to see it than to see the cat scratch on the wall a vindictive caricature of the dog. The childish common sense would keep the most evolutionary child from expecting to see anything like that; yet in the traces of the rude and recently evolved ancestors of humanity he would have seen exactly that. It must surely strike him as strange that men so remote from him should be so near, and that beasts so near to him should be so remote. To his simplicity it must seem at least odd that he could not find any trace of the beginning of any arts among any animals. That is the simplest lesson to learn in the cavern of the coloured pictures; only it is too simple to be learnt. It is the simple truth that man does differ from the brutes in kind and not in degree; and the proof of it is here; that it sounds like a truism to say that the most primitive man drew a picture of a monkey and that it sounds like a joke to say that the most intelligent monkey drew a picture of a man. Something of division and disproportion has appeared; and it is unique. Art is the signature of man.

That is the sort of simple truth with which a story of the beginnings ought really to begin. The evolutionist stands staring in the painted cavern at the things that are too large to be seen and too simple to be understood. He tries to deduce all sorts of other indirect and doubtful things from the details of the pictures, because he cannot see the primary significance of the whole; thin and theoretical deductions about the absence of religion or the presence of superstition; about tribal government and hunting and human sacrifice and heaven knows what. In the next chapter I shall try to trace in a little more detail the much disputed question about these prehistoric origins of human ideas and especially of the religious idea. Here I am only taking this one case of the cave as a sort of symbol of the simpler sort of truth with which the story ought to start. When all is said the main fact that the record of the reindeer men attests, along with all other records, is that the reindeer man could draw and the reindeer could not. If the reindeer man was as much an animal as the reindeer, it was all the more extraordinary that he could do what all other animals could not. If he was an ordinary product of biological growth like any other beast or bird, then it is all the more extraordinary that he was not in the least like any other beast or bird. He seems rather more supernatural as a natural product than as a supernatural one.

But I have begun this story in the cave, like the cave of the speculations of Plato, because it is a sort of model of the mistake of merely evolutionary introductions and prefaces. It is useless to begin by saying that everything was slow and smooth and a mere matter of development and degree. For in the plain matter like the pictures there is in fact not a trace of any such development or degree. Monkeys did not begin pictures and men finish them; Pithecanthropus did not draw a reindeer badly and Homo Sapiens draw it well. The higher animals did not draw better and better portraits; the dog did not paint better in his best period than in his early bad manner as a jackal; the wild horse was not an Impressionist and the race horse a Post-Impressionist. All we can say of this notion of reproducing things in shadow or representative shape is that it exists nowhere in nature except in man; and that we cannot even talk about it without treating man as something separate from nature. In other words, every sane sort of history must begin with man as man, a thing standing absolute and alone. How he came there, or indeed how anything else came there, is a thing for theologians and philosophers and scientists and not for historians. But an excellent test case of this isolation and mystery is the matter of the impulse of art. This creature was truly different from all other creatures; because he was a creator as well as a creature. Nothing in that sense could be made in any other image but the image of man. But the truth is so true that, even in the absence of any religious belief, it must be assumed in the form of some moral or metaphysical principle. In the next chapter we shall see how this principle applies to all the historical hypotheses and evolutionary ethics now in fashion; to the origins of tribal government or mythological belief. But the clearest and most convenient example to start with is this popular one of what the cave-man really did in his cave. It means that somehow or other a new thing had appeared in the cavernous night of nature, a mind that is like a mirror. It is like a mirror because it is truly a thing of reflection. It is like a mirror because in it alone all the other shapes can be seen like shining shadows in a vision. Above all, it is like a mirror because it is the only thing of its kind. Other things may resemble it or resemble each other in various ways; other things may excel it or excel each other in various ways; just as in the furniture of a room a table may be round like a Mirror or a cupboard may be larger than a mirror. But the mirror is the only thing that can contain them all. Man is the microcosm; man is the measure of all things; man is the image of God. These are the only real lessons to be learnt in the cave and it is time to leave it for the open road.

It will be well in this place, however, to sum up once and for all what is meant by saying that man is at once the exception to everything and the mirror and the measure of all things. But to see man as he is, it is necessary once more to keep close to that simplicity that can clear itself of accumulated clouds of sophistry. The simplest truth about man is that he is a very strange being; almost in the sense of being a stranger on the earth. In all sobriety, he has much more of the external appearance of one bringing alien habits from another land than of a mere growth of this one. He has an unfair advantage and an unfair disadvantage. He cannot sleep in his own skin; he cannot trust his own instincts. He is at once a creator moving miraculous hands and fingers and a kind of cripple. He is wrapped in artificial bandages called clothes; he is propped on artificial crutches called furniture. His mind has the same doubtful liberties and the same wild limitations. Alone among the animals, he is shaken with the beautiful madness called laughter; as if he had caught sight of some secret in the very shape of the universe hidden from the universe itself. Alone among the animals he feels the need

of averting his thoughts from the root realities of his own
bodily being; of hiding them as in the presence of some
higher possibility which creates the mystery of shame.
Whether we praise these things as natural to man or abuse
them as artificial in nature, they remain in the same sense
unique. This is realised by the whole popular instinct called
religion, until disturbed by pedants, especially the laborious
pedants of the Simple Life. The most sophisticate of all
sophists are gymnosophists.

It is not natural to see man as a natural product. It is
not sense to call man a common object of the country or
the seashore. It is not seeing straight to see him as an animal. It is not sane. It sins against the light; against that
broad daylight of proportion which is the principle of all
reality. It is reached by stretching a point, by making out a
case, by artificially selecting a certain light and shade, by
bringing into prominence the lesser or lower things which
may happen to be similar. The solid thing standing in the
sunlight, the thing we can walk round and see from all
sides, is quite different. It is also quite extraordinary; and
the more sides we see of it the more extraordinary it
seems. It is emphatically not a thing that follows or flows
naturally from anything else. If we imagine that an inhuman or impersonal intelligence could have felt from the
first the general nature of the non-human world sufficiently to see that things would evolve in whatever way
they did evolve, there would have been nothing whatever
in all that natural world to prepare such a mind for such an
unnatural novelty. To such a mind, man would most certainly not have seemed something like one herd out of a
hundred herds finding richer pasture; or one swallow out
of a hundred swallows making a summer under a strange
sky. It would not be in the same scale and scarcely in the
same dimension. We might as truly say that it would not be
in the same universe. It would be more like seeing one cow
out of a hundred cows suddenly jump over the moon or
one pig out of a hundred pigs grow wings in a flash and
fly. It would not be a question of the cattle finding their

own grazing-ground but of their building their own cattle-sheds, not a question of one swallow making a summer but of his making a summer-house. For the very fact that birds do build nests is one of those similarities that sharpen the startling difference. The very fact that a bird can get as far as building a nest, and cannot get any farther, proves that he has not a mind as man has a mind; it proves it more completely than if he built nothing at all. If he built nothing at all, he might possibly be a philosopher of the Quietist or Buddhist school, indifferent to all but the mind within. But when he builds as he does build and is satisfied and sings aloud with satisfaction, then we know there is really an invisible veil like a pane of glass between him and us, like the window on which a bird will beat in vain. But suppose our abstract onlooker saw one of the birds begin to build as men build. Suppose in an incredibly short space of time there were seven styles of architecture for one style of nest. Suppose the bird carefully selected forked twigs and pointed leaves to express the piercing piety of Gothic, but turned to broad foliage and black mud when he sought in a darker mood to call up the heavy columns of Bel and Ashtaroth; making his nest indeed one of the hanging gardens of Babylon. Suppose the bird made little clay statues of birds celebrated in letters or politics and stuck them up in front of the nest. Suppose that one bird out of a thousand birds began to do one of the thousand things that man had already done even in the morning of the world; and we can be quite certain that the onlooker would not regard such a bird as a mere evolutionary variety of the other birds; he would regard it as a very fearful wild-fowl indeed; possibly as a bird of ill-omen, certainly as an omen. That bird would tell the augurs, not of something that would happen, but of something that had happened. That something would be the appearance of a mind with a new dimension of depth; a mind like that of man. If there be no God, no other mind could conceivably have foreseen it.

Now as a matter of fact, there is a not a shadow of evidence that *this* thing was evolved at all. There is not a particle of proof that *this* transition came slowly or even that it came naturally. In a strictly scientific sense we simply know nothing whatever about how it grew, or whether it grew, or what it is. There may be a broken trail of stones and bones faintly suggesting the development of the human body. There is nothing even faintly suggesting such a development of this human mind. It was not and it was; we know not in what instant or in what infinity of years. Something happened; and it has all the appearance of a transaction outside time. It has therefore nothing to do with history in the ordinary sense. The historian must take it or something like it for granted; it is not his business as a historian to explain it. But if he cannot explain it as a historian, he will not explain it as a biologist. In neither case is there any disgrace to him in accepting it without explaining it; for it is a reality, and history and biology deal with realities. He is quite justified in calmly confronting the pig with wings and the cow that jumped over the moon, merely because they have happened. He can reasonably accept man as a freak, because he accepts man as a fact. He can be perfectly comfortable in a crazy and disconnected world, or in a world that can produce such a crazy and disconnected thing. For reality is a thing in which we can all repose, even if it hardly seems related to anything else. The thing is there; and that is enough for most of us. But if we do indeed want to know how it can conceivably have come there, if we do indeed wish to see it related realistically to other things, if we do insist on seeing it evolved before our very eyes from an environment nearer to its own nature, then assuredly it is to very different things that we must go. We must stir very strange memories and return to very simple dreams, if we desire some origin that can make man other than a monster. We shall have discovered very different causes before he becomes a creature of causation; and invoked other authority to turn him into something reasonable, or even into anything probable That way lies all that is at once awful and familiar and forgotten, with dreadful faces thronged and fiery arms. We can accept man as a fact, if we are content with an unexplained fact. We can accept him as an animal, if we can live with a fabulous animal. But if we must needs have sequence and necessity, then indeed we must provide a prelude and crescendo of mounting miracles, that ushered in with unthinkable thunders in all the seven heavens, of another order, a man may be an ordinary thing.

2
PROFESSORS AND PREHISTORIC MEN

SCIENCE IS WEAK about these prehistoric things in a way that has hardly been noticed. The science whose modern marvels we all admire succeeds by incessantly adding to its data. In all practical inventions, in most natural discoveries, it can always increase evidence by experiment. But it cannot experiment in making men; or even in watching to see what the first men make. An inventor can advance step by step in the construction of an airplane even if he is only experimenting with sticks and scraps of metal in his own backyard. But he cannot watch the Missing Link evolving in his own backyard. If he has made a mistake in his calculations, the airplane will correct it by crashing to the ground. But if he has made a mistake about the arboreal habitat of his ancestor, he cannot see his arboreal ancestor falling off the tree. He cannot keep a caveman like a cat in the backyard and watch him to see whether he does really practice cannibalism or carry off his mate on the principles of marriage by capture. He cannot keep a tribe of primitive men like a pack of hounds and notice how far they are influenced by the herd instinct. If he sees a particular bird behave in a particular way, he can get other birds and see if they behave in that way; but if he finds a skull, or the scrap of a skull in the hollow of a hill, he cannot multiply it into a vision of the valley of dry bones. In dealing with a past that has almost entirely perished he can only go by evidence and not by experiment. And there is hardly enough evidence to be even evidential. Thus while most science moves in a sort of curve, being constantly corrected by new evidence, this science flies off into space in a straight line uncorrected by anything. But the habit of forming conclusions, as they can really be formed in more fruitful fields, is so fixed in the Scientific mind that it cannot resist talking like this. It talks about the idea suggested by one scrap of bone as if it were something like the airplane which is constructed at last out of whole scrap heaps of scraps of metal. The trouble with the professor of the prehistoric is that he cannot scrap his scrap. The marvellous and triumphant airplane is made out of a hundred mistakes. The student of origins can only make one mistake and stick to it.

We talk very truly of the patience of science; but in this department it would be truer to talk of the impatience of science. Owing to the difficulty above described, the theorist is in far too much of a hurry. We have a series of hypotheses so hasty that they may well be called fancies, and cannot in any case be further corrected by facts. The most empirical anthropologist is here as limited as an antiquary. He can only cling to a fragment of the past and has no way of increasing it for the future. He can only clutch his fragment of fact, almost as the primitive man clutched his fragment of flint. And indeed he does deal with it in much the same way and for much the same reason. It is his tool and his only tool. It is his weapon and his only weapon. He often wields it with a fanaticism far in excess of anything shown by men of science when they can collect more facts from experience and even add new facts by experiment. Sometimes the professor with his bone becomes almost as dangerous as a dog with his bone. And the dog at least does not deduce a theory from it, proving that mankind is going to the dogs – or that it came from them.

For instance, I have pointed out the difficulty of keeping a monkey and watching it evolve into a man. Experimental evidence of such an evolution being impossible, the professor is not content to say (as most of us would be ready to say) that such an evolution is likely enough anyhow. He produces his little bone, or little collection of bones, and deduces the most marvellous things from it. He found in Java a piece of a skull, seeming by its contour to be smaller than the human. Somewhere near it he found an upright thigh-bone and in the same scattered fashion some teeth that were not human. If they all form part of one creature, which is doubtful, our conception of the creature would be almost equally doubtful. But the effect on popular science was to produce a complete and even complex figure, finished down to the last details of hair and habits. He was given a name as if he were an ordinary historical character. People talked of Pithecanthropus as of Pitt or Fox or Napoleon. Popular histories published portraits of 'him like the portraits of Charles the First and George the Fourth. A detailed drawing was reproduced, carefully shaded, to show that the very hairs of his head were all numbered. No uninformed person looking at its carefully lined face and wistful eyes would imagine for a moment that this was the portrait of a thigh bone; or of a few teeth and a fragment of a cranium. In the same way people talked about him as if he were an individual whose influence and character were familiar to us all. I have just read a story in a magazine about Java and how modern white inhabitants of that island are prevailed on to misbehave themselves by the personal influence of poor old Pithecanthropus. That the modern inhabitants of Java misbehave themselves I can very readily believe; but I do not imagine that they need any encouragement from the discovery of a few highly doubtful bones. Anyhow, those bones are far too few and fragmentary and dubious to fill up the whole of the vast void that does in reason and in reality lie between man and his bestial ancestors, if they were his ancestors. On the assumption of that evolutionary connection (a connection which I am not in the least concerned to deny), the really arresting and remarkable fact is the comparative absence of any such remains recording that connection at that point. The sincerity of Darwin really admitted this; and that is how we came to use such a term as the Missing Link. But the dogmatism of Darwinian has been too strong for agnosticism of Darwin; and men have fallen into turning this entirely negative term into a positive image. They talk of searching for the habits and habitat of the Missing Link; as if one were to talk of being on friendly terms with the gap in a narrative or the hole in an argument, of taking a walk with a *non sequitur* or dining with an undistributed middle.

In this sketch, therefore, of man in his relation to certain religious and historical problems, I shall waste no further space on these speculations on the nature of man before he became man. His body may have been evolved from the brutes; but we know nothing of any such transition that throws the smallest light upon his soul as it has shown itself in history. Unfortunately the same school of writers pursue the same style of reasoning when they come to the first real evidence about the first real men. Strictly speaking of course we know nothing about prehistoric man, for the simple reason that he was prehistoric. The history of the prehistoric man is a very obvious contradiction in terms. It is the sort of unreason in which only rationalists are allowed to indulge. If a parson had casually observed that the Flood was antediluvian, it is possible that he might be a little chaffed about his logic. If a bishop were to say that Adam was Pre-Adamite, we might think it a little odd. But we are not supposed to notice such verbal trifles when sceptical historians talk of the part of history that is prehistoric. The truth is that they are using the terms historic and prehistoric without any clear test or definition in their minds. What they mean is that there are traces of human lives before the beginning of human stories; and in that sense we do at least know that humanity was before history.

Human civilisation is older than human records. That is the sane way of stating our relations to these remote things. Humanity has left examples of its other arts earlier than the art of writing; or at least of any writing that we can read. But it is certain that the primitive arts were arts; and it is in every way probable that the primitive civilisations were civilisations. The man left a picture of the reindeer, but he did not leave a narrative of how he hunted the

reindeer; and therefore what we say of him is hypothesis
and not history. But the art he did practice was quite artistic; his drawing was quite intelligent and there is no reason
to doubt that his story of the hunt would be quite intelligent, only if it exists it is not intelligible. In short, the prehistoric period need not mean the primitive period, in the
sense of the barbaric or bestial period. It does not mean
the time before civilisation or the time before arts and
crafts. It simply means the time before any connected nar-
ratives that we can read. This does indeed make all the
practical difference between remembrance and forgetful-
ness; but it is perfectly possible that there were all sorts of
forgotten forms of civilisation, as well as all sorts of forgotten forms of barbarism. And in any case everything
indicated that many of these forgotten or half-forgotten
social stages were much more civilised and much less barbaric than is vulgarly imagined today. But even about these
unwritten histories of humanity, when humanity was quite
certainly human, we can only conjecture with the greatest
doubt and caution. And unfortunately doubt and caution
are the last things commonly encouraged by the loose evolutionism of current culture. For that culture is full of curiosity; and the one thing that it cannot endure is the agony
of agnosticism. It was in the Darwinian age that the word
first became known and the thing first became impossible.

It is necessary to say plainly that all this ignorance is
simply covered by impudence. Statements are made so
plainly and positively that men have hardly the moral courage to pause upon them and find that they are without
support. The other day a scientific summary of the state of
a prehistoric tribe began confidently with the words 'They
wore no clothes.' Not one reader in a hundred probably
stopped to ask himself how we should come to know
whether clothes had once been worn by people of whom
everything has perished except a few chips of bone and
stone. It was doubtless hoped that we should find a stone
hat as well as a stone hatchet. It was evidently anticipated
that we might discover an everlasting pair of trousers of

the same substance as the everlasting rock. But to persons of a less sanguine temperament it will be immediately apparent that people might wear simple garments, or even highly ornamental garments, without leaving any more traces of them than these people have left. The plaiting of rushes and grasses, for instance, might have become more and more elaborate without in the least becoming more eternal. One civilisation might specialize in things that happen to be perishable, like weaving and embroidering, and not in things that happen to be more permanent, like architecture and sculpture. There have been plenty of examples of such specialist societies. A man of the future finding the ruins of our factory machinery might as fairly say that we were acquainted with iron and with no other substance; and announce the discovery that the proprietor and manager of the factory undoubtedly walked about naked – or possibly wore iron hats and trousers.

It is not contended here that these primitive men did wear clothes any more than they did weave rushes; but merely that we have not enough evidence to know whether they did or not. But it may be worthwhile to look back for a moment at some of the very few things that we do know and that they did do. If we consider them, we shall certainly not find them inconsistent with such ideas as dress and decoration. We do not know whether they decorated themselves; but we do know that they decorated other things. We do not know whether they had embroideries, and if they had the embroideries could not be expected to have remained. But we do know that they did have pictures; and the pictures have remained. And there remains with them as already suggested the testimony to something that is absolute and unique; that belongs to man and to nothing else except man; that is a difference of kind and not a difference of degree. A monkey does not draw clumsily and a man cleverly; a monkey does not begin the art of representation and a man carry it to perfection. A monkey does not do it at all; he does not begin to do it at all; he does not begin to begin to do it at all. A line of some kind is crossed before the first faint line can begin.

Another distinguished writer, again, in commenting on the cave drawings attributed to the Neolithic men of the reindeer period, said that none of their pictures appeared to have any religious purpose; and he seemed almost to infer that they had no religion. I can hardly imagine a thinner thread of argument than this which reconstructs the very inmost moods of the prehistoric mind from the fact that somebody who has scrawled a few sketches on a rock, from what motive we do not know, for what purpose we do not know, acting under what customs or conventions we do not know, may possibly have found it easier to draw reindeer than to draw religion. He may have drawn it because it was his religious symbol. He may have drawn it because it was not his religious symbol. He may have drawn anything except his religious symbol. He may have drawn his real religious symbol somewhere else; or it may have been deliberately destroyed when it was drawn. He may have done or not done half a million things; but in any case it is an amazing leap of logic to infer that he had no religious symbol, or even to infer from his having no religious symbol that he had no religion. Now this particular case happens to illustrate the insecurity of these guesses very clearly. For a little while afterwards, people discovered not only paintings but sculptures of animals in the caves. Some of these were said to be damaged with dints or holes supposed to be the marks of arrows; and the damaged images were conjectured to be the remains of some magic rite of killing the beasts in effigy; while the undamaged images were explained in connection with another magic rite invoking fertility upon the herds. Here again there is something faintly humorous about the scientific habit of having it both ways. If the image is damaged it proves one superstition and if it is undamaged it proves another. Here again there is a rather reckless jumping to conclusions; it has hardly occurred to the speculators that a crowd of hunters imprisoned in winter in a cave might conceivably have aimed at a mark for fun, as a sort of primitive parlour game. But in any case, if it was done out of superstition, what has become of the thesis that it had nothing to do with religion? The truth is that all this guesswork has nothing to do with anything. It is not half such a good parlour game as shooting arrows at a carved reindeer for it is shooting them into the air.

Such speculators rather tend to forget, for instance, that men in the modern world also sometimes make marks in caves. When a crowd of trippers is conducted through the labyrinth of the Marvellous Grotto or the Magic Stalactite Cavern, it has been observed that hieroglyphics spring into sight where they have passed; initials and inscriptions which the learned refuse to refer to any remote date. But the time will come when these inscriptions will really be of remote date. And if the professors of the future are anything like the professors of the present, they will be able to deduce a vast number of very vivid and interesting things from these cave writings of the twentieth century. If I know anything about the breed, and if they have not fallen away from the full-blooded confidence of their fathers, they will be able to discover the most fascinating facts about us, from the initials left in the Magic Grotto by 'Arry and 'Arriet, possibly in the form of two intertwined A's. From this alone they will know, (1) That as the letters are rudely chipped with a blunt pocketknife, the twentieth century possessed no delicate graving-tools and was unacquainted with the art of sculpture. (2) That as the letters are capital letters, our civilisation never evolved any small letters or anything like a running band. (3) That because initial consonants stand together in an unpronounceable fashion, our language was possibly akin to Welsh or more probably of the early Semitic type that ignored vowels. (4) That as the initials of 'Arry and 'Arriet do not in any special fashion profess to be religious symbols, our civilisation possessed no religion. Perhaps the last is about the nearest to the truth; for a civilisation that had religion would have a little more reason.

It is commonly affirmed, again, that religion grew in a

very slow and evolutionary manner; and even that it grew
not from one cause, but from a combination that might be
called a coincidence. Generally speaking, the three chief
elements in the combination are, first, the fear of the chief
of the tribe (whom Mr. Wells insists on calling, with regret-
table familiarity, the Old Man), second, the phenomena of
dreams, and third, the sacrificial associations of the harvest
and the resurrection symbolised in the growing corn I may
remark in passing that it seems to me very doubtful psychology to refer one living and single spirit to three dead
and disconnected causes, if they were merely dead and disconnected causes. Suppose Mr. Wells, in one of his fascinating novels of the future, were to tell us that there would
arise among men a new and as yet nameless passion, of
which men will dream as they dream of first love, for
which they will die as they die for a flag and a fatherland. I
think we should be a little puzzled if he told us that this
singular sentiment would be a combination of the habit of
smoking Woodbines, the increase of the income tax and
the pleasure of a motorist in exceeding the speed limit. We
could not easily imagine this, because we could not imagine any connection between the three or any common feeling that could include them all. Nor could anyone imagine
any connection between corn and dreams and an old chief
with a spear, unless there was already a common feeling to
include them all. But if there was such a common feeling it
could only be the religious feeling; and these things could
not be the beginnings of a religious feeling that existed
already. I think anybody's common sense will tell him that
it is far more likely that this sort of mystical sentiment did
exist already, and that in the light of it dreams and kings
and cornfields could appear mystical then, as they can appear mystical now.

For the plain truth is that all this is a trick of making
things seem distant and dehumanised, merely by pretending not to understand things that we do understand. It is
like saying that prehistoric men had an ugly and uncouth
habit of opening their mouths wide at intervals and stuff-

ing strange substances into them, as if we had never heard of eating. It is like saying that the terrible Troglodytes of the Stone Age lifted alternate legs in rotation, as if we had never heard of walking. If it were meant to touch the mystical nerve and awaken us to the wonder of walking and eating, it might be a legitimate fancy. As it is here intended to kill the mystical nerve and deaden us to the wonder of religion, it is irrational rubbish. It pretends to find something incomprehensible in the feelings that we all comprehend. Who does *not* find dreams mysterious and feel that they lie on the dark borderland of being? Who does *not* feel the death and resurrection of the growing things of the earth as something near to the secret of the Universe? Who does *not* understand that there must always be the savour of something sacred about authority and the solidarity that is the soul of the tribe? If there be any anthropologist who really finds these things remote and impossible to realise, we can say nothing of that scientific gentleman except that he has not got so large and enlightened a mind as a primitive man. To me it seems obvious that nothing but a spiritual sentiment already active could have clothed these separate and diverse things with sanctity. To say that religion came *from* reverencing a chief or sacrificing at a harvest is to put a highly elaborate cart before a really primitive horse. It is like saying that the impulse to draw pictures came from the contemplation of the pictures of reindeer in the cave. In other words, it is explaining painting by saying that it arose out of the work of painters; or accounting for art by saying that it arose out of art. It is even more like saying that the thing we call poetry arose as the result of certain customs; such as that of an ode being officially composed to celebrate the advent of spring; or that of a young man rising at a regular hour to listen to the skylark and then writing his report on a piece of paper. It is quite true that young men often become poets in the spring; and it is quite true that when once there are poets, no mortal power can restrain them from writing about the skylark. But the poems did not exist before the poets. The

poetry did not arise out of the poetic forms. In other
words, it is hardly an adequate explanation of how a thing
appeared for the first time to say it existed already. Similarly, we cannot say that religion arose out of the religious
forms because that is only another way of saying that it
only arose when it existed already. It needed a certain sort
of mind to see that there was anything mystical about the
dreams or the dead, as it needed a particular sort of mind
to see that there was anything poetical about the skylark or
the spring. That mind was presumably what we call the
human mind, very much as it exists to this day; for mystics
still meditate upon death and dreams as poets still write
about spring and skylarks. But there is not the faintest hint
to suggest that anything short of the human mind we
know feels any of these mystical associations at all. A cow
in a field seems to derive no lyrical impulse or instruction
from her unrivalled opportunities for listening to the skylark. And similarly there is no reason to suppose that live
sheep will ever begin to use dead sheep as the basis of a
system of elaborate ancestor-worship. It is true that in the
spring a young quadruped's fancy may lightly turn to
thoughts of love, but no succession of springs has ever led
it to turn however lightly to thoughts of literature. And in
the same way, while it is true that a dog has dreams, while
most other quadrupeds do not seem even to have that, we
have waited a long time for the dog to develop his dreams
into an elaborate system of religious ceremonial. We have
waited so long that we have really ceased to expect it; and
we no more look to see a dog apply his dreams to ecclesiastical construction than to see him examine his dreams by
the rules of psychoanalysis. It is obvious, in short, that for
some reason or other these natural experiences, and even
natural excitements, never do pass the line that separates
them from creative expression like art and religion, in any
creature except man. They never do, they never have, and
it is now to all appearance very improbable that they ever
will. It is not impossible, in the sense of self-contradictory,
that we should see cows fasting from grass every Friday or

going on their knees as in the old legend about Christmas
Eve. It is not in that sense impossible that cows should
contemplate death until they can lift up a sublime psalm of
lamentation to the tune the old cow died of. It is not in
that sense impossible that they should express their hopes
of a heavenly career in a symbolical dance, in honour of
the cow that jumped over the moon. It may be that the
dog will at last have laid in a sufficient store of dreams to
enable him to build a temple to Cerberus as a sort of ca-
nine trinity. It may be that his dreams have already begun
to turn into visions capable of verbal expression Dog Star
as the spiritual home for lost dogs. These things are logically possible, in the sense that it is logically difficult to
prove the universal negative which we call an impossibility.
But all that instinct for the probable, which we call common sense, must long ago have told us that the animals are
not to all appearance evolving in that sense; and that, to
say the least, we are not likely to have any personal evidence of their passing from the animal experience to the
human experiments. But spring and death and even
dreams, considered merely as experiences, are their experiences as much as ours. The only possible conclusion is that
these experiences, considered as experiences, do not gen-
erate anything like a religious sense in any mind except a
mind like ours. We come back to the fact of a certain kind
of mind was already alive and alone. It was unique and it
could make creeds as it could make cave drawings. The
materials for religion had lain there for countless ages like
the materials for everything else; but the power of religion
was in the mind. Man could already see in these things the
riddles and hints and hopes that he still sees in them. He
could not only dream but dream about dreams. He could
not only see the dead but see the shadow of death; and was
possessed with that mysterious mystification that forever
finds death incredible.

It is quite true that we have even these hints chiefly
about man when he unmistakably appears as man. We
cannot affirm this or anything else about the alleged animal

originally connecting man and the brutes. But that is only because he is not an animal but an allegation. We cannot be certain that Pithecanthropus ever worshipped, because we cannot be certain that be ever lived. He is only a vision called up to fill the void that does in fact yawn between the first creatures who were certainly men and any other creatures that are certainly apes or other animals. A few very doubtful fragments are scraped together to suggest such an intermediate creature because it is required by a certain philosophy; but nobody supposes that these are sufficient to establish anything philosophical even in support of that philosophy. A scrap of skull found in Java cannot establish anything about religion or about the absence of religion. If there ever was any such ape-man, he may have exhibited as much ritual in religion as a man or as much simplicity in religion as an ape. He may have been a mythologist or he may have been a myth. It might be interesting to inquire whether this mystical quality appeared in a transition from the ape to the man, if there were really any types of the transition to inquire about. In other words, the Missing Link might or might not be mystical if he were not missing. But compared with the evidence we have of real human beings, we have no evidence that he was a human being or a half human being or a being at all. Even the most extreme evolutionists do not attempt to deduce any evolutionary views about the origin of religion from him. Even in trying to prove that religion grew slowly from rude or irrational sources, they begin their proof with the first men who were men. But their own proof only proves that the men who were already men were already mystics. They used the rude and irrational elements as only men and mystics can use them. We come back once more to the simple truth; that at some time too early for these critics to trace, a transition had occurred to which bones and stones cannot in their nature bear witness; and man became a living soul.

Touching this matter of the origin of religion, the truth is that those who are thus trying to explain it are trying to explain it away. Subconsciously they feel that it looks less formidable when thus lengthened out into a gradual and almost invisible process. But in fact this perspective entirely falsifies the reality of experience. They bring together two things that are totally different, the stray hints of evolutionary origins and the solid and self-evident block of humanity, and try to shift their standpoint till they see them in a single foreshortened line. But it is an optical illusion. Men do not in fact stand related to monkeys or missing links in any such chain as that in which men stand related to men. There may have been intermediate creatures whose faint traces can be found here and there in the huge gap. Of these beings, if they ever existed, it may be true that they were things very unlike men or men very unlike ourselves. But of prehistoric men, such as those called the cave-men or the reindeer men, it is not true in any sense whatever. Prehistoric men of that sort were things exactly like men and men exceedingly like ourselves. They only happened to be men about whom we do not know much, for the simple reason that they have left no records or chronicles; but all that we do know about them makes them just as human and ordinary as men in a medieval manor or a Greek city.

Looking from our human standpoint up the long perspective of humanity, we simply recognise this thing as human. If we had to recognise it as animal we should have had to recognise it as abnormal. If we chose to look through the other end of the telescope, as I have done more than once in these speculations, if we chose to project the human figure forward out of an inhuman world, we could only say that one of the animals had obviously gone mad. But seeing the thing from the right end, or rather from the inside, we know it is sanity; and we know that these primitive men were sane. We hail a certain human freemasonry wherever we see it, in savages, in foreigners or in historical characters. For instance, all we can infer from primitive legend, and all we know of barbaric life, supports a certain moral and even mystical idea of

which the commonest symbol is clothes. For clothes are
very literally investments and man wears them because he
is a priest. It is true that even as an animal he is here different from the animals. Nakedness is not nature to him; it
is not his life but rather his death; even in the vulgar sense
of his death of cold. But clothes are worn for dignity or
decency or decoration where they are not in any way
wanted for warmth. It would sometimes appear that they
are valued for ornament before they are valued for use. It
would almost always appear that they are felt to have some
connection with decorum. Conventions of this sort vary a
great deal with various times and places; and there are
some who cannot get over this reflection and for whom it
seems a sufficient argument for letting all conventions
slide. They never tire of repeating, with simple wonder,
that dress is different in the Cannibal Islands and in Cam-
den Town; they cannot get any further and throw up the
whole idea of decency in despair. They might as well say
that because there have been hats of a good many different
shapes, and some rather eccentric shapes, therefore hats
do not matter or do not exist. They would probably say
that there is no such thing as sunstroke or going bald. Men
have felt everywhere that certain forms were necessary to
fence off and protect certain private things from contempt
or coarse misunderstanding; and the keeping of those
forms, whatever they were, made for dignity and mutual
respect. The fact that they mostly refer, more or less remotely, to the relations of the sexes illustrates the two facts
that must be put at the very beginning of the record of the
race. The first is the fact that original sin is really original.
Not merely in theology but in history it is a thing rooted in
the origins. Whatever else men have believed, they have all
believed that there is something the matter with mankind.
This sense of sin has made it impossible to be natural and
have no clothes, just as it has made it impossible to be
natural and have no laws. But above all it is to be found in
that other fact, which is the father and mother of all laws
as it is itself founded on a father and mother; the thing that

is before all thrones and even all commonwealths.

That fact is the family. Here again we must keep the enormous proportions of a normal thing clear of various modifications and degrees and doubts more or less reasonable, like clouds clinging about a mountain. It may be that what we call the family had to fight its way from or through various anarchies and aberrations; but it certainly survived them and is quite as likely as not to have also preceded them. As we shall see in the case of communism and nomadism, more formless things could and did lie on the flank of societies that had taken a fixed form; but there is nothing to show that the form did not exist before the formlessness. What is vital is that form is more important than formlessness; and that the material called mankind has taken this form. For instance, of the rules revolving round sex, which were recently mentioned, none is more curious than the savage custom commonly called the *couvade*. That seems like a law out of topsy-turveydom; by which the father is treated as if he were the mother. In any case, it clearly involves the mystical sense of sex; but many have maintained that it is really a symbolic act by which the father accepts the responsibility of fatherhood. In that case that grotesque antic is really a very solemn act; for it is the foundation of all we call the family and all we know as human society. Some groping in these dark beginnings have said that mankind was once under a matriarchy; I suppose that under a matriarchy it would not be called mankind but womankind. But others have conjectured that what is called matriarchy was simply moral anarchy, in which the mother alone remained fixed because all the fathers were fugitive and irresponsible. Then came the moment when the man decided to guard and guide what he had created. So he became the head of the family, not as a bully with a big club to beat women with, but rather as a respectable person trying to be a responsible person. Now all that might be perfectly true, and might even have been the first family act, and it would still be true that man then for the first time acted like a man, and therefore for the first time became fully a man. But it might quite as well be true that the matriarchy or moral anarchy, or whatever we call it, was only one of the hundred social dissolutions or barbaric backslidings which may have occurred at intervals in prehistoric as they certainly did in historic times. A symbol like the *couvade*, if it was really such a symbol, may have commemorated the suppression of a heresy rather than the first rise of a religion. We cannot conclude with any certainty about these things, except in their big results in the building of mankind, but we can say in what style the bulk of it and the best of it is built. We can say that the family is the unit of the state; that it is the cell that makes up the formation. Round the family do indeed gather the sanctities that separate men from ants and bees. Decency is the curtain of that tent; liberty is the wall of that city; property is but the family farm; honour is but the family flag. In the practical proportions of human history, we come back to that fundamental of the father and the mother and the child. It has been said already that if this story cannot start with religious assumptions, it must none the less start with some moral or metaphysical assumptions, or no sense can be made of the story of man. And this is a very good instance of that alternative necessity. If we are not of those who begin by invoking a divine Trinity, we must none the less invoke a human Trinity; and see that triangle repeated everywhere in the pattern of the world. For the highest event in history, to which all history looks forward and leads up, is only something that is at once the reversal and the renewal of that triangle. Or rather it is the one triangle superimposed so as to intersect the other, making a sacred pentacle of which, in a mightier sense than that of the magicians, the fiends are afraid. The old Trinity was of father and mother and child and is called the human family. The new is of child and mother and father and has the name of the Holy Family. It is in no way altered except in being entirely reversed; just as the world which is transformed was not in the least different, except in being turned upside-down.

3
THE ANTIQUITY OF CIVILISATION

THE MODERN MAN looking at the most ancient origins has been like a man watching for daybreak in a strange land; and expecting to see that dawn breaking behind bare uplands or solitary peaks. But that dawn is breaking behind the black bulk of great cities long built and lost for us in the original night; colossal cities like the houses of giants, in which even the carved ornamental animals are taller than the palm-trees; in which the painted portrait can be twelve times the size of the man; with tombs like mountains of man set four-square and pointing to the stars; with winged and bearded bulls standing and staring enormous at the gates of temples; standing still eternally as if a stamp would shake the world. The dawn of history reveals a humanity already civilised. Perhaps it reveals a civilisation already old. And among other more important things, it reveals the folly of most of the generalisations about the previous and unknown period when it was really young. The two first human societies of which we have any reliable and detailed record are Babylon and Egypt. It so happens that these two vast and splendid achievements of the genius of the ancients bear witness against two of the commonest and crudest assumptions of the culture of the moderns. If we want to get rid of half the nonsense about nomads and cave-men and the old man of the forest, we need only look steadily at the two solid and stupendous facts called Egypt and Babylon.

Of course most of these speculators who are talking about primitive men are thinking about modern savages. They prove their Progressive evolution by assuming that a great part of the human race has not progressed or evolved; or

even changed in any way at all. I do not agree with their
theory of change; nor do I agree with their dogma of
things unchangeable. I may not believe that civilised man
has had so rapid and recent a progress; but I cannot quite
understand why uncivilised man should be so mystically
immortal and immutable. A somewhat simpler mode of
thought and speech seems to me to be needed throughout
this inquiry. Modern savages cannot be exactly like primitive man, because they are not primitive. Modern savages
are not ancient because they are modern. Something has
happened to their race as much as to ours, during the
thousands of years of our existence and endurance on the
earth. They have had some experiences, and have presumably acted on them if not profited by them, like the
rest of us. They have had some environment and even
some change of environment and have presumably
adapted themselves to it in a proper and decorous evolutionary manner. This would be true even if the experiences
were mild or the environment dreary; for there is an effect
in mere time when it takes the moral form of monotony.
But it has appeared to a good many intelligent and well
informed people quite as probable that the experience of
the savages has been that of a decline from civilisation.
Most of those who criticise this view do not seem to have
any very clear notion of what a decline from civilisation
would be like. Heaven help them, it is likely enough that
they will soon find out. They seem to be content if cave-
men and cannibal islanders have some things in common,
such as certain particular implements. But it is obvious on
the face of it that any peoples reduced for any reason to a
ruder life would have some things in common. If we lost
all our firearms we should make bows and arrows; but we
should not necessarily resemble in every way the first men
who made bows and arrows. It is said that the Russians in
their great retreat were so short of armament that they
fought with clubs cut in the wood. But a professor of the
future would err in supposing that the Russian army of
1936 was a naked Scythian tribe that had never been out of

the wood. It is like saying that a man in his second childhood must exactly copy his first. A baby is bald like an old man; but it would be an error for one ignorant of infancy to infer that the baby had a long white beard. Both a baby and an old man walk with difficulty; but he who shall expect the old gentleman to lie on his back and kick joyfully instead, will be disappointed.

It is therefore absurd to argue that the first pioneers of humanity must have been identical with some of the last and most stagnant leavings of it. There were almost certainly some things, there were probably many things, in which the two were widely different or flatly contrary. An example of the way in which this distinction works, and an example essential to our argument here, is that of the nature and origin of government. I have already alluded to Mr. H. G. Wells and the Old Man, with whom he appears to be on such intimate terms. If we considered the cold facts of prehistoric evidence for this portrait of the prehistoric chief of the tribe, we could only excuse it by saying that its brilliant and versatile author simply forgot for a moment that he was supposed to be writing a history, and dreamed he was writing one of his own very wonderful and imaginative romances. At least I cannot imagine how he can possibly know that the prehistoric ruler was called the Old Man or that court etiquette requires it to be spelt with capital letters. He says of the same potentate, 'No one was allowed to touch his spear or to sit in his seat.' I have difficulty in believing that anybody has dug up a prehistoric spear with a prehistoric label, 'Visitors are Requested not to Touch,' or a complete throne with the inscription, 'Reserved for the Old Man.' But it may be presumed that the writer, who can hardly be supposed to be merely making up things out of his own head, was merely taking for granted this very dubious parallel between the prehistoric and the civilised man. It may be that in certain savage tribes the chief is called the Old Man and nobody is allowed to touch his spear or sit on his seat. It may be that in those cases he is surrounded with superstitious and traditional terrors; and it may be that in those cases, for all I know, he is despotic and tyrannical. But there is not a grain of evidence that primitive government was despotic and tyrannical. It may have been, of course, for it may have been anything or even nothing; it may not have existed at all. But the despotism in certain dingy and decayed tribes in the twentieth century does not prove that the first men were ruled despotically. It does not even suggest it; it does not even begin to hint at it. If there is one fact we really can prove, from the history that we really do know, it is that despotism can be a development, often a late development and very often indeed the end of societies that have been highly democratic. A despotism may almost be defined as a tired democracy. As fatigue falls on a community, the citizens are less inclined for that eternal vigilance which has truly been called the price of liberty; and they prefer to arm only one single sentinel to watch the city while they sleep. It is also true that they sometimes needed him for some sudden and militant act of reform; it is equally true that he often took advantage of being the strong man armed to be a tyrant like some of the Sultans of the East. But I cannot see why the Sultan should have appeared any earlier in history than many other human figures. On the contrary, the strong man armed obviously depends upon the superiority of his armour; and armament of that sort comes with more complex civilisation. One man may kill twenty with a machine gun; it is obviously less likely that he could do it with a piece of flint. As for the current cant about the strongest man ruling by force and fear, it is simply a nursery fairytale about a giant with a hundred hands. Twenty men could hold down the strongest strong man in any society, ancient or modern. Undoubtedly they might *admire*, in a romantic and poetical sense, the man who was really the strongest; but that is quite a different thing, and is as purely moral and even mystical as the admiration for the purest or the wisest. But the spirit that endures the mere cruelties and caprices of an established despot is the spirit of an ancient and settled and probably stiffened society, not the spirit of a new one. As his name implies, the Old Man is the ruler of an old humanity.

It is far more probable that a primitive society was something like a pure democracy. To this day the comparatively simple agricultural communities are by far the purest democracies. Democracy is a thing which is always breaking down through the complexity of civilisation. Anyone who likes may state it by saying that democracy is the foe of civilisation. But he must remember that some of us really prefer democracy to civilisation, in the sense of preferring democracy to complexity. Anyhow, peasants tilling patches of their own land in a rough equality and meeting to vote directly under a village tree are the most truly self-governing of men. It is surely as likely as not that such a simple idea was found in the first condition of even simpler men. Indeed the despotic vision is exaggerated even if we do not regard the men as men. Even on an evolutionary assumption of the most materialistic sort, there is really no reason why men should not have had at least as much camaraderie as rats or rooks. Leadership of some sort they doubtless had, as have the gregarious animals; but leadership implies no such irrational servility as that attributed to the superstitious subjects of the Old Man. There was doubtless somebody corresponding, to use Tennyson's expression, to the many-wintered crow that leads the clanging rookery home. But I fancy that if that venerable fowl began to act after the fashion of some Sultans in ancient and decayed Asia, it would become a very clanging rookery and the many-wintered crow would not see many more winters. It may be remarked, in this connection, but even among animals it would seem that something else is respected more than bestial violence, if it be only the familiarity which in men is called tradition or the experience which in men is called wisdom. I do not know if crows really follow the oldest crow, but if they do they are certainly not following the strongest crow. And I do know in the human case that if some ritual of seniority keeps sav-

ages reverencing somebody called the Old Man, then at
least they have not our own servile sentimental weakness
for worshipping the Strong Man.

It may be said then that primitive government, like
primitive art and religion and everything else, is very im-
perfectly known or rather guessed at; but that it is at least
as good a guess to suggest that it was as popular as a Bal-
kan or Pyrenean village as that it was as capricious and
secret as a Turkish divan. Both the mountain democracy
and the oriental palace are modern in the sense that they
are still there, or are some sort of growth of history; but of
the two the palace has much more the look of being an
accumulation and a corruption, the village much more the
look of being a really unchanged and primitive thing. But
my suggestions at this point do not go beyond expressing a
wholesome doubt about the current assumption. I think it
interesting, for instance, that liberal institutions have been
traced even by moderns back to barbarian or undeveloped
states, when it happened to be convenient for the support
of some race or nation or philosophy. So the Socialists
profess that their ideal of communal property existed in
very early times. So the Jews are proud of the Jubilees or
juster redistributions under their ancient law. So the Teu-
tonists boasted of tracing parliaments and juries and various popular things among the Germanic tribes of the
north. So the Celtophiles and those testifying to the
wrongs of Ireland have pleaded the more equal justice of
the clan system, to which the Irish chiefs bore witness before Strongbow. The strength of the case varies in the different cases; but as there is some case for all of them, I
suspect there is some case for the general proposition that
popular institutions of some sort were by no means un-
common in early and simple societies. Each of these separate schools was making the admission to prove a particular modern thesis; but taken together they suggest a more
ancient and general truth, that there was something more
in prehistoric councils than ferocity and fear. Each of these
separate theorists had his own axe to grind, but he was

willing to use a stone axe; and he manages to suggest that the stone axe might have been as republican as the guillotine.

But the truth is that the curtain rises upon the play already in progress. In one sense it is a true paradox that there was history before history. But it is not the irrational paradox implied in prehistoric history; for it is a history we do not know. Very probably it was exceedingly like the history we do know, except in the one detail that we do not know it. It is thus the very opposite of the pretentious prehistoric history, which professes to trace everything in a consistent course from the amoeba to the anthropoid and from the anthropoid to the agnostic. So far from being a question of our knowing all about queer creatures very different from ourselves, they were very probably people very like ourselves, except that we know nothing about them. In other words, our most ancient records only reach back to a time when humanity had long been human, and even long been civilised. The most ancient records we have not only mention but take for granted things like kings and priests and princes and assemblies of the people; they describe communities that are roughly recognisable as communities in our own sense. Some of them are despotic; but we cannot tell that they have always been despotic. Some of them may be already decadent and nearly all are mentioned as if they were old. We do not know what really happened in the world before those records; but the little we do know would leave us anything but astonished if we learnt that it was very much like what happens in this world now. There would be nothing inconsistent or confounding about the discovery that those unknown ages were full of republics collapsing under monarchies and rising again as republics, empires expanding and finding colonies and then losing colonies, kingdoms combining again into world states and breaking up again into small nationalities, classes selling themselves into slavery and marching out once more into liberty; all that procession of humanity which may or may not be a progress but most

assuredly a romance. But the first chapters of the romance
have been torn out of the book; and we shall never read
them.

It is so also with the more special fancy about evolution
and social stability. According to the real records available,
barbarism and civilisation were not successive states in the
progress of the world. They were conditions that existed
side by side, as they still exist side by side. There were civilisations then as there are civilisations now; there are savages now as there were savages then. It is suggested that all
men passed through a nomadic stage; but it is certain that
there are some who have never passed out of it, and it
seems not unlikely that there were some who never passed
into it. It is probable that from very primitive times the
static tiller of the soil and the wandering shepherd were
two distinct types of men; and the chronological rear-
rangement of them is but a mark of that mania for progressive stages that has largely falsified history. It is suggested that there was a communist stage, in which private
property was everywhere unknown, a whole humanity living on the negation of property; but the evidences of this
negation are themselves rather negative. Redistributions of
property, jubilees, and agrarian laws, occur at various intervals and in various forms; but that humanity inevitably
passed through a communist stage seems as doubtful as
the parallel proposition that humanity will inevitably return
to it. It is chiefly interesting as evidence that the boldest
plans for the future invoke the authority of the past; and
that even a revolutionary seeks to satisfy himself that he is
also a reactionary. There is an amusing parallel example in
the case of what is called feminism. In spite of all the
pseudo-scientific gossip about marriage by capture and the
cave-man beating the cave-woman with a club, it may be
noted that as soon as feminism became a fashionable cry,
it was insisted that human civilisation in its first stage had
been a matriarchy. Apparently it was the cave-woman who
carried the club. Anyhow all these ideas are little better
than guesses; they have a curious way of following the for-

tune of modern theories and fads. In any case they are not history in the sense of record; and we may repeat that when it comes to record, the broad truth is that barbarism and civilisation have always dwelt side by side in the world, the civilisation sometimes spreading to absorb the barbarians, sometimes decaying into relative barbarism, and in almost all cases possessing in a more finished form certain ideas and institutions which the barbarians possess in a ruder form; such as government or social authority, the arts and especially the decorative arts, mysteries and taboos of various kinds especially surrounding the matter of sex, and some form of that fundamental thing which is the chief concern of this enquiry; the thing that we call religion.

Now Egypt and Babylon, those two primeval monsters, might in this matter have been specially provided as models. They might almost be called working models to show how these modern theories do not work. The two great truths we know about these two great cultures happen to contradict flatly the two current fallacies which have just been considered. The story of Egypt might have been invented to point the moral that man does not necessarily begin with despotism because he is barbarous, but very often finds his way to despotism because he is civilised. He finds it because he is experienced; or, what is often much the same thing, because he is exhausted. And the story of Babylon might have been invented to point the moral that man need not be a nomad or a communist before he becomes a peasant or a citizen; and that such cultures are not always in successive stages but often contemporary states. Even touching these great civilisations with which our written history begins there is a temptation of course to be too ingenious or too cocksure. We can read the bricks of Babylon in a very different sense from that in which we guess about the Cup and Ring stones; and we do definitely know what is meant by the animals in the Egyptian hieroglyphic as we know nothing of the animals in the Neolithic cave. But even here the admirable archaeologists who have

deciphered line after line of miles of hieroglyphics may be
tempted to read too much between the lines; even the real
authority on Babylon may forget how fragmentary is his
hard-won knowledge; may forget that Babylon has only
heaved half a brick at him, though half a brick is better
than no cuneiform. But some truths, historic and not prehistoric, dogmatic and not evolutionary, facts and not fancies, do indeed emerge from Egypt and Babylon; and these
two truths are among them.

Egypt is a green ribbon along the river edging the dark
red desolation of the desert. It is a proverb, and one of
vast antiquity, that it is created by the mysterious bounty
and almost sinister benevolence of the Nile. When we first
hear of Egyptians they are living as in a string of riverside
villages, in small and separate but cooperative communities
along the bank of the Nile. Where the river branched into
the broad Delta there was traditionally the beginning of a
somewhat different district or people; but this need not
complicate the main truth. These more or less independent
though interdependent peoples were considerably civilised
already. They had a sort of heraldry; that is, decorative art
used for symbolic and social purposes; each sailing the
Nile under its own ensign representing some bird or animal. Heraldry involves two things of enormous importance to normal humanity; the combination of the two
making that noble thing called cooperation; on which rest
all peasantries and peoples that are free. The art of heraldry
means independence; an image chosen by the imagination
to express the individuality. The science of heraldry means
interdependence; an agreement between different bodies
to recognise different images; a science of imagery. We
have here therefore exactly that compromise of cooperation between free families or groups which is the
most normal mode of life for humanity and is particularly
apparent wherever men own their own land and live on it.
With the very mention of the images of bird and beast the
student of mythology will murmur the word 'totem' almost
in his sleep. But to my mind much of the trouble arises

from his habit of saying such words as if in his sleep. Throughout this rough outline I have made a necessarily inadequate attempt to keep on the inside rather than the outside of such things; to consider them where possible in terms of thought and not merely in terms of terminology. There is very little value in talking about totems unless we have some feeling of what it really felt like to have a totem. Granted that they had totems and we have no totems; was it because they had more fear of animals or more familiarity with animals? Did a man whose totem was a wolf feel like a werewolf or like a man running away from a werewolf? Did he feel like Uncle Remus about Brer Wolf or like St. Francis about his brother the wolf, or like Mowgli about his brothers the wolves? Was a totem a thing like the British lion or a thing like the British bull-dog? Was the worship of a totem like the feeling of blacks about Mumbo jumbo, or of children about jumbo? I have never read any book of folklore, however learned, that gave me any light upon this question, which I think by far the most important one. I will confine myself to repeating that the earliest Egyptian communities had a common understanding about the images that stood for their individual states; and that this amount of communication is prehistoric in the sense that it is already there at the beginning of history. But as history unfolds itself, this question of communication is clearly the main question of these riverside communities. With the need of communication comes the need of a common government and the growing greatness and spreading shadow of the king. The other binding force besides the king, and perhaps older than the king, is the priesthood; and the priesthood has presumably even more to do with these ritual symbols and signals by which men can communicate. And here in Egypt arose probably the primary and certainly the typical invention to which we owe all history, and the whole difference between the historic and the prehistoric: the archetypal script, the art of writing.

The popular pictures of these primeval empires are not

half so popular as they might be. There is shed over them
the shadow of an exaggerated gloom, more than the normal and even healthy sadness of heathen men. It is part of
the same sort of secret pessimism that loves to make
primitive man a crawling creature, whose body is filth and
whose soul is fear. It comes of course from the fact that
men are moved most by their religion; especially when it is
irreligion. For them anything primary and elemental must
be evil. But it is the curious consequence that while we
have been deluged with the wildest experiments in primitive romance, they have all missed the real romance of being primitive. They have described scenes that are wholly
imaginary, in which the men of the Stone Age are men of
stone like walking statues; in which the Assyrians or Egyptians are as stiff or as painted as their own most archaic art.
But none of these makers of imaginary scenes have tried to
imagine what it must really have been like to see those
things as fresh which we see as familiar. They have not
seen a man discovering fire like a child discovering fire-
works. They have not seen a man playing with the wonderful invention called the wheel, like a boy playing at putting
up a wireless station. They have never put the spirit of
youth into their descriptions of the youth of the world. It
follows that amid all their primitive or prehistoric fancies
there are no jokes. There are not even practical jokes, in
connection with the practical inventions. And this is very
sharply defined in the particular case of hieroglyphics; for
there seems to be serious indication that the whole high
human art of scripture or writing began with a joke.

There are some who will learn with regret that it seems
to have begun with a pun. The king or the priests or some
responsible persons, wishing to send a message up the
river in that inconveniently long and narrow territory, hit
on the idea of sending it in picture-writing, like that of the
Red Indian. Like most people who have written picture
writing for fun he found the words did not always fit. But
when the word for taxes sounded rather like the word for
pig, he boldly put down a pig as a bad pun and chanced it.

So a modern hieroglyphist might represent 'at once' by unscrupulously drawing a hat followed by a series of upright numerals. It was good enough for the Pharaohs and ought to be good enough for him. But it must have been great fun to write or even to read these messages, when writing and reading were really a new thing. And if people must write romances about ancient Egypt (and it seems that neither prayers nor tears nor curses can withhold them from the habit), I suggest that scenes like this would really remind us that the ancient Egyptians were human beings. I suggest that somebody should describe the scene of the great monarch sitting among his priests, and all of them roaring with laughter and bubbling over with suggestions as the royal puns grew more and more wild and indefensible. There might be another scene of almost equal excitement about the decoding of this cipher; the guesses and clues and discoveries having all the popular thrill of a detective story. That is how primitive romance and primitive history really ought to be written. For whatever was the quality of the religious or moral life of remote times, and it was probably much more human than is conventionally supposed, the scientific interest of such a time must have been intense. Words must have been more wonderful than wireless telegraphy; and experiments with common things a series of electric shocks. We are still waiting for somebody to write a lively story of primitive life. The point is in some sense a parenthesis here; but it is connected with the general matter of political development by the institution which was most active in these first and most fascinating of all the fairy-tales of science.

It is admitted that we owe most of this science to the priests. Modern writers like Mr. Wells cannot be accused of any weakness of sympathy with a pontifical hierarchy but they agree at least in recognising what pagan priesthoods did for the arts and sciences. Among the more ignorant of the enlightened there was indeed a convention of saying that priests had obstructed progress in all ages; and a politician once told me in a debate that I was resisting modern reforms exactly as some ancient priest probably resisted the discovery of wheels. I pointed out, in reply, that it was far more likely that the ancient priest made the discovery of the wheels. It is overwhelmingly probable that the ancient priest had a great deal to do with the discovery of the art of writing. It is obvious enough in the fact that the very word hieroglyphic is akin to the word hierarchy. The religion of these priests was apparently a more or less tangled polytheism of a type that is more particularly described elsewhere. It passed through a period when it co-operated with the king, another period when it was temporarily destroyed by the king, who happened to be a prince with a private theism of his own, and a third period when it practically destroyed the king and ruled in his stead. But the world has to thank it for many things which it considers common and necessary; and the creators of those common things ought really to have a place among the heroes of humanity. If we were at rest in a real paganism, instead of being restless in a rather irrational reaction from Christianity, we might pay some sort of pagan honour to these nameless makers of mankind. We might have veiled statues of the man who first found fire or the man who first made a boat or the man who first tamed a horse. And if we brought them garlands or sacrifices, there would be more sense in it than in disfiguring our cities with cockney statues of stale politicians and philanthropists. But one of the strange marks of the strength of Christianity is that, since it came, no pagan in our civilisation has been able to be really human.

The point is here, however, that the Egyptian government, whether pontifical or royal, found it more and more necessary to establish communication; and there always went with communication a certain element of coercion. It is not necessarily an indefensible thing that the state grew more despotic as it grew more civilised; it is arguable that it had to grow more despotic in order to grow more civilised. That is the argument for autocracy in every age; and the interest lies in seeing it illustrated in the earliest age. But it is emphatically not true that it was most despotic in the earliest age and grew more liberal in a later age; the practical process of history is exactly the reverse. It is not true that the tribe began in the extreme of terror of the Old Man and his seat and spear; it is probable, at least in Egypt, that the Old Man was rather a New Man armed to attack new conditions. His spear grew longer and longer and his throne rose higher and higher, as Egypt rose into a complex and complete civilisation. That is what I mean by saying that the history of the Egyptian territory is in this the history of the earth; and directly denies the vulgar assumption that terrorism can only come at the beginning and cannot come at the end. We do not know what was the very first condition of the more or less feudal amalgam of land-owners, peasants and slaves in the little commonwealth beside the Nile; but it may have been a peasantry of an even more popular sort. What we do know is that it was by experience and education that little commonwealths lose their liberty; that absolute sovereignty is something not merely ancient but rather relatively modern and it is at the end of the path called progress that men return to the king.

Egypt exhibits, in that brief record of its remotest beginnings, the primary problem of liberty and civilisation. It is the fact that men actually lose variety by complexity. We have not solved the problem properly any more than they did; but it vulgarizes the human dignity of the problem itself to suggest that even tyranny has no motive save in tribal terror. And just as the Egyptian example refutes the fallacy about despotism and civilisation, so does the Babylonian example refute the fallacy about civilisation and barbarism. Babylon also we first hear of when it is already civilised; for the simple reason that we cannot hear of anything until it is educated enough to talk. It talks to us in what is called cuneiform; that strange and stiff triangle symbolism that contrasts with the picturesque alphabet of Egypt. However relatively rigid Egyptian art may be, there is always something different from the Babylonian spirit which was too rigid to have any art. There is always a living grace in the lines of the lotus and something of rapidity as well as rigidity in the movement of the arrows and the birds. Perhaps there is something of the restrained but living curve of the river, which makes us in talking of the serpent of old Nile almost think of the Nile as a serpent. Babylon was a civilisation of diagrams rather than of drawings. Mr. W. B. Yeats who has a historical imagination to match his mythological imagination (and indeed the former is impossible without the latter) wrote truly of the men who watched the stars 'from their pedantic Babylon.' The cuneiform was cut upon bricks, of which all their architecture was built up; the bricks were of baked mud, and perhaps the material had something in it forbidding the sense of form to develop in sculpture or relief. Theirs was a static but a scientific civilisation, far advanced in the machinery of life and in some ways highly modern. It is said that they had much of the modern cult of the higher spinsterhood and recognised an official class of independent working women There is perhaps something in that mighty stronghold of hardened mud that suggests the utilitarian activity of a huge hive. But though it was huge it was human; we see many of the same social problems as in ancient Egypt or modern England; and whatever its evils this also was one of the earliest masterpieces of man. It stood of course in the triangle formed by the almost legendary rivers of Tigris and Euphrates and the vast agriculture of its empire on which its towns depended, was perfected by a highly scientific system of canals. It had by tradition a high intellectual life, though rather philosophic than artistic; and there presided over its primal foundation those figures who have come to stand for the stargazing wisdom of antiquity; the teachers of Abraham; the Chaldees.

Against this solid society, as against some vast bare wall of brick, there surged age after age the nameless armies of the Nomads. They came out of the deserts where the nomadic life had been lived from the beginning and where it is still lived today. It is needless to dwell on the nature of that life; it was obvious enough and even easy enough to follow a herd or a flock which generally found its own grazing-ground and to live on the milk or meat it, provided. Nor is there any reason to doubt that this habit of life could give almost every human thing except a home. Many such shepherds or herdsmen may have talked in the earliest times of all the truths and enigmas of the Book of Job; and of these were Abraham and his children, who have given to the modern world for an endless enigma the almost monomaniac monotheism of the Jews. But they were a wild people without comprehension of complex social organisation; and a spirit like the wind within them made them wage war on it again and again. The history of Babylonia is largely the history of its defence against the desert hordes; who came on at intervals of a century or two and generally retreated as they came. Some say that an admixture of nomad invasion built at Nineveh the arrogant kingdom of the Assyrians, who carved great monsters upon their temples, bearded bulls with wings like cherubim, and who sent forth many military conquerors who stamped the world as if with such colossal hooves. Assyria was an imperial interlude but it was an interlude. The main story of all that land is the war between the wandering peoples and the state that was truly static. Presumably in prehistoric times, and certainly in historic times, those wanderers went westward to waste whatever they could find. The last time they came they found Babylon vanished; but that was in historic times and the name of their leader was Mahomet.

Now it is worthwhile to pause upon that story because, as has been suggested, it directly contradicts the impression still current, that nomadism is merely a prehistoric thing and social settlement a comparatively recent thing. There is nothing to show that the Babylonians had ever wandered; there is very little to show that the tribes of the desert ever settled down. Indeed it is probable that this notion of a nomadic stage followed by a static stage has

already been abandoned by the sincere and genuine scholars to whose researches we all owe so much. But I am not
at issue in this book with sincere and genuine scholars, but
with a vast and vague public opinion which has been prematurely spread from certain imperfect investigations, and
which has made fashionable a false notion of the whole
history of humanity. It is the whole vague notion that a
monkey evolved into a man and in the same way a barbarian evolved into a civilised man, and therefore at every
stage we have to look back to barbarism and forward to
civilisation. Unfortunately this notion is in a double sense
entirely in the air. It is an atmosphere in which men live
rather than a thesis which they defend. Men in that mood
are more easily answered by objects than by theories and it
will be well if anyone tempted to make that assumption, in
some trivial turn of talk or writing can be checked for a
moment by shutting his eyes and seeing for an instant vast
and vaguely crowded like a populous precipice the wonder
of the Babylonian wall.

One fact does certainly fall across us like its shadow.
Our glimpses of both these early empires show that the
first domestic relation had been complicated by something
which was less human but was often regarded as equally
domestic. The dark giant called Slavery had been called up
like a genie and labouring on gigantic works of brick and
stone. Here again we must not too easily assume that what
was backward was barbaric in the matter of manumission
the earlier servitude seems in some ways more liberal than
the later perhaps more liberal than the servitude of the
future. To insure food for humanity by forcing part of it to
work was after all a very human expedient; which is why it
will probably be tried again. But in one sense there is a
significance in the old Slavery. It stands for one fundamental fact about all antiquity before Christ something to be
assumed from first to last. It is the insignificance of the
individual before the State. It was as true of the most democratic City State in Hellas as of any despotism in Babylon. It is one of the signs of this spirit that a whole class of

individuals could be insignificant or even invisible. It must be normal because it was needed for what would now be called 'social service.' Somebody said, 'The Man is nothing and the Work is all,' meaning it for a breezy Carlylean commonplace. It was the sinister motto of the heathen Servile State. In that sense there is truth in the traditional vision of vast pillars and pyramids going up under those everlasting skies forever by the labour of numberless and nameless men toiling like ants and dying like flies, wiped out by the work of their own hands.

But there are two other reasons for beginning with the two fixed points of Egypt and Babylon. For one thing they are fixed in tradition as the types of antiquity; and history without tradition is dead. Babylon is still the burden of a nursery rhyme, and Egypt (with its enormous population of princesses awaiting reincarnation) is still the topic of an unnecessary number of novels. But a tradition is generally a truth so long as the tradition is sufficiently popular even if it is almost vulgar. And there is a significance in this Babylonian and Egyptian element in nursery rhymes and novels; even the newspapers, normally so much behind the times, have already got as far as the reign of Tutankhamen. The first reason is full of the common sense of popular legend; it is the simple fact that we do know more of these traditional things than of other contemporary things and that we always did. All travellers from Herodotus to Lord Carnarvon follow this route. Scientific speculations of to-day do indeed spread out a map of the whole primitive world with streams of racial emigration or admixture marked in dotted lines everywhere over spaces which the unscientific medieval mapmaker would have been content to call 'Terra incognita,' if he did not fill the inviting blank with a picture of a dragon to indicate the probable reception given to pilgrims. But these speculations are only speculations at the best and at the worst the dotted lines can be far more fabulous than the dragon.

There is unfortunately one fallacy here into which it is very easy for men to fall even those who are most intelli-

gent and perhaps especially those who are most imaginative. It is the fallacy of supposing that because an idea is
greater in the sense of larger therefore it is greater in the
sense of more fundamental and fixed and certain. If a man
lives alone in a straw hut in the middle of Tibet he may be
told that he is living in the Chinese Empire and the Chinese Empire is certainly a splendid and spacious and impressive thing. Or alternatively he may be told that he is
living in the British Empire and be duly impressed. But the
curious thing is that in certain mental states he can feel
much more certain about the Chinese Empire that he cannot see than about the straw hut that he can see. He has
some strange magical juggle in his mind which his argument begins with the empire though his experience begins
with the hut. Sometimes he goes mad and appears to be
proving that a straw hut cannot exist in the domains of the
Dragon Throne; that it is impossible for such a civilisation
as he enjoys to contain such a hovel as he inhabits, but his
insanity arises from the intellectual slip of supposing that
because China is a large and all embracing hypothesis
therefore it is something more than a hypothesis. Now
modern people are perpetually arguing in this way and they
extend it to things much less real and certain than the Chinese Empire. They seem to forget, for instance, that a man
is not even certain of the Solar System as he is certain of
the South Downs. The Solar System is a deduction and
doubtless a true deduction; but the point is that it is a very
vast and far reaching deduction and therefore he forgets
that it is a deduction at all and treats it as a first principle.
He *might* discover that the whole calculation is a miscalcu-
lation and the sun and stars and street lamps would look
exactly the same. But he has forgotten that it is a calculation and is already to contradict the sun if it does not fit
into the system. If this is a fallacy even in the case of facts
pretty well ascertained such as the Solar System and the
Chinese Empire it is an even more devastating fallacy in
connection with theories and other things that are not
really ascertained at all. Thus history, especially prehistoric

history, has a horrible habit of beginning with certain generalisations about races. I will not describe the disorder and misery this inversion produced in modern politics. Because the race is vaguely supposed to have produced the nation, men talk as if the nation were something vaguer than the race. Because they themselves invented a reason to explain a result they almost deny the result in order to justify the reason. They first treat a Celt as an axiom and then treat an Irishman as an inference. And then they are surprised that a great fighting, roaring Irishman is angry at being treated as an inference. They cannot see that the Irish are Irish whether or no there ever were any Celts. And what misleads them once more is the *size* of the theory; the sense that the fancy is bigger than the fact. A great scattered Celtic race is supposed to contain the Irish so of course the Irish must depend for their very existence upon it. The same confusion of course has eliminated the English and the Germans by swamping them in the Teutonic race; and some tried to prove from the races being at one that the nations could not be at war. But I only give these vulgar and hackneyed examples in passing as more familiar examples of the fallacy; the matter at issue here is not its application to these modern things but rather to the most ancient things. But the more remote and unrecorded was the racial problem, the more fixed was this curious inverted certainty in the Victorian man of science. To this day it gives a man of those scientific traditions the same sort of shock to question these things which were only the last inferences when he turned them into first principles. He is still more certain that he is an Aryan even than that he is an Anglo-Saxon, just as he is more certain that be is an Anglo-Saxon than that he is an Englishman. He has never really discovered that he is a European. But he has never doubted that be is an Indo-European. These Victorian theories have shifted a great deal in their shape and scope but this habit of a rapid hardening of a hypothesis into a theory and of a theory into an assumption has hardly yet gone out of fashion. People cannot easily get rid of the mental confusion of feeling that the foundations of history must surely be secure; that the first steps must be safe; that the biggest generalisation must be obvious. But though the contradiction may seem to them a paradox, this is the very contrary of the truth. It is the large thing that is secret and invisible; it is the small thing that is evident and enormous.

Every race on the face of the earth has been the subject of these speculations and it is impossible even to suggest an outline of the subject. But if we take the European race alone its history, or rather its prehistory, has undergone many retrospective revolutions in the short period of my own lifetime. It used to be called the Caucasian race and I read in childhood an account of its collision with the Mongolian race; it was written by Bret Harte and opened with the query 'Or is the Caucasian played out?' Apparently the Caucasian was played out, for in a very short time he had been turned into the Indo-European man; sometimes, I regret to say, proudly presented as the Indo-Germanic man. It seems that the Hindu and the German have similar words for mother or father; there were other similarities between Sanskrit and various Western tongues and with that all superficial differences between a Hindu and a German seemed suddenly to disappear. Generally this composite person was more conveniently described as the Aryan and the really important point was that he had marched westward out of those high lands of India where fragments of his language could still be found. When I read this as a child I had the fancy that after all the Aryan need not have marched westward and left his language behind him; he might also have marched eastward and taken his language with him. If I were to read it now I should content myself with confessing my ignorance of the whole matter. But as a matter of fact I have great difficulty in reading it now because it is not being written now. It looks as if the Aryan is also played out. Anyhow he has not merely changed his name 'but changed his address; his starting place and his route of travel. One new theory maintains that our race did not come to its present home from the East but from the South. Some say the Europeans did not come from Asia but from Africa. Some have even had the wild idea that the Europeans came from Europe or rather that they never left it.

Then there is a certain amount of evidence of a more or less prehistoric pressure from the North such as that which seems to have brought the Greeks to inherit the Cretan culture and so often brought the Gauls over the hills into the fields of Italy. But I merely mention this example of European ethnology to point out that the learned have pretty well boxed the compass by this time and that I who am not one of the learned, cannot pretend for a moment to decide where such doctors disagree. But I can use my own common sense and I sometimes fancy that theirs is a little rusty from want of use. The first act of common sense is to recognise the difference between a cloud and a mountain. And I will affirm that nobody knows any of these things, in the sense that we all know of the existence of the Pyramids of Egypt.

The truth, it may be repeated, is that what we really see, as distinct from what we may reasonably guess, in this earliest phase of history is darkness covering the earth and great darkness the peoples, with a light or two gleaming here and there on chance patches of humanity; and that two of these flames do burn upon two of these tall primeval towns; upon the high terraces of Babylon and the huge pyramids of the Nile. There are indeed other ancient lights, or lights that may be conjectured to be very ancient, in very remote parts of that vast wilderness of night. Far away to the east there is a high civilisation of vast antiquity in China; there are the remains of civilisations in Mexico and South America and other places, some of them apparently so high in civilisation as to have reached the most refined forms of devil-worship. But the difference lies in the element of tradition; the tradition of these lost cultures has been broken off, and though the tradition of China still lives, it is doubtful whether we know anything about it. Moreover, a man trying to measure the Chinese antiquity has to use Chinese traditions of measurement; and he has a strange sensation of having passed into another world under other laws of time and space. Time is telescoped outwards and centuries assume the slow and stiff movement of aeons; the white man trying to see it as the yellow man sees, feels as if his head were turning round and wonders wildly whether it is growing a pigtail. Anyhow he cannot take in a scientific sense that queer perspective that leads up to the primeval pagoda of the first of the Sons of Heaven. He is in the real antipodes; the only true alternative world to Christendom; and he is after a fashion walking upside down. I have spoken of the medieval mapmaker and his dragon; but what medieval traveller, however much interested in monsters, would expect to find a country where a dragon is a benevolent and amiable being? Of the more serious side of Chinese tradition something will be said in another connection; but here I am only talking of tradition and the test of antiquity. And I only mention China as an antiquity that is not for us reached by a bridge of tradition; and Babylon and Egypt as Antiquities that are. Herodotus is a human being, in a sense in which a Chinaman in a billy-cock hat, sitting opposite to us in a London teashop, is hardly human. We feel as if we knew what David and Isaiah felt like, in a way in which we never were quite certain what Li Hung Chang felt like. The very sins that snatched away Helen or Bathsheba have passed into a proverb of private human weakness, of pathos and even of pardon. The very virtues of the Chinaman have about them something terrifying. This is the difference made by the destruction or preservation of a continuous historical inheritances from ancient Egypt to modern Europe. But when we ask what was that world that we inherit, and why those particular people and places seem to belong to it, we are led to the central fact of civilised history.

That centre was the Mediterranean; which was not so much a piece of water as a world. But it was a world with something of the character of such a water; for it became

more and more a place of unification in which the streams
of strange and very diverse cultures met. The Nile and the
Tiber alike flow into the Mediterranean; so did the Egyptian and the Etrurian contribute to a Mediterranean civilisation The glamour of the great sea spread indeed very far
inland and the unity was felt among the Arabs alone in the
deserts and the Gauls beyond the northern hills. But the
gradual building up of a common culture running round all
the coasts of this inner sea is the main business of antiquity. As will be seen, it was sometimes a bad business as
well as a good business. In that *orbis terrarum* or circle of
lands there were the extremes of evil and of piety, there
were contrasted races and still more contrasted religions. It
was the scene of an endless struggle between Asia and
Europe from the flight of the Persian ships at Salamis to
the flight of the Turkish ships at Lepanto. It was the scene,
as will be more especially suggested later, of a supreme
spiritual struggle between the two types of paganism, confronting each other in the Latin and the Phoenician cities;
in the Roman forum and the Punic mart. It was the world
of war and peace, the world of good and evil, the world of
all that matters most; with all respect to the Aztecs and the
Mongols of the Far East, they did not matter as the Mediterranean tradition mattered and still matters. Between it
and the Far East there were, of course, interesting cults
and conquests of various kinds, more or less in touch with
it and in proportion as they were so intelligible also to us.
The Persian came riding in to make an end of Babylon and
we are told in a Greek story how these barbarians learned
to draw the bow and tell the truth. Alexander the great
Greek marched with his Macedonians into the sunrise and
brought back strange birds coloured like the sunrise clouds
and strange flowers and jewels from the gardens and treas-
uries of nameless kings. Islam went eastward into that
world and made it partly imaginable to us; precisely because Islam itself was born in that circle of lands that
fringed our own ancient and ancestral sea. In the Middle
Ages the empire of the Moguls increased its majesty with-

out losing its mystery; the Tartars conquered China and
the Chinese apparently took very little notice of them. All
these things are interesting in themselves; but it is impossible to shift the centre of gravity to the inland spaces of
Asia from the inland sea of Europe. When all is said, if
there were nothing in the world but what was said and
done and written and built in the lands lying round the
Mediterranean, it would still be in all the most vital and
valuable things the world in which we live. When that
southern culture spread to the northwest it produced many
very wonderful things; of which doubtless we ourselves are
the most wonderful. When it spread thence to colonies
and new countries, it was still the same culture so long as it
was culture at all. But round that little sea like a lake were
the things themselves, apart from all extensions and echoes
and commentaries on the things; the Republic and the
Church; the Bible and the heroic epics; Islam and Israel
and the memories of the lost empires; Aristotle and the
measure of all things. It is because the first light upon *this*
world is really light, the daylight in which we are still walking today, and not merely the doubtful visitation of strange
stars, that I have begun here with noting where that light
first falls on the towered cities of the eastern Mediterranean.

But though Babylon and Egypt have thus a sort of first
claim, in the very fact of being familiar and traditional, fascinating riddles to us but also fascinating riddles to our
fathers, we must not imagine that they were the only old
civilisations on the southern sea; or that all the civilisation
was merely Sumerian or Semitic or Coptic, still less merely
Asiatic or African. Real research is more and more exalting
the ancient civilisation of Europe and especially of what
we may still vaguely call the Greeks. It must be understood
in the sense that there were Greeks before the Greeks, as
in so many of their mythologies there were gods before the
gods. The island of Crete was the centre of the civilisation
now called Minoan, after the Minos who lingered in ancient legend and whose labyrinth was actually discovered

by modern archaeology. This elaborate European society, with its harbour and its drainage and its domestic machinery, seems to have gone down before some invasion of its northern neighbours, who made or inherited the Hellas we know in history. But that earlier period did not pass till it had given to the world gifts so great that the world has ever since been striving in vain to repay them, if only by plagiarism.

Somewhere along the Ionian coast opposite Crete and the islands was a town of some sort, probably of the sort that we should call a village or hamlet with a wall. It was called Ilion but it came to be called Troy, and the name will never perish from the earth. A poet who may have been a beggar and a ballad-monger, who may have been unable to read and write, and was described by tradition as blind, composed a poem about the Greeks going to war with this town to recover the most beautiful woman in the world. That the most beautiful woman in the world lived in that one little town sounds like a legend; that the most beautiful poem in the world was written by somebody who knew of nothing larger than such little towns is a historical fact. It is said that the poem came at the end of the period; that the primitive culture brought it forth in its decay; in which case one would like to have seen that culture in its prime. But anyhow it is true that this, which is our first poem, might very well be our last poem too. It might well be the last word as well as the first word spoken by man about his mortal lot, as seen by merely mortal vision. If the world becomes pagan and perishes, the last man left alive would do well to quote the Iliad and die.

But in this one great human revelation of antiquity there is another element of great historical importance; which has hardly I think been given its proper place in history. The poet has so conceived the poem that his sympathies apparently, and those of his reader certainly, are on the side of the vanquished rather than of the victor. And this is a sentiment which increases in the poetical tradition even as the poetical origin itself recedes. Achilles had some status as a sort of demigod in pagan times; but he disappears altogether in later times. But Hector grows greater as the ages pass; and it is his name that is the name of a Knight of the Round Table and his sword that legend puts into the band of Roland, laying about him with the weapon of the defeated Hector in the last ruin and splendour of his own defeat. The name anticipates all the defeats through which our race and religion were to pass; that survival of a hundred defeats that is its triumph.

The tale of the end of Troy shall have no ending; for it is lifted up forever into living echoes, immortal as our hopelessness and our hope. Troy standing was a small thing that may have stood nameless for ages. But Troy falling has been caught up in a flame and suspended in an immortal instant of annihilation; and because it was destroyed with fire the fire shall never be destroyed. And as with the city so with the hero; traced in archaic lines in that primeval twilight is found the first figure of the Knight. There is a prophetic coincidence in his title; we have spoken of the word chivalry and how it seems to mingle the horseman with the horse. It is almost anticipated ages before in the thunder of the Homeric hexameter, and that long leaping word with which the Iliad ends. It is that very unity for which we can find no name but the holy centaur of chivalry. But there are other reasons for giving in this glimpse of antiquity the flame upon the sacred town. The sanctity of such towns ran like a fire round the coasts and islands of the northern Mediterranean; the high-fenced hamlet for which heroes died. From the smallness of the city came the greatness of the citizen. Hellas with her hundred statues produced nothing statelier than that walking statue; the ideal of the self-commanding man. Hellas of the hundred statues was one legend and literature; and all that labyrinth of little walled nations resounding with the lament of Troy.

A later legend, an afterthought but not an accident, said that stragglers from Troy founded a republic on the Italian shore. It was true in spirit that republican virtue had such a root. A mystery of honour, that was not born of Babylon or the Egyptian pride, there shone like the shield of Hector, defying Asia and Africa; till the light of a new day was loosened, with the rushing of the eagles and the coming of the name; the name that came like a thunderclap when the world woke to Rome.

4
GOD AND COMPARATIVE RELIGION

I WAS ONCE ESCORTED over the Roman foundations of an ancient British city by a professor, who said something that seems to me a satire on a good many other professors. Possibly the professor saw the joke, though he maintained an iron gravity, and may or may not have realised that it was a joke against a great deal of what is called comparative religion. I pointed out a sculpture of the head of the sun with the usual halo of rays, but with the difference that the face in the disc, instead of being boyish like Apollo, was bearded like Neptune or Jupiter. 'Yes,' he said with a certain delicate exactitude, 'that is supposed to represent the local god Sul. The best authorities identify Sul with Minerva; but this has been held to show that the identification is not complete.'

That is what we call a powerful understatement. The modern world is madder than any satires on it; long ago Mr. Belloc made his burlesque don say that a bust of Ariadne had been proved by modern research to be a Silenus. But that is not better than the real appearance of Minerva as the Bearded Woman of Mr. Barnum. Only both of them are very like many identifications by 'the best authorities' on comparative religion; and when Catholic creeds are identified with various wild myths, I do not laugh or curse or misbehave myself; I confine myself decorously to saying that the identification is not complete.

In the days of my youth the Religion of Humanity was a term commonly applied to Comtism, the theory of certain rationalists who worshipped corporate mankind as a Supreme Being. Even in the days of my youth, I remarked that there was something slightly odd about despising and dismissing the doctrine of the Trinity as a mystical and even maniacal contradiction; and then asking us to adore a deity who is a hundred million persons in one God, neither confounding the persons nor dividing the substance.

But there is another entity, more or less definable and much more imaginable than the many-headed and monstrous idol of mankind. And it has a much better right to be called, in a reasonable sense, the religion of humanity. Man is not indeed the idol; but man is almost everywhere the idolater. And these multitudinous idolatries of mankind have something about them in many ways more human and sympathetic than modern metaphysical abstractions. If an Asiatic god has three heads and seven arms, there is at least in it an idea of material incarnation bringing an unknown power nearer to us and not further away. But if our friends Brown, Jones, and Robinson, when out for a Sunday walk, were transformed and amalgamated into an Asiatic idol before our eyes, they would surely seem farther away. If the arms of Brown and the legs of Robinson waved from the same composite body, they would seem to be waving something of a sad farewell. If the heads of all three gentlemen appeared smiling on the same neck, we should hesitate even by what name to address our new and somewhat abnormal friend. In the many headed and many handed Oriental idol there, is a certain sense of mysteries becoming at least partly intelligible; of formless forces of nature taking some dark but material form, but though this be true of the multiform god it is not so of the multiform man. The human beings become less human by becoming less separate; we might say less human in being less lonely. The human beings become less intelligible as they become less isolated; we might say with strict truth that the closer they are to us the farther they are away. An Ethical Hymn book of this humanitarian sort of religion was carefully selected and expurgated on the principle of preserving anything human and eliminating anything divine. One consequence was that a hymn appeared in the amended form of 'Nearer Mankind to Thee, Nearer to Thee.' It always suggested to the sensations of a strap-hanger during a crush on the Tube. But it is strange and wonderful how far away the souls of men can seem, when their bodies are so near as all that.

The human unity with which I deal here is not to be confounded with this modern industrial monotony and herding, which is rather a Congestion than a communion. It is a thing to which human groups left to themselves, and even human individuals left to themselves, have every-where tended by an instinct that may truly be called hu-man. Like all healthy human things, it has varied very much within the limits of a general character, for that is characteristic of everything belonging to that ancient land of liberty that lies before and around the servile industrial town. Industrialism actually boasts that its products are all of one pattern; that men in Jamaica or Japan can break the same seal and drink the same bad whiskey, that a man at the North Pole and another at the South might recognise the same optimistic label on the same dubious tinned salmon. But wine, the gift of gods to men, can vary with every valley and every vineyard, can turn into a hundred wines without any wine once reminding us of whiskey; and cheeses can change from county to county without forget-ting the difference between chalk and cheese. When I am speaking of this thing, therefore, I am speaking of some-thing that doubtless includes very wide differences; never-theless I will here maintain that it is one thing. I will main-tain that most of the modern botheration comes from not realising that it is really one thing. I will advance the thesis that before all talk about comparative religion and the separate religious founders of the world, the first essential is to recognise this thing as a whole, as a thing almost na-tive and normal to the great fellowship that we call man-kind. This thing is paganism; and I propose to show in these pages that it is the one real rival to the Church of Christ.

Comparative religion is very comparative indeed. That is, it is so much a matter of degree and distance and difference that it is only comparatively successful when it tries to compare. When we come to look at it closely we find it comparing things that are really quite incomparable. We are accustomed to see a table or catalogue of the world's great religions in parallel columns, until we fancy they are really parallel. We are accustomed to see the names of the great religious founders all in a row: Christ; Mahomet; Buddha; Confucius. But in truth this is only a trick; another of these optical illusions by which any objects may be put into a particular relation by shifting to a particular point of sight. Those religions and religious founders, or rather those whom we choose to lump together as religions and religious founders, do not really show any common character. The illusion is partly produced by Islam coming immediately after Christianity in the list; as Islam did come after Christianity and was largely an imitation of Christianity. But the other eastern religions, or what we call religions, not only do not resemble the Church but do not resemble each other. When we come to Confucianism at the end of the list, we come to something in a totally different world of thought. To compare the Christian and Confucian religions is like comparing a theist with an English squire or asking whether a man is a believer in immortality or a hundred-per-cent American. Confucianism may be a civilisation but it is not a religion.

In truth the Church is too unique to prove herself unique. For most popular and easy proof is by parallel and here there is no parallel. It is not easy, therefore, to expose the fallacy by which a false classification is created to swamp a unique thing when it really is a unique thing. As there is nowhere else exactly the same fact so there is nowhere else exactly the same fallacy. But I will take the nearest thing I can find to such a solitary social phenomenon in order to show how it is thus swamped and assimilated. I imagine most of us would agree that there is something unusual and unique about the position of the Jews. There is nothing that is quite in the same sense an international nation; an ancient culture scattered in different countries but still distinct and indestructible. Now this business is like an attempt to make a list of Nomadic Nations in order to soften the strange solitude of the Jew. It would be easy enough to do it by the same process of putting a plausible approximation first and then tailing off to totally different things thrown in somehow to make up the list. Thus in the new list of nomadic nations the Jews would be followed by the Gypsies; who at least are really nomadic if they are not really national. Then the professor of the new science of Comparative Nomadics could pass easily on to something different; even if it was very different. He could remark on the wandering adventure of the English who had scattered their colonies over so many seas and call *them* nomads. It is quite true that a great many Englishmen seem to be strangely restless in England. It is quite true that not all of them have left their country for their country's good. The moment we mention the wandering empire of the English, we must add the strange exiled empire of the Irish. For it is a curious fact, to be noted in our imperial literature, that the same ubiquity and unrest which is a proof of English enterprise and triumph is a proof of Irish futility and failure. Then the professor of Nomadism would look round thoughtfully and remember that there was great talk recently of German waiters, German barbers, German clerks, Germans naturalising themselves in England and the United States and the South American republics. The Germans would go down as the fifth nomadic race; the words Wanderlust and FolkWandering would come in very useful here. For there really have been historians who explained the Crusades by suggesting that the Germans were found wandering (as the police say) in what happened to be the neighbourhood of Palestine. Then the professor, feeling he was now near the end, would make a last leap in desperation. He would recall the fact that the French army has captured nearly every capital in Europe, that it marched across countless conquered lands under Charlemagne or Napoleon; and *that* would be wanderlust and *that* would be the note of a no-

madic race. Thus he would have his six nomadic nations all
compact and complete and would feel that the Jew was no
longer a sort of mysterious and even mystical exception.
But people with more common sense would probably realise that he had only extended nomadism by extending the
meaning of nomadism; and that he had extended that until
it really had no meaning at all. It is quite true that the
French soldier has made some of the finest marches in all
military history. But it is equally true, and far more self-
evident, that if the French peasant is not a rooted reality
there is no such thing as a rooted reality in the world; or in
other words, if he is a nomad there is nobody who is not a
nomad.

Now that is the sort of trick that has been tried in the
case of comparative religion and the world's religious
founders all standing respectably in a row. It seeks to classify Jesus as the other would classify Jews, by inventing a
new class for the purpose and filling up the rest of it with
stop-gaps and second-rate copies. I do not mean that these
other things are not often great things in their own real
character and class. Confucianism and Buddhism are great
things, but it is not true to call them Churches; just as the
French and English are great peoples, but it is nonsense to
call them nomads. There are some points of resemblance
between Christendom and its imitation in Islam; for that
matter there are some points of resemblance between Jews
and Gypsies. But after that the lists are made up of anything that comes to hand; of anything that can be put in
the same catalogue without being in the same category.

In this sketch of religious history, with all decent defer-
ence to men much more learned than myself, I propose to
cut across and disregard this modern method of classification, which I feel sure has falsified the facts of history. I
shall here submit an alternative classification of religion or
religions, which I believe would be found to cover all the
facts and, what is quite as important here, all the fancies.
Instead of dividing religion geographically and as it were
vertically, into Christian, Moslem, Brahmin, Buddhist, and

so on, I would divide it psychologically and in some sense horizontally, into the strata of spiritual elements and influences that could sometimes exist in the same country, or even in the same man. Putting the Church apart for the moment, I should be disposed to divide the natural religion of the mass of mankind under such headings as these: God; the Gods; the Demons; the Philosophers. I believe some such classification will help us to sort out the spiritual experiences of men much more successfully than the conventional business of comparing religions and that many famous figures will naturally fall into their place in this way who are only forced into their place in the other. As I shall make use of these titles or terms more than once in narrative and allusion, it will be well to define at this stage for what I mean them to stand. And I will begin with the first, the simplest and the most sublime, in this chapter.

In considering the elements of pagan humanity, we must begin by an attempt to describe the indescribable. Many get over the difficulty of describing it by the expedient of denying it, or at least ignoring it; but the whole point of it is that it was something that was never quite eliminated even when it was ignored. They are obsessed by their evolutionary monomania that every great thing grows from a seed, or something smaller than itself. They seem to forget that every seed comes from a tree, or from something larger than itself. Now there is very good ground for guessing that religion did not originally come from some detail that was forgotten because it was too small to be traced. Much more probably it was an idea that was abandoned because it was too large to be managed. There is very good reason to suppose that many people did begin with the simple but overwhelming idea of one God who governs all and afterwards fell away into such things as demon-worship almost as a sort of secret dissipation. Even the test of savage beliefs, of which the folk-lore students are so fond, is admittedly often found to support such a view. Some of the very rudest savages, primitive in every sense in which anthropologists use the word, the Australian aborigines for instance, are found to have a pure monotheism with a high moral tone. A missionary was preaching to a very wild tribe of polytheists, who had told him all their polytheistic tales, and telling them in return of the existence of the one good God who is a spirit and judges men by spiritual standards. And there was a sudden buzz, of excitement among these stolid barbarians, as at somebody who was letting out a secret, and they cried to each other, 'Atahocan! He is speaking of Atahocan!'

Probably it was a point of politeness and even decency among those polytheists not to speak of Atahocan. The name is not perhaps so much adapted as some of our own to direct and solemn religious exhortation; but many other social forces are always covering up and confusing such simple ideas. Possibly the old god stood for an old morality found irksome in more expansive moments; possibly intercourse with demons was more fashionable among the best people, as in the modern fashion of Spiritualism. Anyhow, there are any number of similar examples. They all testify to the unmistakable psychology of a thing taken for granted as distinct from a thing talked about. There is a striking example in a tale taken down word for word from a Red Indian in California, which starts out with hearty legendary and literary relish: 'The sun is the father and ruler of the heavens. He is the big chief. The moon is his wife and the stars are their children'; and so on through a most ingenious and complicated story, in the middle of which is a sudden parenthesis saying that the sun and moon have to do something because 'It is ordered that way by the Great Spirit Who lives above the place of all.' That is exactly the attitude of most paganism towards God. He is something assumed and forgotten and remembered by accident; a habit possibly not peculiar to pagans. Sometimes the higher deity is remembered in the higher moral grades and is a sort of mystery. But always, it has been truly said, the savage is talkative about his mythology and taciturn about his religion. The Australian savages, indeed, exhibit a topsy-turvydom such as the ancients might have thought truly worthy of the antipodes. The savage who thinks nothing of tossing off such a trifle as a tale of the sun and moon being the halves of a baby chopped in two, or dropping into small talk about a colossal cosmic cow milked to make the rain, merely in order to be sociable, will then retire to secret caverns sealed against women and white men, temples of terrible initiation where to the thunder of the bull-roarer and the dripping of sacrificial blood the priest whispers the final secrets, known only to the initiate: that honesty is the best policy, that a little kindness does nobody any harm, that all men are brothers and that there is but one God, the Father Almighty, maker of all things visible and invisible.

In other words, we have here the curiosity of religious history that the savage seems to be parading all the most repulsive and impossible parts of his belief and concealing all the most sensible and creditable parts. But the explanation is that they are not in that sense parts of his belief; or at least not parts of the same sort of belief. The myths are merely tall stories, though as tall as the sky, the waterspout, or the tropic rain. The mysteries are true stories, and are taken secretly that they may be taken seriously. Indeed it is only too easy to forget that there is a thrill in theism. A novel in which a number of separate characters all turned out to be the same character would certainly be a sensational novel. It is so with the idea that sun and tree and river are the disguises of one god and not of many. Alas, we also find it only too easy to take Atahocan for granted. But whether he is allowed to fade into a truism or preserved as a sensation by being preserved as a secret, it is clear that he is always either an old truism or an old tradition. There is nothing to show that he is an improved product of the mere mythology and everything to show that be preceded it. He is worshipped by the simplest tribes with no trace of ghosts or grave offerings or any of the complications in which Herbert Spencer and Grant Allen sought the origin of the simplest of all ideas. Whatever else there was, there was never any such thing as the

Evolution of the Idea of God. The idea was concealed, was avoided, was almost forgotten, was even explained away; but it was never evolved.

There are not a few indications of this change in other places. It is implied for instance in the fact that even polytheism seems often the combination of several monotheisms. A god will gain only a minor seat on Mount Olympus, when he had owned earth and heaven and all the stars while he lived in his own little valley. Like many a small nation melting in a great empire, he gives up local universality only to come under universal limitation. The very name of Pan suggests that he became a god of the wood when he had been a god of the world. The very name of Jupiter is almost a pagan translation of the words 'Our Father which art in heaven.' As with the Great Father symbolised by the sky, so with the Great Mother whom we still call Mother Earth. Demeter and Ceres and Cybele often seem to be almost incapable of taking over the whole business of godhood, so that men should need no other gods. It seems reasonably probable that a good many men did have no other gods but one of these, worshipped as the author of all.

Over some of the most immense and populous tracts of the world, such as China, it would seem that the simpler idea of the Great Father has never been very much complicated with rival cults, though it may have in some sense ceased to be a cult itself. The best authorities seem to think that though Confucianism is in one sense agnosticism, it does not directly contradict the old theism, precisely because it has become a rather vague theism. It is one in which God is called Heaven as in the case of polite persons tempted to swear in drawing rooms. But Heaven is still overhead, even if it is very far overhead. We have all the impression of a simple truth that has receded until it was remote without ceasing to be true. And this phrase alone would bring us back to the same idea even in the pagan mythology of the West. There is surely something of this very notion of the withdrawal of some higher power,

in all those mysterious and very imaginative myths about
the separation of earth and sky. In a hundred forms we are
told that heaven and earth were once lovers, or were once
at one, when some upstart thing, often some undutiful
child, thrust them apart; and the world was built on an
abyss; upon a division and a parting. One of its grossest
versions was given by Greek civilisation in the myth of
Uranus and Saturn. One of its most charming versions was
that of some savage Negroes who say that a little pepper-
plant grew taller and taller and lifted the whole sky like a
lid, a beautiful barbaric vision of daybreak for some of our
painters who love that tropical twilight. Of myths, and the
highly mythical explanations which the moderns offer of
myths, something will be said in another section; for I
cannot but think that most mythology is on another and
more superficial plane. But in this primeval vision of the
rending of one world into two there surely something
more of ultimate ideas. As to what it means, a man will
learn far more about it by lying on his back in a field and
merely looking at the sky than by reading all the libraries
even of the most learned and valuable folklore. He will
know what is meant by saying that the sky ought to be
nearer to us than it is, that perhaps it was once nearer than
it is, that it is not a thing merely alien and abysmal but in
some fashion sundered from us and saying farewell. There
will creep across his mind the curious suggestion that after
all, perhaps, the myth-maker was not merely a mooncalf or
village idiot thinking he could cut up the clouds like a cake,
but had in him something more than it is fashionable to
attribute to the Troglodyte, that it is just possible that
Thomas Hood was not talking like a Troglodyte when he
said that, as time went on, the tree-tops only told him he
was further off from heaven than when he was a boy. But
anyhow the legend of Uranus the Lord of Heaven de-
throned by Saturn the Time Spirit would mean something
to the author of that poem. And it would mean, among
other things, this banishment of the first fatherhood.
There is the idea of God in the very notion that there were

gods before the gods. There is an idea of greater simplicity in all the allusions to that more ancient order. The suggestion is supported by the process of propagation we see in historic times. Gods and demigods and heroes breed like herrings before our very eyes, and suggest of themselves that the family may have had one founder; mythology grows more and more complicated, and the very complication suggests that at the beginning it was more simple. Even on the external evidence, of the sort called scientific, there is therefore a very good case for the suggestion that man began with monotheism before it developed or degenerated into polytheism. But I am concerned rather with an internal than an external truth; and, as I have already said, the internal truth is almost indescribable. We have to speak of something of which it is the whole point that people did not speak of it; we have not merely to translate from a strange tongue or speech, but from a strange silence.

I suspect an immense implication behind all polytheism and paganism. I suspect we have only a hint of it here and there in these savage creeds or Greek origins. It is not exactly what we mean by the presence of God; in a sense it might more truly be called the absence of God. But absence does not mean nonexistence; and a man drinking the toast of absent friends does not mean that from his life all friendship is absent. It is a void but it is not a negation; it is something as positive as an empty chair. It would be an exaggeration to say that the pagan saw higher than Olympus, to an empty throne. It would be nearer the truth to take the gigantic imagery of the Old Testament, in which the prophet saw God from behind; it was as if some immeasurable presence had turned its back on the world. Yet the meaning will again be missed if it is supposed to be anything so conscious and vivid as the monotheism of Moses and his people. I do not mean that the pagan peoples were in the least overpowered by this idea merely because it is overpowering. On the contrary, it was so large that they all carried it lightly, as we all the load of the sky.

Gazing at some detail like a bird or a cloud, we can all ignore its awful blue background; we can neglect the sky;
and precisely because it bears down upon us with an annihilating force it is felt as nothing. A thing of this kind can
only be an impression and a rather subtle impression; but
to me it is a very strong impression made by pagan literature and religion. I repeat that in our special sacramental
sense there is, of course, the absence of the presence of
God. But there is in a very real sense the presence of the
absence of God. We feel it in the unfathomable sadness of
pagan poetry for I doubt if there was ever in all the marvellous manhood of antiquity a man who was happy as St.
Francis was happy. We feel it in the legend of a Golden
Age and again in the vague implication that the gods themselves are ultimately related to something else, even when
that Unknown God has faded into a Fate. Above all we
feel it in those immortal moments when the pagan literature seems to return to a more innocent antiquity and
speak with a more direct voice, so that no word is worthy
of it except our own monosyllable. We cannot say anything
but 'God' in a sentence like that of Socrates bidding farewell to his judges: 'I go to die and you remain to live; and
God alone knows which of us goes the better way.' We
can use no other word even for the best moments of Marcus Aurelius: 'Can say dear city of Cecrops, and canst thou
not say dear city of God?' We can use no other word in
that mighty line which Virgil spoke to all who suffer with
the veritable cry of a Christian before Christ: 'O, you that
have borne things more terrible to this also God shall give
an end.'

   In short there is a feeling that there is something higher
than the gods; but because it is higher it is also further
away. Not yet could even Virgil have read the riddle and
the paradox of that other divinity, who is both higher and
nearer. For them what was truly divine was very distant, so
distant that they dismissed it more and more from their
minds. It had less and less to do with the mere mythology
of which I shall write later. Yet even in this there was a

sort of tacit admission of its intangible purity, when we consider what most of the mythology is like. As the Jews would not degrade it by images, so the Greeks did not degrade it even by imaginations. When the gods were more and more remembered only by pranks and profligacies, it was relatively a movement of reverence. It was an act of piety to forget God. In other words, there is something in the whole tone of the time suggesting that men had accepted a lower level, and still were half conscious that it was a lower level. It is hard to find words for these things; yet the one really just word stands ready. These men were conscious of the Fall if they were conscious of nothing else; and the same is true of all heathen humanity. Those who have fallen may remember the fall, even when they forget the height. Some such tantalising blank or break in memory is at the back of all pagan sentiment. There is such a thing as the momentary power to remember that we forget. And the most ignorant of humanity know by the very look of earth that they have forgotten heaven. But it remains true that even for these men there were moments like the memories of childhood, when they heard themselves talking with a simpler language; there were moments when the Roman, like Virgil in the line already quoted, cut his way with a sword-stroke of song out of the tangle of the mythologies; the motley mob of gods and goddesses sank suddenly out of sight and the Sky-Father was alone in the sky.

This latter example is very relevant to the next step in the process. A white light as of a lost morning still lingers on the figure of Jupiter, of Pan or of the elder Apollo; and it may well be, as already noted, that each was once a divinity as solitary as Jehovah or Allah. They lost this lonely universality by a process it is here very necessary to note; a process of amalgamation very like what was afterwards called syncretism. The whole pagan world set itself to build a Pantheon. They admitted more and more gods, gods not only of the Greeks but of the barbarians; gods not only of Europe but of Asia and Africa. The more the merrier, though some of the Asian and African ones were not very merry. They admitted them to equal thrones with their own; sometimes they identified them with their own. They may have regarded it as an enrichment of their religious life; but it meant the final loss of all that we now call religion. It meant that ancient light of simplicity, that had a single source like the sun, finally fades away in a dazzle of conflicting lights and colours. God is really sacrificed to the Gods; in a very literal sense of the flippant phrase, they have been too many for him.

Polytheism, therefore, was really a sort of pool; in the sense of the pagans having consented to the pooling of their pagan religions. And this point is very important in many controversies ancient and modern. It is regarded as a liberal and enlightened thing to say that the god of the stranger may be as good as our own; and doubtless the pagans thought themselves very liberal and enlightened when they agreed to add to the gods of the city or the hearth some wild and fantastic Dionysus coming down from the mountains or some shaggy and rustic Pan creeping out of the woods. But exactly what it lost by these larger ideas is the largest idea of all. It is the idea of the fatherhood that makes the whole world one. And the converse is also true. Doubtless those more antiquated men of antiquity who clung to their solitary statues and their single sacred names were regarded as superstitious savages benighted and left behind. But these superstitious savages were preserving something that is much more like the cosmic power as conceived by philosophy, or even as conceived by science. This paradox by which the rude reactionary was a sort of prophetic progressive has one consequence very much to the point. In a purely historical sense and apart from any other controversies in the same connection, it throws light, a single and a steady light, that shines from the beginning on a little and lonely people. In this paradox as in some riddle of religion of which the answer was sealed up for centuries, lies the mission and the meaning of the Jews.

It is true in this sense humanly speaking, that the world owes God to the Jews. It owes that truth to much that is blamed in the Jews, possibly to much that is blameable in the Jews. We have already noted the nomadic position of the Jews amid the other pastoral peoples upon the fringe of the Babylonian Empire, and something of that strange erratic course of theirs blazed across the dark territory of extreme antiquity, as they passed from the seat of Abraham and the shepherd princes into Egypt and doubled back into the Palestinian bills and held them against the Philistines from Crete and fell into captivity in Babylon; and yet again returned to their mountain city by the Zionist policy of the Persian conquerors; and so continued that amazing romance of restlessness of which we have not yet seen the end. But through all their wanderings, and especially through all their early wanderings, they did indeed carry the fate of the world in that wooden tabernacle, that held perhaps a featureless symbol and certainly an invisible god. We may say that one most essential feature was that it was featureless. Much as we may prefer that creative liberty which the Christian culture has declared and by which it has eclipsed even the arts of antiquity, we must not underrate the determining importance at the time of the Hebrew inhibition of images. It is a typical example of one of those limitations that did in fact preserve and perpetuate enlargement, like a wall built round a wide open space. The God who could not have a statue remained a spirit. Nor would his statue in any case have had the disarming dignity and grace of the Greek statues then or the Christian statues afterwards. He was living in a land of monsters. We shall have occasion to consider more fully what those monsters were, Moloch and Dagon and Tanit the terrible goddess. If the deity of Israel had ever had an image, he would have had a phallic image. By merely giving him a body they would have brought in all the worst elements of mythology; all the polygamy of polytheism; the vision of the harem in heaven. This point about the refusal of art is the first example of the limitations which are often ad-

versely criticised, only because the critics themselves are
limited. But an even stronger case can be found in the
other criticism offered by the same critics. It is often said
with a sneer that the God of Israel was only a God of Battles, 'a mere barbaric Lord of Hosts' pitted in rivalry
against other gods only as their envious foe. Well it is for
the world that he was a God of Battles. Well it is for us
that he was to all the rest only a rival and a foe. In the ordinary way, it would have been only too easy for them to
have achieved the desolate disaster of conceiving him as a
friend. It would have been only too easy for them to have
seen him stretching out his hands in love and reconciliation, embracing Baal and kissing the painted face of As-
tarte, feasting in fellowship with the gods; last god to sell
his crown of stars for the Soma of the Indian pantheon or
the nectar of Olympus or the mead of Valhalla. It would
have been easy enough for his worshippers, to follow the
enlightened course of Syncretism and the pooling of all the
pagan traditions. It is obvious indeed that his followers
were always sliding down this easy slope; and it required
the almost demoniac energy of certain inspired demagogues who testified to the divine unity in words that are
still like winds of inspiration and ruin. The more we really
understand of the ancient conditions that contributed to
the final culture of the Faith, the more we shall have a real
and even a realistic reverence for the greatness of the
Prophets of Israel. As it was, while the whole world melted
into this mass of confused mythology, this Deity who is
called tribal and narrow, precisely because he was what is
called tribal and narrow, preserved the primary religion of
all mankind. He was tribal enough to be universal. He was
as narrow as the universe.

In a word, there was a popular pagan god called Jupi-
ter-Ammon. There was never a god called Jehovah-
Ammon. There was never a god called Jehovah-Jupiter. If
there had there would certainly have been another called
Jehovah-Molach. Long before the liberal and enlightened
amalgamators had got so far afield as Jupiter, the image of

the Lord of Hosts would have been deformed out of all suggestion of monotheistic maker and ruler and would have become an Idol far worse than any savage fetish; for he might have been as civilised as the gods of Tyre and Carthage. What at that civilisation meant we shall consider more fully in the chapter that follows; when we note how the power of demons nearly destroyed Europe and even the heathen health of the world. But the world's destiny would have been distorted still more fatally if monotheism had failed in the Mosaic tradition. I hope in a subsequent section to show that I am not without sympathy with all that health in the heathen world that made its fairy-tales and its fanciful romances of religion. But I hope also to show that these were bound to fail in the long run and the world would have been lost if it had been unable to return to that great original simplicity of a single authority in all things. That we do preserve something of that primary simplicity, that poets and philosophers can still indeed in some sense say a Universal Prayer, that we live in a large and serene world under a sky that stretches paternally over all the peoples of the earth, that philosophy and philanthropy are truisms in a religion of reasonable men, all that we do most truly owe, under heaven, to a secretive and restless nomadic people; who bestowed on men the supreme and serene blessing of a jealous God.

The unique possession was not available or accessible to the pagan world, because it was also the possession of a jealous people. The Jews were unpopular, partly because of this narrowness already noted in the Roman world, partly perhaps because they had already fallen into that habit of merely handling things for exchange instead of working to make them with their hands. It was partly also because polytheism had become a sort of jungle in which solitary monotheism could be lost; but it is strange to realise how completely it really was lost. Apart from more disputed matters, there were things in the tradition of Israel which belong to all humanity now, and might have belonged to all humanity then. They had one of the colossal cornerstones of the world: the Book of Job. It obviously stands over against the Iliad and the Greek tragedies; and even more than they it was an early meeting and parting of poetry and philosophy in the morning of the world. It is a solemn and uplifting sight to see those two eternal fools, the optimist and the pessimist, destroyed in the dawn of time. And the philosophy really perfects the pagan tragic irony precisely because it is more monotheistic and therefore more mystical. Indeed the Book of Job avowedly only answers mystery with mystery. Job is comforted with riddles; but he is comforted. Herein is indeed a type, in the sense of a prophecy, of things speaking with authority. For when he who doubts can only say 'I do not understand,' it is true that he who knows can only reply or repeat 'You do not understand.' And under that rebuke there is a sudden hope in the heart; and the sense of something that would be worth understanding. But this mighty monotheistic poem remained unremarked by the whole world of antiquity, which thronged with polytheistic poetry. It is a sign of the way in which the Jews stood apart and kept their tradition unshaken and unshared, that they should have kept a thing like The Book of Job out of the whole intellectual world of antiquity. It is as if the Egyptians had modestly concealed the Great Pyramid. But there were other reasons for a cross-purpose and an impasse, characteristic of the whole of the end of paganism. After all, the tradition of Israel had only got hold of one-half of the truth, even if we use the popular paradox and call it the bigger half. I shall try to sketch in the next chapter that love of locality and of personality that ran through mythology; here it need only be said that there was a truth in it that could not be left out, though it were a lighter and less essential truth. The sorrow of Job had to be joined with the sorrow of Hector; and while the former was the sorrow of the universe the latter was the sorrow of the city; for Hector could only stand pointing to heaven as the pillar of holy Troy. When God speaks out of the whirlwind he may well speak in the wilderness. But the monotheism of the nomad was not

enough for all that varied civilisation of fields and fences
and walled cities and temples and towns; and the turn of
these things also was to come, when the two could be
combined in a more definite and domestic religion. Here
and there in all that pagan crowd could be found a philosopher whose thoughts ran on pure theism; but he never
had, or supposed that he had, the power to change the
customs of the whole populace. Nor is it easy even in such
philosophies to find a true definition of this deep business
of the relation of polytheism and theism. Perhaps the
nearest we can come to striking the note, or giving the
thing a name, is in something far away from all that civilisation and more remote from Rome than the isolation of
Israel. It is in a saying I once heard from some Hindu tradition, that gods as well as men are only the dreams of
Brahma; and will perish when Brahma wakes. There is indeed in such an image something of the soul of Asia which
is less sane than the soul of Christendom. We should call it
despair, even if they would call it peace. This note of nihil-
ism can be considered later in a fuller comparison between
Asia and Europe. It is enough to say here that there is
more of disillusion in that idea of a divine awakening than
is implied for us in the passage from mythology to religion.
But the symbol is very subtle and exact in one respect; that
it does suggest the disproportion and even disruption between the very ideas of mythology and religion; the chasm
between the two categories. It is really the collapse of
comparative religion that there is no comparison between
God and the gods. There is no more comparison than
there is between a man and the men who walked about in
his dreams. Under the next heading some attempt will be
made to indicate the twilight of that dream in which the
gods walk about like men. But if anyone fancies the contrast of monotheism and polytheism is only a matter of
some people having one god and others a few more, for
him it will be far nearer the truth to plunge into the elephantine extravagance of Brahmin cosmology; that he may
feel a shudder going through the veil of things, the many-

handed creators, and the throned and haloed animals and all the network of entangled stars and rulers of the night, as the awful eyes of Brahma open like dawn upon the death of all.

5

MAN AND MYTHOLOGIES

WHAT ARE HERE called the Gods might almost alternatively be called the Day-Dreams. To compare them to dreams is not to deny that dreams can come true. To compare them to travellers' tales is not to deny that they may be true tales, or at least truthful tales. In truth they are the sort of tales the traveller tells to himself. All this mythological business belongs to the poetical part of men. It seems strangely forgotten nowadays that a myth is a work of imagination and therefore a work of art. It needs a poet to make it. It needs a poet to criticise it. There are more poets than non-poets in the world, as is proved by the popular origin of such legends. But for some reason I have never heard explained, it is only the minority of un-poetical people who are allowed to write critical studies of these popular poems. We do not submit a sonnet to a mathematician or a song to a calculating boy; but we do indulge the equally fantastic idea that folklore can be treated as a science. Unless these things are appreciated artistically they are not appreciated at all. When the Professor is told by the Polynesian that once there was nothing except a great feathered serpent, unless the learned man feels a thrill and a half temptation to wish it were true, he is no judge of such things at all. When he is assured, on the best Red Indian authority, that a primitive hero carried the sun and moon and stars in a box, unless he clasps his hands and almost kicks his legs as a child would at such a charming fancy, he knows nothing about the matter. This test is not nonsensical; primitive children and barbaric children do laugh and kick like other children; and we must have a certain simplicity to re-picture the childhood of the world. When Hiawatha was told by his nurse that a warrior threw his grandmother up to the moon, he laughed like any English child told by his nurse that a cow jumped over the moon. The child sees the joke as well as most men, and better than some scientific men. But the ultimate test even of the fantastic is the appropriateness of the inappropriate. And the test must appear merely arbitrary because it is merely artistic. If any student tells me that the infant Hiawatha only laughed out of respect for the tribal custom of sacrificing the aged to economical housekeeping, I say he did not. If any scholar tells me that the cow jumped over the moon only because a heifer was sacrificed to Diana, I answer that it did not. It happened because it is obviously the right thing for a cow to jump over the moon. Mythology is a lost art, one of the few arts that really are lost; but it is an art. The horned moon and the horned mooncalf make a harmonious and almost a quiet pattern. And throwing your grandmother into the sky is not good behaviour, but it is perfectly good taste.

Thus scientists seldom understand, as artists understand, that one branch of the beautiful is the ugly. They seldom allow for the legitimate liberty of the grotesque. And they will dismiss a savage myth as merely coarse and clumsy and an evidence of degradation, because it has not all the beauty of the herald Mercury new lighted on a heaven-kissing hill; when it really has the beauty of the Mock Turtle or the Mad Hatter. It is the supreme proof of a man being prosaic that be always insists on poetry being poetical. Sometimes the humour is in the very subject as well as the style of the fable. The Australian aborigines, regarded as the rudest of savages, have a story about a giant frog who had swallowed the sea and all the waters of the world; and who was only forced to spill them by being made to laugh. All the animals with all their antics passed before him and, like Queen Victoria, he was not amused. He collapsed at last before an eel who stood delicately balanced on the tip of its tail, doubtless with a rather desperate dignity. Any amount of fine fantastic literature might be made out of that fable. There is philosophy in that vision of the dry world before the beatific Deluge of laughter. There is imagination in the mountainous monster erupting like an aqueous volcano; there is plenty of fun in the thought of his goggling visage as the pelican or the penguin passed by. Anyhow the frog laughed; but the folklore student remains grave.

Moreover, even where the fables are inferior as art, they cannot be properly judged by science; still less properly judged as science. Some myths are very crude and queer like the early drawings of children; but the child is trying to draw. It is none the less an error to treat his drawing as if it were a diagram, or intended to be a diagram. The student cannot make a scientific statement about the savage, because the savage is not making a scientific statement about the world. He is saying something quite different; what might be called the gossip of the gods. We may say, if we like, that it is believed before there is time to examine it. It would be truer to say it is accepted before there is time to believe it.

I confess I doubt the whole theory of the dissemination myths or (as it commonly is) of one myth. It is true that something in our nature and conditions makes many stories similar but each of them may be original. One man does not borrow the story from the other man, though he may tell it from the same motive as the other man. It would be easy to apply the whole argument about legend to literature; and turn it into a vulgar monomania of plagiarism. I would undertake to trace a notion like that of the Golden Bough through individual modern novels as easily as through communal and antiquated myths. I would undertake to find something like a bunch of flowers figuring again and again from the fatal bouquet of Becky Sharpe to the spray of roses sent by the princess of Ruritania. But though these flowers may spring from the same soil, it is not the same faded flower that is flung from hand to hand. Those flowers are always fresh.

The true origin of all the myths has been discovered

much too often. There are too many keys to mythology, as
there too many cryptograms in Shakespeare. Everything is
phallic; everything is totemistic; everything is seed-time
and harvest everything is ghosts and grave-offerings; everything is the golden bough of sacrifice; everything is the
sun and moon; everything is everything. Every folk-lore
student who knew a little more than his own monomania,
every man of wider reading and critical culture like Andrew
Lang, has practically confessed that the bewilderment of
these things left his brain spinning. Yet the whole trouble
comes from a man trying to look at these stories from the
outside, as if they were scientific objects. He has only to
look at them from the inside, and ask himself bow be
would begin a story. A story may start with anything and
go anywhere. It may start with a bird without the bird being a totem; it may start with the sun without being a solar
myth. It is said there are only ten plots in the world; and
there will certainly be common and recurrent elements. Set
ten thousand children talking at once, and telling tarradid-
dles about what they did in the wood, and it will not be
hard to find parallels suggesting sun-worship or animal-
worship. Some of the stories may be pretty and some silly
and some perhaps dirty; but they can only be judged as
stories. In the modern dialect, they can only be judged aes-
thetically. It is strange that aesthetics, or mere feeling,
which is now allowed to usurp where it has no rights at all,
to wreck reason with pragmatism and morals with anarchy,
is apparently not allowed to give a purely aesthetic judgment on what is obviously a purely aesthetic question. We
may be fanciful about everything except fairy-tales.

Now the first fact is that the most simple people have
the most subtle ideas. Everybody ought to know that, for
everybody has been a child. Ignorant as a child is, he
knows more than be can say and feels not only atmospheres but fine shades. And in this matter there are several
fine shades. Nobody understands it who has not had what
can only be called the ache of the artist to find some sense
and some story in the beautiful things he sees; his hunger

for secrets and his anger at any tower or tree escaping with its tale untold. He feels that nothing is perfect unless it is personal. Without that the blind unconscious beauty of the world stands in its garden like a headless statue. One need only be a very minor poet to have wrestled with the tower or the tree until it spoke like a titan or a dryad. It is often said that pagan mythology was a personification of the powers of nature. The phrase is true in a sense, but it is very unsatisfactory; because it implies that the forces are abstractions and the personification is artificial. Myths are not allegories. Natural powers are not in this case abstractions. It is not as if there were a God of Gravitation. There may be a genius of the waterfall; but not of mere falling, even less than of mere water. The impersonation is not of something impersonal. The point is that the personality perfects the water with significance. Father Christmas is not an allegory of snow and holly; he is not merely the stuff called snow afterwards artificially given a human form, like a snow man. He is something that gives a new meaning to the white world and the evergreens, so that the snow itself seems to be warm rather than cold. The test, therefore, is purely imaginative. But imaginative does not mean imaginary. It does not follow that it is all what the moderns call subjective, when they mean false. Every true artist does feel, consciously or unconsciously, that he is touching transcendental truths; that his images are shadows of things seen through the veil. In other words, the natural mystic does know that there is something *there*; something behind the clouds or within the trees; but he believes that the pursuit of beauty is the way to find it; that imagination is a sort of incantation that can call it up.

Now we do not comprehend this process in ourselves, far less in our most remote fellow-creatures. And the danger of these things being classified is that they may seem to be comprehended. A really fine work of folklore, like *The Golden Bough*, will leave too many readers with the idea, for instance, that this or that story of a giant's or wizard's heart in a casket or a cave only means some stupid and

static superstition called the external soul. But we do not
know what these things mean, simply because we do not
know what we ourselves mean when we are moved by
them. Suppose somebody in a story says 'Pluck this flower
and a princess will die in a castle beyond the sea,' we do
not know why something stirs in the subconsciousness, or
why what is impossible seems almost inevitable. Suppose
we read, 'And in the hour when the King extinguished the
candle his ships were wrecked far away on the coast of
Hebrides.' We do not know why the imagination has accepted that image before the reason can reject it; or why
such correspondences seem really to correspond to something in the soul. Very deep things in our nature, some dim
sense of the dependence of great things upon small, some
dark suggestion that the things nearest to us stretch far
beyond our power, some sacramental feeling of the magic
in material substances, and many more emotions past finding out, are in an idea like that of the external soul. The
power even in the myths of savages is like the power in the
metaphors of poets. The soul of such a metaphor is often
very emphatically an external soul. The best critics have
remarked that in the best poets the simile is often a picture
that seems quite separate from the text. It is as irrelevant as
the remote castle to the flower or the Hebridean coast to
the candle. Shelley compares the skylark to a young
woman on a turret, to a rose embedded in thick foliage, to
a series of things that seem to be about as unlike a skylark
in the sky as anything we can imagine. I suppose the most
potent piece of pure magic in English literature is the
much quoted passage in Keats's *Nightingale* about the
casements opening on the perilous foam. And nobody no-
tices that the image seems to come from nowhere; that it
appears abruptly after some almost equally irrelevant remarks about Ruth; and that it has nothing in the world to
do with the subject of the poem. If there is one place in
the world where nobody could reasonably expect to find a
nightingale, it is on a window-sill at the seaside. But it is
only in the same sense that nobody would expect to find a

giant's heart in a casket under the sea. Now, it would be very dangerous to classify the metaphors of the poets. When Shelley says that the cloud will rise 'like a child from the womb, like a ghost from the tomb,' it would be quite possible to call the first a case of the coarse primitive birth-myth and the second a survival of the ghost worship which became ancestor-worship. But it is the wrong way of dealing with a cloud; and is liable to leave the learned in the condition of Polonius, only too ready to think it like a weasel, or very like a whale.

Two facts follow from this psychology of day-dreams, which must be kept in mind throughout their development in mythologies and even religions. First, these imaginative impressions are often strictly local. So far from being abstractions turned into allegories, they are often images almost concentrated into idols. The poet feels the mystery of a particular forest not of the science of afforestation or the department of woods and forests. He worships the peak of a particular mountain, not the abstract idea of altitude. So we find the god is not merely water but often one special river; he may be the sea because the sea is single like a stream; the river that runs round the world. Ultimately doubtless many deities are enlarged into elements; but they are something more than omnipresent. Apollo does not merely dwell wherever the sun shines; his home is on the rock of Delphi. Diana is great enough to be in three places at once, earth and heaven and hell, but greater is Diana of the Ephesians. This localised feeling has its lowest form in the mere fetish or talisman, such as millionaires put on their motor-cars. But it can also harden into something like a high and serious religion, where it is connected with high and serious duties; into the gods of the city or even the gods of the hearth.

The second consequence is this; that in these pagan cults there is every shade of sincerity – and insincerity. In what sense exactly did an Athenian really think he had to sacrifice to Pallas Athene? What scholar is really certain of the answer? In what sense did Dr. Johnson really think that he had to touch all the posts in the street or that he had to collect orange-peel? In what sense does a child really think that he ought to step on every alternate paving stone? Two things are at least fairly clear. First, in simpler and less self-conscious times these forms could become more solid without really becoming more serious. Day-dreams could be acted in broad daylight, with more liberty of artistic expression; but still perhaps with something of the light step of the somnambulist. Wrap Dr. Johnson in an antique mantle, crown him (by his kind permission) with a garland, and he will move in state under those ancient skies of morning; touching a series of sacred posts carved with the heads of the strange terminal gods, that stand at the limits of the land and of the life of man. Make the child free of the marbles and mosaics of some classic temple, to play on a whole floor inlaid with squares of black and white; and he will willingly make this fulfilment of his idle and drifting day-dream the clear field for a grave and graceful dance. But the posts and the paving-stones are little more and little less real than they are under modern limits. They are not really much more serious for being taken seriously. They have the sort of sincerity that they always had; the sincerity of art as a symbol that expresses very real spiritualities under the surface of life. But they are only sincere in the same sense as art; not sincere in the same sense as morality. The eccentric's collection of orange-peel may turn to oranges in a Mediterranean festival or to golden apples in a Mediterranean myth. But they are never on the same plane with the difference between giving the orange to a blind beggar and carefully placing the orange-peel so that the beggar may fall and break his leg. Between these two things there is a difference of kind and not of degree. The child does not think it wrong to step on the paving-stone as he thinks it wrong to step on the dog's tail. And it is very certain that whatever jest or sentiment or fancy first set Johnson touching the wooden posts, he never touched wood with any of the feeling with which he stretched out his hands to the timber of that terrible tree, which was the death of God and the life of man.

As already noted, this does not mean that there was no reality or even no religious sentiment in such a mood. As a matter of fact the Catholic Church has taken over with uproarious success the whole of this popular business of giving people local legends and lighter ceremonial movements. In so far as all this sort of paganism was innocent and in touch with nature, there is no reason why it should not be patronised by patron saints as much as by pagan gods. And in any case there are degrees of seriousness in the most natural make-believe. There is all the difference between fancying there are fairies in the wood, which often only means fancying a certain wood as fit for fairies, and really frightening ourselves until we walk a mile rather than pass a house we have told ourselves is haunted. Behind all these things is the fact that beauty and terror are very real things and related to a real spiritual world; and to touch them at all, even in doubt or fancy, is to stir the deep things of the soul. We all understand that and the pagans understood it. The point is that paganism did not really stir the soul except with these doubts and fancies; with the consequence that we today can have little beyond doubts and fancies about paganism. All the best critics agree that all the greatest poets, in pagan Hellas for example, had an attitude towards their gods which is quite queer and puzzling to men in the Christian era. There seems to be an admitted conflict between the god and the man; but everybody seems to be doubtful about which is the hero and which is the villain. This doubt does not merely apply to a doubter like Euripides in the Bacchae; it applies to a moderate conservative like Sophocles in the Antigone; or even to a regular Tory and reactionary like Aristophanes in the Frogs. Sometimes it would seem that the Greeks believed above all things in reverence, only they had nobody to revere. But the point of the puzzle is this: that all this vagueness and variation arise from the fact that the whole thing began in fancy and in dreaming; and that there are no rules of architecture for a castle in the clouds.

This is the mighty and branching tree called mythology which ramifies round the whole world whose remote branches under separate skies bear like coloured birds the costly idols of Asia and the half-baked fetishes of Africa and the fairy kings and princesses of the folk-tales of the forest and buried amid vines and olives the Lares of the Latins, and carried on the clouds of Olympus the buoyant supremacy of the gods of Greece. These are the myths and he who has no sympathy with myths has no sympathy with men. But he who has most Sympathy with myths will most fully realise that they are not and never were a religion, in the sense that Christianity or even Islam is a religion. They satisfy some of the needs satisfied by a religion; and notably the need for doing certain things at certain dates; the need of the twin ideas of festivity and formality. But though they provide a man with a calendar they do not provide him with a creed. A man did not stand up and say 'I believe in Jupiter and Juno and Neptune,' etc., and she stands up and says 'I believe in God the Father Almighty' and the rest of the Apostles' Creed. Many believed in some and not in others, or more in some and less in others, or only in a very vague poetical sense in any. There was no moment when they were all collected into an orthodox order which men would fight and be tortured to keep intact. Still less did anybody ever say in that fashion: 'I believe in Odin and Thor and Freya,' for outside Olympus even the Olympian order grows cloudy and chaotic. It seems clear to me that Thor was not a god at all but a hero. Nothing resembling a religion would picture anybody resembling a god as groping like a pigmy in a great cavern, that turned out to be the glove of a giant. That is the glorious ignorance called adventure. Thor may have been a great adventurer; but to call him a god is like trying to compare Jehovah with Jack and the Beanstalk. Odin seems to have been a real barbarian chief, possibly of the Dark Ages after Christianity. Polytheism fades away at its fringes into fairy-tales or barbaric memories; it is not a thing like monotheism as held by serious monotheists. Again, it does satisfy the need to cry out on some uplifted name, or some noble memory in moments that are themselves noble and uplifted, such as the birth of a child or the saving of a city. But the name was so used by many to whom it was only a name. Finally it did satisfy, or rather it partially satisfied, a thing very deep in humanity indeed; the idea of surrendering something as the portion of the unknown powers; of pouring out wine upon the ground, of throwing a ring into the sea; in a word, of sacrifice. It is the wise and worthy idea of not taking our advantage to the full; of putting something in the other balance to ballast our dubious pride, of paying tithes to nature for our land. This deep truth of the danger of insolence, or being too big for our boots, runs through all the great Greek tragedies and makes them great. But it runs side by side with an almost cryptic agnosticism about the real nature of the gods to be propitiated. Where that gesture of surrender is most magnificent, as among the great Greeks, there is really much more idea that the man will be the better for losing the ox than that the god will be the better for getting it. It is said that in its grosser forms there are often actions grotesquely suggestive of the god really eating the sacrifice. But this fact is falsified by the error that I put first in this note on mythology. It is misunderstanding the psychology of daydreams. A child pretending there is a goblin in a hollow tree will do a crude and material thing like leaving a piece of cake for him. A poet might do a more dignified and elegant thing, like bringing to the god fruits as well as flowers. But the degree of *seriousness* in both acts may be the same or it may vary in almost any degree. The crude fancy is no more a creed than the ideal fancy is a creed. Certainly the pagan does not disbelieve like an atheist, any more than he believes like a Christian. He feels the presence of powers about which he guesses and invents. St. Paul said that the Greeks had one altar to an unknown god. But in truth all their gods were unknown gods. And the real break in history did come when St. Paul declared to them whom they had worshipped.

The substance of all such paganism may be summa-
rised thus. It is an attempt to reach the divine reality
through the imagination alone; in its own field reason does
not restrain it all. It is vital to the view of all history that
reason is something separate from religion even in the
most rational of these civilisations. It is only as an afterthought, when such cults are decadent or on the defensive,
that a few Neo-Platonists or a few Brahmins are found
trying to rationalise them, and even then only by trying to
allegorise them. But in reality the rivers mythology and
philosophy run parallel and do not mingle till they meet in
the sea of Christendom. Simple secularists still talk as if the
Church had introduced a sort of schism between reason
and religion. The truth is that the Church was actually the
first thing that ever tried to combine reason and religion.
There had never before been any such union of the priests
and the philosophers. Mythology, then, sought God
through the imagination; or sought truth by means of
beauty, in the sense in which beauty includes much of the
most grotesque ugliness. But the imagination has its own
laws and therefore its own triumphs, which neither logi-
cians nor men of science can understand. It remained true
to that imaginative instinct through a thousand extrava-
gances, through every crude cosmic pantomime of a pig
eating the moon or the world being cut out of a cow,
through all the dizzy convolutions and mystic malforma-
tions of Asiatic art, through all the stark and staring rigidity
of Egyptian and Assyrian portraiture, through every kind
of cracked mirror of mad art that seemed to deform the
world and displace the sky, it remained true to something
about which there can be no argument; something that
makes it possible for some artist of some school to stand
suddenly still before that particular deformity and say, 'My
dream has come true.' Therefore do we all in fact feel that
pagan or primitive myths are infinitely suggestive, so long
as we are wise enough not to inquire what they suggest.
Therefore we all feel what is meant by Prometheus stealing
fire from heaven, until some prig of a pessimist or pro-

gressive person explains what it means. Therefore we all
know the meaning of Jack and the Beanstalk, until we are
told. In this sense it is true that it is the ignorant who accept myths, but only because it is the ignorant who appreciate poems. Imagination has its own laws and triumphs;
and a tremendous power began to clothe its images,
whether images in the mind or in the mud, whether in the
bamboo of the South Sea Islands or the marble of the
mountains of Hellas. But there was always a trouble in the
triumph, which in these pages I have tried to analyse in
vain; but perhaps I might in conclusion state it thus.

The crux and crisis is that man found it natural to worship; even natural to worship unnatural things. The pos-
ture of the idol might be stiff and strange; but the gesture
of the worshipper was generous and beautiful. He not only
felt freer when he bent; he actually felt taller when he
bowed. Henceforth anything that took away the gesture of
worship would stunt and even maim him forever. Henceforth being merely secular would be a servitude and an
inhibition. If man cannot pray he is gagged; if he cannot
kneel be is in irons. We therefore feel throughout the
whole of paganism a curious double feeling of trust and
distrust. When the man makes the gesture of salutation
and of sacrifice, when he pours out the libation or lifts up
the sword, he knows he is doing a worthy and a virile
thing. He knows he is doing one of the things for which a
man was made. His imaginative experiment is therefore
justified. But precisely because it began with imagination,
there is to the end something of mockery in it, and especially in the object of it. This mockery, in the more intense
moments of the intellect, becomes the almost intolerable
irony of Greek tragedy. There seems a disproportion between the priest and the altar or between the altar and the
god. The priest seems more solemn and almost more sacred than the god. All the order of the temple is solid and
sane and satisfactory to certain parts of our nature; except
the very centre of it, which seems strangely mutable and
dubious, like a dancing flame. It is the first thought round

which the whole has been built; and the first thought is still
a fancy and almost a frivolity. In that strange place of
meeting, the man seems more statuesque than the statue.
He himself can stand forever in the noble and natural attitude of the statue of the Praying Boy. But whatever name
be written on the pedestal, whether Zeus or Ammon or
Apollo, the god whom he worships is Proteus.

The Praying Boy may be said to express a need rather
than to satisfy a need. It is by a normal and necessary action that his hands are lifted; but it is no less a parable that
his hands are empty. About the nature of that need there
will be more to say, but at this point it may be said that
perhaps after all this true instinct, that prayer and sacrifice
are a liberty and an enlargement, refers back to that vast
and half-forgotten conception of universal fatherhood,
which we have already seen everywhere fading from the
morning sky. This is true; and yet it is not all the truth.
There remains an indestructible instinct, in the poet as represented by the pagan, that he is not entirely wrong in lo-
calising his God. It is something in the soul of poetry if
not of piety. And the greatest of poets, when he defined
the poet, did not say that he gave us the universe or the
absolute or the infinite; but, in his own larger language, a
local habitation and a name. No poet is merely a pantheist;
those who are counted most pantheistic, like Shelley, start
with some local and particular image as the pagans did.
After all, Shelley wrote of the skylark because it was a skylark. You could not issue an imperial or international translation of it for use in South Africa, in which it was changed
to an ostrich. So the mythological imagination moves as it
were in circles, hovering either to find a place or to return
to it. In a word, mythology is a *search*; it is something that
combines a recurrent desire with a recurrent doubt, mixing
a most hungry sincerity in the idea of seeking for a place
with a most dark and deep and mysterious levity about all
the places found. So far could the lonely imagination lead,
and we must turn later to the lonely reason. Nowhere
along this road did the two ever travel together.

That is where all these things differed from religion or the reality in which these different dimensions met in a sort of solid. They differed from the reality not in what they looked like but in what they were. A picture may look like a landscape, may look in every detail exactly like a landscape. The only detail in which it differs is that it is not a landscape. The difference is only that which divides a portrait of Queen Elizabeth from Queen Elizabeth. Only in this mythical and mystical world the portrait could exist before the person; and the portrait was therefore more vague and doubtful. But anybody who has felt and fed on the atmosphere of these myths will know what I mean, when I say that in one sense they did not really profess to be realities. The pagans had dreams about realities; and they would have been the first to admit, in their own words, that some came through the gate of ivory and others through the gate of horn. The dreams do indeed tend to be very vivid dreams when they touch on those tender or tragic things, which can really make a sleeper awaken with the sense that his heart has been broken in his sleep. They tend continually to hover over certain passionate themes of meeting and parting, of a life that ends in death or a death that is the beginning of life. Demeter wanders over a stricken world looking for a stolen child; Isis stretches out her arms over the earth in vain to gather the limbs of Osiris; and there is lamentation upon the hills for Atys and through the woods for Adonis. There mingles with all such mourning the mystical and profound sense that death can be a deliverer and an appeasement; that such death gives us a divine blood for a renovating river and that all good is found in gathering the broken body of the god. We may truly call these fore-shadowing; so long as we remember that fore-shadowing are shadows. And the metaphor of a shadow happens to hit very exactly the truth that is very vital here. For a shadow is a shape but not texture. These things are something *like* the real thing; and to say that they were like is to say that they were different. Saying something is like a dog is another way of

saying it is not a dog; and it is in this sense of identity that
a myth is not a man. Nobody really thought of Isis as a
human being; nobody really thought of Demeter as a historical character, nobody thought of Adonis as the founder
of a Church. There was no idea that any one of them had
changed the world; but rather that their recurrent death
and life bore the sad and beautiful burden of the change-
lessness of the world. Not one of them was a revolution,
save in the sense of the revolution of the sun and moon.
Their whole meaning is missed if we do not see that they
mean the shadows that we are and the shadows that we
pursue. In certain sacrificial and communal aspects they
naturally suggest what sort of a god might satisfy men; but
they do not profess to be satisfied. Anyone who says they
do is a bad judge of poetry.

Those who talk about pagan Christs have less sympathy
with paganism than with Christianity. Those who call these
cults 'religions', and 'compare' them with the certitude and
challenge of the Church have much less appreciation than
we have of what made heathenism human, or of why classic literature is still something that hangs in the air like a
song. It is no very human tenderness for the hungry to
prove that hunger is the same as food. It is no very genial
understanding of youth to argue that hope destroys the
need for happiness. And it is utterly unreal to argue that
these images in the mind, admired entirely in the abstract,
were even in the same world with a living man and a living
polity that were worshipped because they were concrete.
We might as well say that a boy playing at robbers is the
same as a man in his first day in the trenches; or that a
boy's first fancies about 'the not impossible she' are the
same as the sacrament of marriage. They are fundamentally
different exactly where they are superficially similar; we
might almost say they are not the same even when they are
the same. They are only different because one is real and
the other is not. I do not mean merely that I myself believe
that one is true and the other is not. I mean that one was
never meant to be true in the same sense as the other. The

sense in which it was meant to be true I have tried to suggest vaguely here, but it is undoubtedly very subtle and almost indescribable. It is so subtle that the students who profess to put it up as a rival to our religion miss the whole meaning and purport of their own study. We know better than the scholars, even those of us who are no scholars, what was in that hollow cry that went forth over the dead Adonis and why the Great Mother had a daughter wedded to death. We have entered more deeply than they into the Eleusinian Mysteries and have passed a higher grade, where gate within gate guarded the wisdom of Orpheus. We know the meaning of all the myths. We know the last secret revealed to the perfect initiate. And it is not the voice of a priest or a prophet saying, 'These things are.' It is the voice of a dreamer and an idealist crying, 'Why cannot these things be?'

6
THE DEMONS AND PHILOSOPHERS

I HAVE DWELT AT some little length on this imaginative
sort of paganism, which has crowded the world with temples and is everywhere the parent of popular festivity. For
the central history of civilisation, as I see it, consists of two
further stages before the final stage of Christendom. The
first was the struggle between this paganism and something less worthy than itself, and the second the process by
which it grew in itself less worthy. In this very varied and
often very vague polytheism there was a weakness of
original sin. Pagan gods were depicted as tossing men like
dice; and indeed they are loaded dice. About sex especially
men are born unbalanced; we might almost say men are
born mad. They scarcely reach sanity till they reach sanctity. This disproportion dragged down the winged fancies;
and filled the end of paganism with a mere filth and litter
of spawning gods. But the first point to realise is that this
sort of paganism had an early collision with another sort of
paganism; and that the issue of that essentially spiritual
struggle really determined the history of the world. In order to understand it we must pass to a review of the other
kind of paganism. It can be considered much more briefly;
indeed there is a very real sense in which the less that is
said about it the better. If we have called the first sort of
mythology the day-dream, we might very well call the second sort of mythology the nightmare.

Superstition recurs in all ages, and especially in rationalistic ages. I remember defending the religious tradition
against a whole luncheon table of distinguished agnostics;
and before the end of our conversation every one of them
had procured from his pocket or exhibited on his watch

chain some charm or talisman from which he admitted that he was never separated. I was the only person present who had neglected to provide himself with a fetish. Superstition recurs in a rationalist age because it rests on something which, if not identical with rationalism, is not unconnected with scepticism. It is at least very closely connected with agnosticism. It rests on something that is really a very human and intelligible sentiment, like the local invocations of the *numen* in popular paganism. But it is an agnostic sentiment, for it rests on two feelings: first that we do not really know the laws of the universe; and second that they may be very different to all that we call reason. Such men realise the real truth that enormous things do often turn upon tiny things. When a whisper comes, from tradition or what not, that one particular tiny thing is the key or clue, something deep and not altogether senseless in human nature tells them that it is not unlikely. This feeling exists in both the forms of paganism here under consideration. But when we come to the second form of it, we find it transformed and filled with another and more terrible spirit.

In dealing with the lighter thing called mythology, I have said little about the most disputable aspect of it; the extent to which such invocation of the spirits of the sea or the elements can indeed call spirits from the vast deep; or rather (as the Shakespearean scoffer put it), whether the spirits come when they are called. I believe that I am right in thinking that this problem, practical as it sounds, did not play a dominant part in the poetical business of mythology. But I think it even more obvious, on the evidence, that things of that sort have sometimes appeared, even if they were only appearances. But when we come to the world of superstition, in a more subtle sense, there is a shade of difference; a deepening and a darkening shade. Doubtless most popular superstition is as frivolous as any popular mythology. Men do not believe as a dogma that God would throw a thunderbolt at them for walking under a ladder; more often they amuse themselves with the not very laborious exercise of walking round it. There is no more in it than what I have already adumbrated; a sort of airy agnosticism about the possibilities of so strange a world. But there is another sort of superstition that does definitely look for results; what might be called a realistic superstition. And with that the question of whether spirits do answer or do appear becomes much more serious. As I have said, it seems to me pretty certain that they sometimes do; but about that there is a distinction that has been the beginning of much evil in the world.

Whether it be because the Fall has really brought men nearer to less desirable neighbours in the spiritual world, or whether it is merely that the mood of men eager or greedy finds it easier to imagine evil, I believe that the black magic of witchcraft has been much more practical and much less poetical than the white magic of mythology. I fancy the garden of the witch has been kept much more carefully than the woodland of the nymph. I fancy the evil field has even been more fruitful than the good. To start with, some impulse, perhaps a sort of desperate impulse, drove men to the darker powers when dealing with practical problems. There was a sort of secret and perverse feeling that the darker powers would really do things; that they had no nonsense about them. And indeed that popular phrase exactly expresses the point. The gods of mere mythology had a great deal of nonsense about them. They had a great deal of good nonsense about them; in the happy and hilarious sense in which we talk of the nonsense of Jabberwocky or the Land where the Jumblies live. But the man consulting a demon felt as many a man has felt in consulting a detective, especially a private detective; that it was dirty work but the work would really be done. A man did not exactly go into the wood to meet a nymph; he rather went with the hope of meeting a nymph. It was an adventure rather than an assignation. But the devil really kept his appointments and even in one sense kept his promises; even if a man sometimes wished afterwards, like Macbeth, that he had broken them.

In the accounts given us of many rude or savage races we gather that the cult of demons often came after the cult of deities, and even after the cult of one single and supreme deity. It may be suspected that in almost all such places the higher deity is felt to be too far off for appeal in certain petty matters, and men invoke the spirits because they are in a more literal sense familiar spirits. But with the idea of employing the demons who get things done, a new idea appears more worthy of the demons. It may indeed be truly described as the idea of being worthy of the demons; of making oneself fit for their fastidious and exacting society. Superstition of the lighter sort toys with the idea that some trifle, some small gesture such as throwing the salt, may touch the hidden spring that works the mysterious machinery of the world. And there is after all something in the idea of such an Open Sesame. But with the appeal to lower spirits comes the horrible notion that the gesture must not only be very small but very low; that it must be a monkey trick of an utterly ugly and unworthy sort. Sooner or later a man deliberately sets himself to do the most disgusting thing he can think of. It is felt that the extreme of evil will extort a sort of attention or answer from the evil powers under the surface of the world. This is the meaning of most of the cannibalism in the world. For most cannibalism is not a primitive or even a bestial habit. It is artificial and even artistic; a sort of art for art's sake. Men do not do it because they do not think it horrible; but, on the contrary, because they do think it horrible. They wish, in the most literal sense, to sup on horrors. That is why it is often found that rude races like the Australian natives are not cannibals, while much more refined and intelligent races, like the New Zealand Maories, occasionally are. They are refined and intelligent enough to indulge sometimes in a self-conscious diabolism. But if we could understand their minds, or even really understand their language, we should probably find that they were not acting as ignorant, that is as innocent cannibals. They are not doing it because they do not think it wrong, but precisely because they do think it wrong. They are acting like a Parisian decadent at a Black Mass. But the Black Mass has to hide underground from the presence of the real Mass. In other words, the demons have really been in hiding since the coming of Christ on earth. The cannibalism of the higher barbarians is in hiding from the civilisation of the white man. But before Christendom, and especially outside Europe, this was not always so. In the ancient world the demons often wandered abroad like dragons. They could be positively and publicly enthroned as gods. Their enormous images could be set up in public temples in the centre of populous cities. And all over the world the traces can be found of this striking and solid fact, so curiously overlooked by the moderns who speak of all such evil as primitive and early in evolution, that as a matter of fact some of the very highest civilisations of the world were the very places where the horns of Satan were exalted, not only to the stars but in the face of the sun.

Take for example the Aztecs and American Indians of the ancient empires of Mexico and Peru. They were at least as elaborate as Egypt or China and only less lively than that central civilisation which is our own. But those who criticise that central civilisation (which is always their own civilisation) have a curious habit of not merely doing their legitimate duty in condemning its crimes, but of going out of their way to idealize its victims. They always assume that before the advent of Europe there was nothing anywhere but Eden. And Swinburne, in that spirited chorus of the nations in 'Songs Before Sunrise', used an expression about Spain in her South American conquests which always struck me as very strange. He said something about 'her sins and sons through sinless lands dispersed,' and how they 'made accursed the name of man and thrice accursed the name of God.' It may be reasonable enough that he should say the Spaniards were sinful, but why in the world should he say that the South Americans were sinless? Why should he have supposed that continent to be exclusively populated by archangels or saints perfect in

heaven? It would be a strong thing to say of the most respectable neighbourhood; but when we come to think of
what we really do know of that society the remark is rather
funny. We know that the sinless priests of this sinless people worshipped sinless gods, who accepted as the nectar
and ambrosia of their sunny paradise nothing but incessant
human sacrifice accompanied by horrible torments. We
may note also in the mythology of this American civilisation that element of reversal or violence against instinct of
which Dante wrote; which runs backwards everywhere
through the unnatural religion of the demons. It is notable
not only in ethics but in aesthetics. A South American idol
was made as ugly as possible, as a Greek image was made
as beautiful as possible. They were seeking the secret of
power, by working backwards against their own nature and
the nature of things. There was always a sort of yearning to
carve at last, in gold or granite or the dark-red timber of
the forests, a face at which the sky itself would break like a
cracked mirror.

In any case it is clear enough that the painted and
gilded civilisation of tropical America systematically indulged in human sacrifice. It is by no means clear, so far as
I know, that the Eskimos ever indulged in human sacrifice.
They were not civilised enough. They were too closely imprisoned by the white winter and the endless dark. Chill
penury repressed their noble rage and froze the genial current of the soul. It was in brighter days and broader daylight that the noble rage was found unmistakably raging. It
was in richer and more instructed lands that the genial current flowed on the altars, to be drunk by great gods wear-
ing goggling and grinning masks and called on in terror or
torment by long cacophonous names that sound like
laughter in hell. A warmer climate and a more scientific
cultivation were needed to bring forth these blooms; to
draw up towards the sun the large leaves and flamboyant
blossoms that gave their gold and crimson and purple to
that garden, which Swinburne compares to the Hesperides.
There was at least no doubt about the dragon.

I do not raise in this connection the special controversy about Spain and Mexico; but I may remark in passing that it resembles exactly the question that must in some sense be raised afterwards about Rome and Carthage. In both cases there has been a queer habit among the English of always siding against the Europeans, and representing the rival civilisation, in Swinburne's phrase, as sinless; when its sins were obviously crying or rather screaming to heaven. For Carthage also was a high civilisation, indeed a much more highly civilised civilisation. And Carthage also founded that civilisation on a religion of fear, sending up everywhere the smoke of human sacrifice. Now it is very right to rebuke our own race or religion for falling short of our own standards and ideals. But it is absurd to pretend that they fell lower than the other races and religions that professed the very opposite standards and ideals. There is a very real sense in which the Christian is worse than the heathen, the Spaniard worse than the Red Indian, or even the Roman potentially worse than the Carthaginian. But there is only one sense in which he is worse; and that is not in being positively worse. The Christian is only worse because it is his business to be better.

This inverted imagination produces things of which it is better not to speak. Some of them indeed might almost be named without being known; for they are of that extreme evil which seems innocent to the innocent. They are too inhuman even to be indecent. But without dwelling much longer in these dark corners, it may be noted as not irrelevant here that certain anti-human antagonisms seem to recur in this tradition of black magic. There may be suspected as running through it everywhere, for instance, a mystical hatred of the idea of childhood. People would understand better the popular fury against the witches, if they remembered that the malice most commonly attributed to them was preventing the birth of children. The Hebrew prophets were perpetually protesting against the Hebrew race relapsing into an idolatry that involved such a war upon children; and it is probable enough that this abominable apostasy from the God of Israel has occasionally appeared in Israel since, in the form of what is called ritual murder; not of course by any representative of the religion of Judaism, but by individual and irresponsible diabolists who did happen to be Jews. This sense that the forces of evil especially threaten childhood is found again in the enormous popularity of the Child Martyr of the Middle Ages. Chaucer did but give another version of a very national English legend, when he conceived the wickedest of all possible witches as the dark alien woman watching behind her high lattice and hearing, like the babble of a brook down the stony street, the singing of little St. Hugh.

Anyhow the part of such speculations that concerns this story centred especially round that eastern end of the Mediterranean, where the nomads had turned gradually into traders and had begun to trade with the whole world. Indeed in the sense of trade and travel and colonial extension, it already had something like an empire of the whole world. Its purple dye, the emblem of its rich pomp and luxury, had steeped the wares which were sold far away amid the last crags of Cornwall and the sails that entered the silence of tropic seas amid all the mystery of Africa. It might be said truly to have painted the map purple. It was already a worldwide success, when the princes of Tyre would hardly have troubled to notice that one of their princesses had condescended to marry the chief of some tribe called Judah; when the merchants of its African outpost would only have curled their bearded and Semitic lips with a slight smile at the mention of a village called Rome. And indeed no two things could have seemed more distant from each other, not only in space but in spirit, than the monotheism of the Palestinian tribe and the very virtues of the small Italian republic. There was but one thing between them; and the thing which divided them has united them. Very various and incompatible were the things that could be loved by the consuls of Rome and the prophets of Israel; but they were at one in what they hated. It is very easy in both cases to represent that hatred as something merely hateful. It is easy enough to make a merely harsh and inhuman figure either of Elijah raving above the slaughter of Carmel or Cato thundering against the amnesty of Africa. These men had their limitations and their local passions; but this criticism of them is unimaginative and therefore unreal. It leaves out something, something immense and intermediate, facing east and west and calling up this passion in its eastern and western enemies; and that something is the first subject of this chapter.

The civilisation that centred in Tyre and Sidon was above all things practical. It has left little in the way of art and nothing in the way of poetry. But it prided itself upon being very efficient; and it followed in its philosophy and religion that strange and sometimes secret train of thought which we have already noted in those who look for immediate effects. There is always in such a mentality an idea that there is a short cut to the secret of all success; something that would shock the world by this sort of shameless thoroughness. They believed, in the appropriate modern phrase, in people who delivered the goods. In their dealings with their god Moloch, they themselves were always careful to deliver the goods. It was an interesting transaction, upon which we shall have to touch more in the rest of the narrative; it is enough to say here that it involved the theory I have suggested, about a certain attitude towards children. This was what called up against it in simultaneous fury the servant of one God in Palestine and the guardians of all the household gods in Rome. This is what challenged two things naturally so much divided by every sort of distance and disunion, whose union was to save the world.

I have called the fourth and final division of the spiritual elements into which I should divide heathen humanity by the name of The Philosophers. I confess that it covers in my mind much that would generally be classified otherwise; and that what are here called philosophies are very often called religions. I believe however that my own description will be found to be much the more realistic and not the less respectful. But we must first take philosophy in its purest and clearest form that we may trace its normal outline; and that is to be found in the world of the purest and clearest outlines, that culture of the Mediterranean of which we have been considering the mythologies and idolatries in the last two chapters.

Polytheism, or that aspect of paganism, was never to the pagan what Catholicism is to the Catholic. It was never a view of the universe satisfying all sides of life; a complete and complex truth with something to say about everything. It was only a satisfaction of one side of the soul of man, even if we call it the religious side; and I think it is truer to call it the imaginative side. But this it did satisfy; in the end it satisfied it to satiety. All that world was a tissue of inter-woven tales and cults, and there ran in and out of it, as we have already seen, that black thread among its more blame-less colours; the darker paganism that was really diabolism. But we all know that this did not mean that all pagan men thought of nothing but pagan gods. Precisely because my-thology only satisfied one mood, they turned in other moods to something totally different. But it is very impor-tant to realise that it was totally different. It was too differ-ent to be inconsistent. It was so alien that it did not clash. While a mob of people were pouring on a public holiday to the feast of Adonis or the games in honour of Apollo, this or that man would prefer to stop at home and think out a little theory about the nature of things. Sometimes his hobby would even take the form of thinking about the nature of God; or even in that sense about the nature of the gods. But he very seldom thought of pitting his nature of the gods against the gods of nature.

It is necessary to insist on this abstraction in the first student of abstractions. He was not so much antagonistic as absentminded. His hobby might be the universe; but at first the hobby was as private as if it had been numismatics or playing draughts. And even when his wisdom came to be a public possession, and almost a political institution, it was very seldom on the same plane as the popular and re-

ligious institutions. Aristotle, with his colossal common
sense, was perhaps the greatest of all philosophers; certainly the most practical of all philosophers. But Aristotle
would no more have set up the Absolute side by side with
the Apollo of Delphi, as a similar or rival religion, than
Archimedes would have thought of setting up the Lever as
a sort of idol or fetish to be substituted for the Palladium
of the city. Or we might as well imagine Euclid building an
altar to an isosceles triangle, or offering sacrifices to the
square of the hypotenuse. The one man meditated on
metaphysics as the other man did on mathematics; for the
love of truth or for curiosity or for the fun of the thing.
But that sort of fun never seems to have interfered very
much with the other sort of fun; the fun of dancing or
singing to celebrate some rascally romance about Zeus
becoming a bull or a swan. It is perhaps the proof of a certain superficiality and even insincerity about the popular
polytheism, that men could be philosophers and even
sceptics without disturbing it. These thinkers could move
the foundations of the world without altering even the outline of that coloured cloud that hung above it in the air.

For the thinkers did move the foundations of the
world; even when a curious compromise seemed to prevent them from moving the foundations of the city. The
two great philosophers of antiquity do indeed appear to us
as defenders of sane and even of sacred ideas; their maxims often read like the answers to sceptical questions too
completely answered to be always recorded. Aristotle an-
nihilated a hundred anarchists and nature worshipping
cranks by the fundamental statement that man is a political
animal. Plato in some sense anticipated the Catholic realism, as attacked by the heretical nominalism, by insisting
on the equally fundamental fact that ideas are realities; that
ideas exist just as men exist. Plato however seemed sometimes almost to fancy that ideas exist as men do not exist;
or that the men need hardly be considered where they conflict with the ideas. He had something of the social sentiment that we call Fabian in his ideal of fitting the citizen to

the city, like an imaginary head to an ideal hat; and great and glorious as he remains, he has been the father of all faddists. Aristotle anticipated more fully the sacramental sanity that was to combine the body and the soul of things; for he considered the nature of men as well as the nature of morals, and looked to the eyes as well as to the light. But though these great men were in that sense constructive and conservative, they belonged to a world where thought was free to the point of being fanciful. Many other great intellects did indeed follow them, some exalting an abstract vision of virtue, others following more rationalistically the necessity of the human pursuit of happiness. The former had the name of Stoics; and their name has passed into a proverb for what is indeed one of the main moral ideals of mankind: that of strengthening the mind itself until it is of a texture to resist calamity or even pain. But it is admitted that a great number of the philosophers degenerated into what we still call sophists. They became a sort of professional sceptics who went about asking uncomfortable questions, and were handsomely paid for making themselves a nuisance to normal people. It was perhaps an accidental resemblance to such questioning quacks that was responsible for the unpopularity of the great Socrates; whose death might seem to contradict the suggestion of the permanent truce between the philosophers and the gods. But Socrates did not die as a monotheist who denounced polytheism; certainly not as a prophet who denounced idols. It is clear to anyone reading between the lines that there was some notion, right or wrong, of a purely personal influence affecting morals and perhaps politics. The general compromise remained; whether it was that the Greeks thought their myths a joke or that they thought their theories a joke. There was never any collision in which one really destroyed the other, and there was never any combination in which one was really reconciled with the other. They certainly did not work together; if anything the philosopher was a rival of the priest. But both seemed to have accepted a sort of separation of functions and remained parts of the same social system. Another important tradition descends from Pythagoras; who is significant because he stands nearest to the Oriental mystics who must be considered in their turn. He taught a sort of mysticism of mathematics, that number is the ultimate reality; but he also seems to have taught the transmigration of souls like the Brahmins; and to have left to his followers certain traditional tricks of vegetarianism and water-drinking very common among the eastern sages, especially those who figure in fashionable drawing-rooms like those of the later Roman Empire. But in passing to eastern sages, and the somewhat different atmosphere of the east, we may approach a rather important truth by another path.

One of the great philosophers said that it would be well if philosophers were kings, or kings were philosophers. He spoke as of something too good to be true; but, as a matter of fact, it not infrequently was true. A certain type, perhaps too little noticed in history, may really be called the royal philosopher. To begin with, apart from actual royalty, it did occasionally become possible for the sage, though he was not what we call a religious founder, to be something like a political founder. And the great example of this, one of the very greatest in the world, will with the very thought of it carry us thousands of miles across the vast spaces of Asia to that very wonderful and in some ways that very wise world of ideas and institutions, which we dismiss somewhat cheaply when we talk of China. Men have served many very strange gods; and trusted themselves loyally to many ideals and even idols. China is a society that has really chosen to believe in intellect. It has taken intellect seriously; and it may be that it stands alone in the world. From a very early age it faced the dilemma of the king and the philosopher by actually appointing a philosopher to advise the king. It made a public institution out of a private individual, who had nothing in the world to do but to be intellectual. It had and has, of course, many other things on the same pattern. It creates all ranks and privileges by public examination; it has nothing that we call an aristocracy; it is a democracy dominated by an intelligent-sia. But the point here is that it had philosophers to advise kings; and one of those philosophers must have been a great philosopher and a great statesman.

Confucius was not a religious founder or even a religious teacher; possibly not even a religious man. He was not an atheist; he was apparently what we call an agnostic. But the really vital point is that it is utterly irrelevant to talk about his religion at all. It is like talking of theology as the first thing in the story of how Rowland Hill established the postal system or Baden-Powell organised the Boy Scouts. Confucius was not there to bring a message from heaven to humanity, but to organise China; and be must have organised it exceedingly well. It follows that he dealt much with morals; but he bound them up strictly with manners. The peculiarity of his scheme, and of his country, in which it contrasts with its great pendant the system of Christendom, is that he insisted on perpetuating an external life with all its forms, that outward continuity might preserve internal peace. Anyone who knows how much habit has to do with health, of mind as well as body, will see the truth in his idea. But he will also see that the ancestor worship and the reverence for the Sacred Emperor were habits and not creeds. It is unfair to the great Confucius to say he was a religious founder. It is even unfair to him to say he was not a religious founder. It is as unfair as going out of one's way to say that Jeremy Bentham was not a Christian martyr.

But there is a class of most interesting cases in which philosophers were kings, and not merely the friends of kings. The combination is not accidental. It has a great deal to do with this rather elusive question of the function of the philosopher. It contains in it some hint of why philosophy and mythology seldom came to an open rupture. It was not only because there was something a little frivolous about the mythology. It was also because there was something a little supercilious about the philosopher. He despised the myths, but he also despised the mob; and thought they suited each other. The pagan philosopher was seldom a man of the people, at any rate in spirit; he was seldom a democrat and often a bitter critic of democracy. He had about him an air of aristocratic and humane leisure; and his part was most easily played by men who happened to be in such a position. It was very easy and natural for a prince or a prominent person to play at being as philosophical as Hamlet or Theseus in the *Midsummer Night's Dream*. And from very early ages we find ourselves in the presence of these princely intellectuals. In fact, we find one of them in the very first recorded ages of the world; sitting on that primeval throne that looked over ancient Egypt.

The most intense interest of the incident of Akenahten, commonly called the Heretic Pharaoh, lies in the fact that he was the one example, at any rate before Christian times, of one of these royal philosophers who set himself to fight popular mythology in the name of private philosophy. Most of them assumed the attitude of Marcus Aurelius, who is in many ways the model of this sort of monarch and sage. Marcus Aurelius has been blamed for tolerating the pagan amphitheatre or the Christian martyrdoms. But it was characteristic; for this sort of man really thought of popular religion just as he thought of popular circuses. Of him Professor Phillimore has profoundly said 'a great and good man – and he knew it.' The heretic Pharaoh had a philosophy more earnest and perhaps more humble. For there is a corollary to the conception of being too proud to fight. It is that the humble have to do most of the fighting. Anyhow, the Egyptian prince was simple enough to take his own philosophy seriously, and alone among such intellectual princes he effected a sort of *coup d'etat*; hurling down the high gods of Egypt with one imperial gesture and lifting up for all men, like a blazing mirror of monotheistic truth, the disc of the universal sun. He had other interesting ideas often to be found in such idealists. In the sense in which we speak of Little Englander he was a Little Egypter. In art he was a realist because he was an idealist; for realism is more impossible than any other ideal. But after all there falls on him something of the shadow of Marcus Aurelius; stalked by the shadow of Professor Phillimore. What is the matter with this noble sort of prince is that he has nowhere quite escaped being something of a prig. Priggishness is so pungent a smell that it clings amid the faded spices even to an Egyptian mummy. What was the matter with the heretic Pharaoh, as with a good many other heretics, was that he probably never paused to ask himself whether there was *anything* in the popular beliefs and tales of people less educated than himself. And, as already suggested, there was something in them. There was a real human hunger in all that element of feature and locality, that procession of deities like enormous pet animals, in that unwearied watching at certain haunted spots, in all the mazy wandering of mythology. Nature may not have the name of Isis; Isis may not be really looking for Osiris. But it is true that Nature is really looking for something; Nature is always looking for the supernatural. Something much more definite was to satisfy that need; but a dignified monarch with a disc of the sun did not satisfy it. The royal experiment failed amid a roaring reaction of popular superstitions, in which the priests rose on the shoulders of the people and ascended the throne of the kings.

The next great example I shall take of the princely sage is Gautama, the great Lord Buddha. I know he is not generally classed merely with the philosophers; but I gin more and more convinced, from all information that reaches me, that this is the real interpretation of his immense importance. He was by far the greatest and the best of these intellectuals born in the purple. His reaction was perhaps the noblest and most sincere of all the resultant actions of that combination of thinkers and of thrones. For his reaction was renunciation. Marcus Aurelius was content to say, with a refined irony, that even in a palace life could be lived well. The fierier Egyptian king concluded that it could be lived even better after a palace revolution. But the great Gautama was the only one of them who proved he could really do without his palace. One fell back on toleration

and the other on revolution. But after all there is something more absolute about abdication. Abdication is perhaps the one really absolute action of an absolute monarchy. The Indian prince, reared in Oriental luxury and
pomp, deliberately went out and lived the life of a beggar.
That is magnificent, but it is not war; that is, it is not necessarily a Crusade in the Christian sense. It does not decide
the question of whether the life of a beggar was the life of
a saint or the life of a philosopher. It does not decide
whether this great man is really to go into the tub of Dio-
genes or the cave of St. Jerome. Now those who seem to
be nearest to the study of Buddha, and certainly those who
write most clearly and intelligently about him, convince me
for one that he was simply a philosopher who founded a
successful school of philosophy, and was turned into a sort
of *divus* or sacred being merely by the more mysterious and
unscientific atmosphere of all such traditions in Asia. So
that it is necessary to say at this point a word about that
invisible yet vivid borderline that we cross in passing from
the Mediterranean into the mystery of the East.

Perhaps there are no things out of which we get so little of the truth as the truisms; especially when they are
really true. We are all in the habit of saying certain things
about Asia, which are true enough but which hardly help
us because we do not understand their truth; as that Asia is
old or looks to the past or is not progressive. Now it is
true that Christendom is more progressive, in a sense that
has very little to do with the rather provincial notion of an
endless fuss of political improvement. Christendom does
believe, for Christianity does believe, that man can eventu-
ally get somewhere, here or hereafter, or in various ways
according to various doctrines. The world's desire can
somehow be satisfied as desires are satisfied, whether by a
new life or an old love or some form of positive possession and fulfilment. For the rest, we all know there is a
rhythm and not a mere progress in things, that things rise
and fall; only with us the rhythm is a fairly free and incal-
culable rhythm. For most of Asia the rhythm has hardened

into a recurrence. It is no longer merely a rather topsy-turvy sort of world; it is a wheel. What has happened to all those highly intelligent and highly civilised peoples is that they have been caught up in a sort of cosmic rotation of which the hollow hub is really nothing. In that sense the worst part of existence is that it may just as well go on like that forever. That is what we really mean when we say that Asia is old or unprogressive or looking backwards. That is why we see even her curved swords as arcs broken from that blinding wheel; why we see her serpentine ornament as returning everywhere, like a snake that is never slain. It has very little to do with the political varnish of progress; all Asiatics might have top-hats on their heads but if they had this spirit still in their hearts, they would only think the hats would vanish and come round again like the planets; not that running after a hat could lead them to heaven or even to home.

Now when the genius of Buddha arose to deal with the matter this sort of cosmic sentiment was already common to almost everything in the east. There was indeed the jungle of an extraordinarily extravagant and almost asphyxiating mythology. Nevertheless it is possible to have more sympathy with this popular fruitfulness in folk-lore than with some of the higher pessimism that might have withered it. It must always be remembered, however, when all fair allowances are made, that a great deal of spontaneous eastern imagery really is idolatry; the local and literal worship of an idol. This is probably not true of the ancient Brahminical system, at least as seen by Brahmins. But that phrase alone will remind us of a reality of much greater moment. This great reality is the Caste System of ancient India. It may have had some of the practical advantages of the Guild System of Medieval Europe. But it contrasts not only with that Christian democracy, but with every extreme type of Christian aristocracy, in the fact that it does really conceive the social superiority as a spiritual superiority. This not only divides it fundamentally from the fraternity of Christendom, but leaves it standing like a mighty

and terraced mountain of pride between the relatively
egalitarian levels both of Islam and of China. But the fixity
of this formation through thousands of years is another
illustration of that spirit of repetition that has marked time
from time immemorial. Now we may also presume the
prevalence of another idea which we associate with the
Buddhists as interpreted by the Theosophists. As a fact,
some of the strictest Buddhists repudiate the idea and still
more scornfully repudiate the Theosophists. But whether
the idea is in Buddhism, or only in the birthplace of Buddhism, or only in a tradition or a travesty of Buddhism, it
is an idea entirely proper to this principle of recurrence. I
mean of course the idea of Reincarnation.

But Reincarnation is not really a mystical idea. It is not
really a transcendental idea, or in that sense a religious idea.
Mysticism conceives something transcending experience;
religion seeks glimpses of a better good or a worse evil
than experience can give. Reincarnation need only extend
experiences in the sense of repeating them. It is no more
transcendental for a man to remember what he did in
Babylon before he was born than to remember what he
did in Brixton before he had a knock on the head. His successive lives *need* not be any more than human lives, under
whatever limitations burden human life. It has nothing to
do with seeing God or even conjuring up the devil. In
other words, reincarnation as such does not necessarily
escape from the wheel of destiny; in some sense it is the
wheel of destiny. And whether it was something that Buddha founded, or something that Buddha found, or something that Buddha entirely renounced when he found, it is
certainly something having the general character of that
Asiatic atmosphere in which he had to play his part. And
the part be played was that of an intellectual philosopher
with a particular theory about the right intellectual attitude
towards it.

I can understand that Buddhists might resent the view
that Buddhism is merely a philosophy, if we understand by
a philosophy merely an intellectual game such as Greek

sophists played, tossing up worlds and catching them like balls. Perhaps a more exact statement would be that Buddha was a man who made a metaphysical discipline; which might even be called a psychological discipline. He proposed a way of escaping from all this recurrent sorrow; and that was simply by getting rid of the delusion that is called desire. It was emphatically *not* that we should get what we want better by restraining our impatience for part of it, or that we should get it in a better way or in a better world. It was emphatically that we should leave off wanting it. If once a man realised that there is really no reality, that everything, including his soul, is in dissolution at every instant, he would anticipate disappointment and be intangible to change, existing (in so far as he could be said to exist) in a sort of ecstasy of indifference. The Buddhists call this beatitude and we will not stop our story to argue the point; certainly to us it is indistinguishable from despair. I do not see, for instance, why the disappointment of desire should not apply as much to the most benevolent desires as to the most selfish ones. Indeed the Lord of Compassion seems to pity people for living rather than for dying. For the rest, an intelligent Buddhist wrote, 'The explanation of popular Chinese and Japanese Buddhism is that it is not Buddhism.' *That* has doubtless ceased to be a mere philosophy, but only by becoming a mere mythology. One thing is certain; it has never become anything remotely resembling what we call a Church.

It will appear only a jest to say that all religious history has really been a pattern of noughts and crosses. But I do not by noughts mean nothings, but only things that are negative compared with the positive shape or pattern of the other. And though the symbol is of course only a coincidence, it is a coincidence that really does coincide. The mind of Asia can really be represented by a round O if not in the sense of a cipher at least of a circle. The great Asiatic symbol of a serpent with its tail in its mouth is really a very perfect image of a certain idea of unity and recurrence that does indeed belong to the Eastern philosophies and religions. It really is a curve that in one sense includes everything, and in another sense comes to nothing. In that sense it does confess, or rather boast, that all argument is an argument in a circle. And though the figure is but a symbol, we can see how sound is the symbolic sense that produces it, the parallel symbol of the Wheel of Buddha generally called the Swastika. The cross is a thing at right angles pointing boldly in opposite directions; but the Swastika is the same thing in the very act of returning to the recurrent curve. That crooked cross is in fact a cross turning into a wheel. Before we dismiss even these symbols as if they were arbitrary symbols, we must remember how intense was the imaginative instinct that produced them or selected them both in the east and the west. The cross has become something more than a historical memory; it does convey, almost as by a mathematical diagram, the truth about the real point at issue; the idea of a conflict stretching outwards into eternity. It is true, and even tautological, to say that the cross is the crux of the whole matter.

In other words the cross, in fact as well as figure, does really stand for the idea of breaking out of the circle that is everything and nothing. It does escape from the circular argument by which everything begins and ends in the mind. Since we are still dealing in symbols, it might be put in a parable in the form of that story about St. Francis, which says that the birds departing with his benediction could wing their way into the infinities of the four winds of heaven, their tracks making a vast cross upon the sky; for compared with the freedom of that flight of birds, the very shape of the Swastika is like a kitten chasing its tail. In a more popular allegory, we might say that when St. George thrust his spear into the monster's jaws, he broke in upon the solitude of the self-devouring serpent and gave it something to bite besides its own tail. But while many fancies might be used as figures of the truth, the truth itself is abstract and absolute; though it is not very easy to sum up except by such figures. Christianity does appeal to a solid truth outside itself; to something which is in that sense external as well as eternal. It does declare that things are really there; or in other words that things are really things. In this Christianity is at one with common sense; but all religious history shows that this common sense perishes except where there is Christianity to preserve it.

It cannot otherwise exist, or at least endure, because mere thought does not remain sane. In a sense it becomes too simple to be sane. The temptation of the philosophers is simplicity rather than subtlety. They are always attracted by insane simplifications, as men poised above abysses are fascinated by death and nothingness and the empty air. It needed another kind of philosopher to stand poised upon the pinnacle of the Temple and keep his balance without casting himself down. One of these obvious, these too obvious explanations is that everything is a dream and a delusion and there is nothing outside the ego. Another is that all things recur; another, which is said to be Buddhist and is certainly Oriental, is the idea that what is the matter with us is our creation, in the sense of our coloured differentiation and personality, and that nothing will be well till we are again melted into one unity. By this theory, in short, the Creation was the Fall. It is important historically because it was stored up in the dark heart of Asia and went forth at various times in various forms over the dim borders of Europe. Here we can place the mysterious figure of Manes or Manichaeus, the mystic of inversion, whom we should call a pessimist, parent of many sects and heresies; here, in a higher place, the figure of Zoroaster. He has been popularly identified with another of these too simple explanations; the equality of evil and good, balanced and battling in every atom. He also is of the school of sages that may be called mystics; and from the same mysterious Persian garden came upon ponderous wings Mithras, the unknown god, to trouble the last twilight of Rome.

That circle or disc of the sun set up in the morning of the world by the remote Egyptian has been a mirror and a model for all the philosophers. They have made many things out of it, and sometimes gone mad about it, especially when as in these eastern sages the circle became a wheel going round and round in their heads. But the point about them is that they all think that existence can be represented by a diagram instead of a drawing; and the rude drawings of the childish mythmakers are a sort of crude and spirited protest against that view. They cannot believe that religion is really not a pattern but a picture. Still less can they believe that it is a picture of something that really exists outside our minds. Sometimes the philosopher paints the disc all black and calls himself a pessimist; sometimes he paints it all white and calls himself an optimist; sometimes he divides it exactly into halves of black and white and calls himself a dualist, like those Persian mystics to whom I wish there were space to do justice. None of them could understand a thing that began to draw the proportions just as if they were real proportions, disposed in the living fashion which the mathematical draughtsman would call disproportionate. Like the first artist in the cave, it revealed to incredulous eyes the suggestion of a new purpose in what looked like a wildly crooked pattern; he seemed only to be distorting his diagram, when he began for the first time in all the ages to trace the lines of a form – and of a Face.

7

THE WAR OF THE GODS
AND DEMONS

THE MATERIALIST THEORY of history, that all politics and
ethics are the expression of economics, is a very simple
fallacy indeed. It consists simply of confusing the necessary conditions of life with the normal preoccupations of
life, that are quite a different thing. It is like saying that
because a man can only walk about on two legs, therefore
he never walks about except to buy shoes and stockings.
Man cannot live without the two props of food and drink,
which support him like two legs; but to suggest that they
have been the motives of all his movements in history is
like saying that the goal of all his military marches or religious pilgrimages must have been the Golden Leg of Miss
Kilmansegg or the ideal and perfect leg of Sir Willoughby
Patterne. But it is such movements that make up the story
of mankind and without them there would practically be
no story at all. Cows may be purely economic, in the sense
that we cannot see that they do much beyond grazing and
seeking better grazing-grounds; and that is why a history of
cows in twelve volumes would not be very lively reading.
Sheep and goats may be pure economists in their external
action at least; but that is why the sheep has hardly been a
hero of epic wars and empires thought worthy of detailed
narration; and even the more active quadruped has not
inspired a book for boys called Golden Deeds of Gallant
Goats or any similar title. But so far from the movements
that make up the story of man being economic, we may
say that the story only begins where the motive of the
cows and sheep leaves off. It will be hard to maintain that

the Crusaders went from their homes into a howling wilderness because cows go from a wilderness to a more comfortable grazing-ground. It will be hard to maintain that the Arctic explorers went north with the same material motive that made the swallows go south. And if you leave things like all the religious wars and all the merely adventurous explorations out of the human story, it will not only cease to be human at all but cease to be a story at all. The outline of history is made of these decisive curves and angles determined by the will of man. Economic history would not even be history.

But there is a deeper fallacy besides this obvious fact; that men need not live for food merely because they cannot live without food. The truth is that the thing most present to the mind of man is not the economic machinery necessary to his existence; but rather that existence itself; the world which he sees when he wakes every morning and the nature of his general position in it. There is something that is nearer to him than livelihood, and that is life. For once that he remembers exactly what work produces his wages and exactly what wages produce his meals, he reflects ten times that it is a fine day or it is a queer world, or wonders whether life is worth living, or wonders whether marriage is a failure, or is pleased and puzzled with his own children, or remembers his own youth, or in any such fashion vaguely reviews the mysterious lot of man. This is true of the majority even of the wage slaves of our morbid modern industrialism, which by its hideousness and inhumanity has really forced the economic issue to the front. It is immeasurably more true of the multitude of peasants or hunters or fishers who make up the real mass of mankind. Even those dry pedants who think that ethics depend on economics must admit that economics depend on existence. And any number of normal doubts and day-dreams are about existence; not about how we can live, but about why we do. And the proof of it is simple; as simple as suicide. Turn the universe upside down in the mind and you turn all the political economists upside down with it. Suppose that a man wishes to die, and the professor of political economy becomes rather a bore with his elaborate explanations of how he is to live. And all the departures and decisions that make our human past into a story have this character of diverting the direct course of pure economics. As the economist may be excused from calculating the future salary of a suicide, so he may be excused from providing an old age pension for a martyr. As he need not provide for the future of a martyr, so he need not provide for the family of a monk. His plan is modified in lesser and varying degrees by a man being a soldier and dying for his own country, by a man being a peasant and especially loving his own land, by a man being more or less affected by any religion that forbids or allows him to do this or that. But all these come back not to an economic calculation about livelihood but to an elemental outlook upon life. They all come back to what a man fundamentally feels, when he looks forth from those strange windows which we call the eyes, upon that strange vision that we call the world.

No wise man will wish to bring more long words into the world. But it may be allowable to say that we need a new thing; which may be called psychological history. I mean the consideration of what things meant in the mind of a man, especially an ordinary man; as distinct from what is defined or deduced merely from official forms or political pronouncements. I have already touched on it in such a case as the totem or indeed any other popular myth. It is not enough to be told that a tom-cat was called a totem; especially when it was not called a totem. We want to know what it felt like. Was it like Whittington's cat or like a witch's cat? Was its real name Pasht or Puss-In-Boots? That is the sort of thing we need touching the nature of political and social relations. We want to know the real sentiment that was the social bond of many common men, as sane and as selfish as we are. What did soldiers feel when they saw splendid in the sky that strange totem that we call the Golden Eagle of the Legions? What did vassals feel about those other totems, the lions or the leopards upon the shield of their lord? So long as we neglect this subjective side of history, which may more simply be called the inside of history, there will always be a certain limitation on that science which can be better transcended by art. So long as the historian cannot do that, fiction will be truer than fact. There will be more reality in a novel; yes, even in a historical novel.

In nothing is this new history needed so much as in the psychology of war. Our history is stiff with official documents, public or private, which tell us nothing of the thing itself. At the worst we only have the official posters, which could not have been spontaneous precisely because they were official. At the best we have only the secret diplomacy, which could not have been popular precisely because it was secret. Upon one or other of these is based the historical judgment about the real reasons that sustained the struggle. Governments fight for colonies or commercial rights; governments fight about harbours or high tariffs; governments fight for a gold mine or a pearl fishery. It seems sufficient to answer that governments do not fight at all. Why do the fighters fight? What is the psychology that sustains the terrible and wonderful thing called a war? Nobody who knows anything of soldiers believes the silly notion of the dons, that millions of men can be ruled by force. If they were all to slack, it would be impossible to punish all the slackers. And the least little touch of slacking would lose a whole campaign in half a day. What did men really feel about the policy? If it be said that they accepted the policy from the politician, what did they feel about the politician? If the vassals warred blindly for their prince, what did those blind men see in their prince?

There is something we all know which can only be rendered, in an appropriate language, as *realpolitik*. As a matter of fact, it is an almost insanely unreal politik. It is always stubbornly and stupidly repeating that men fight for material ends, without reflecting for a moment that the material ends are hardly ever material to the men who fight. In any case no man will die for practical politics, just as no man will die for pay. Nero could not hire a hundred Christians to be eaten by lions at a shilling an hour, for men will not be martyred for money. But the vision called up by real politik, or realistic politics, is beyond example crazy and incredible. Does anybody in the world believe that a soldier says, 'My leg is nearly dropping off, but I shall go on till it drops; for after all I shall enjoy all the advantages of my government obtaining a warm water port in the Gulf of Finland!' Can anybody suppose that a clerk turned conscript says, 'If I am gassed I shall probably die in torments; but it is a comfort to reflect that should I ever decide to become a pearl-diver in the South Seas, that career is now open to me and my countrymen!' Materialist history is the most madly incredible of all histories, or even of all romances. Whatever starts wars, the thing that sustains wars is something in the soul; that is something akin to religion. It is what men feel about life and about death. A man near to death is dealing directly with an absolute; it is nonsense to say he is concerned only with relative and remote complications that death in any case will end. If he is sustained by certain loyalties, they must be loyalties as simple as death. They are generally two ideas, which are only two sides of one idea. The first is the love of something said to be threatened, if it be only vaguely known as home; the second is dislike and defiance of some strange thing that threatens it. The first is far more philosophical than it sounds though we need not discuss it here. A man does not want his national home destroyed or even changed, because he cannot even remember all the good things that go with it; just as he does not want his house burnt down because he can hardly count all the things he would miss. Therefore he fights for what sounds like a hazy abstraction, but is really a house. But the negative side of it is quite as noble as well as quite as strong. Men fight hardest when they feel that the foe is at once an old enemy and an eternal stranger, that his atmosphere is alien and antagonistic; as the French feel about the Prussian or the Eastern

Christians about the Turk. If we say it is a difference of religion, people will drift into dreary bickerings about sects and dogmas. We will pity them and say it is a difference about death and daylight; a difference that does really come like a dark shadow between our eyes and the day. Men can think of this difference even at the point of death; for it is a difference about the meaning of life.

Men are moved in these things by something far higher and holier than policy; by hatred. When men hung on in the darkest days of the Great War, suffering either in their bodies or in their souls for those they loved, they were long past caring about details of diplomatic objects as motives for their refusal to surrender. Of myself and those I knew best I can answer for the vision that made surrender impossible. It was the vision of the German Emperor's face as he rode into Paris. This is not the sentiment which some of my idealistic friends describe as Love. I am quite content to call it hatred; the hatred of hell and all its works, and to agree that as they do not believe in hell they need not believe in hatred. But in the face of this prevalent prejudice, this long introduction has been unfortunately necessary to ensure an understanding of what is meant by a religious war. There is a religious war when two worlds meet; that is, when two visions of the world meet; or in more modern language when two moral atmospheres meet. What is the one man's breath is the other man's poison; and it is vain to talk of giving a pestilence a place in the sun. And this is what we must understand even at the expense of digression, if we would see what really happened in the Mediterranean; when right athwart the rising of the Republic on the Tiber, a thing overtopping and disdaining it, dark with all the riddles of Asia and trailing all the tribes and dependencies of imperialism, came Carthage riding on the sea.

The ancient religion of Italy was on the whole that mixture which we have considered under the head of mythology; save that where the Greeks had a natural turn for the mythology, the Latins seem to have had a real turn for religion. Both multiplied gods, yet they sometimes seem to have multiplied them for almost opposite reasons. It would seem sometimes as if the Greek polytheism branched and blossomed upwards like the boughs of a tree, while the Italian polytheism ramified downward like the roots. Perhaps it would be truer to say that the former branches lifted themselves lightly, bearing flowers, while the latter hung down, being heavy with fruit. I mean that the Latins seem to multiply gods to bring them nearer to men, while the Greek gods rose and radiated outwards into the morning sky. What strikes us in the Italian cults is their local and especially their domestic character. We gain the impression of divinities swarming about the house like flies; of deities clustering and clinging like bats about the pillars or building like birds under the eaves. We have a vision of a god of roofs and a god of gate-posts, of a god of doors and even a god of drains. It has been suggested that all mythology was a sort of fairy-tale; but this was a particular sort of fairy-tale which may truly be called a fireside tale, or a nursery-tale; because it was a tale of the interior of the home; like those which make chairs and tables talk like elves. The old household gods of the Italian peasants seem to have been great, clumsy. wooden images, more featureless than the figure-head which Quilp battered with the poker. This religion of the home was very homely. Of course there were other less human elements in the tangle of Italian mythology. There were Greek deities superimposed on the Roman; there were here and there uglier things underneath, experiments in the cruel kind of paganism, like the Arician rite of the priest slaying the slayer. But these things were always potential in paganism; they are certainly not the peculiar character of Latin paganism. The peculiarity of that may be roughly covered by saying that if mythology personified the forces of nature, this mythology personified nature as transformed by the forces of man. It was the god of the corn and not of the grass, of the cattle and not the wild things of the forest; in short the cult was literally a culture; as when we speak of it as agriculture.

With this there was a paradox which is still for many the puzzle or riddle of the Latins. With religion running through every domestic detail like a climbing plant, there went what seems to many the very opposite spirit; the spirit of revolt. Imperialists and reactionaries often involve Rome as the very model of order and obedience; but Rome was the very reverse. The real history of ancient Rome is much more like the history of modern Paris. It might be called in modern language a city built out of barricades. It is said that the gate of Janus was never closed because there was an eternal war without; it is almost as true that there was an eternal revolution within. From the first Plebeian riots to the last Servile Wars, the state that imposed peace on the world was never really at peace. The rulers were themselves rebels.

There is a real relation between this religion in private and this revolution in public life. Stories none the less heroic for being hackneyed remind us that the Republic was founded on a tyrannicide that avenged an insult to a wife; that the Tribunes of the people were re-established after another which avenged an insult to a daughter. The truth is that only men to whom the family is sacred will ever have a standard or a status by which to criticise the state. They alone can appeal to something more holy than the gods of the city; the gods of the hearth. That is why men are mystified in seeing that the same nations that are thought rigid in domesticity are also thought restless in politics; for instance the Irish and the French. It is worthwhile to dwell on this domestic point because it is an exact example of what is meant here by the inside of history, like the inside of houses. Merely political histories of Rome may be right enough in saying that this or that was a cynical or cruel act of the Roman politicians; but the spirit that lifted Rome from beneath was the spirit of all the Romans; and it is not a cant to call it the ideal of Cincinnatus passing from the senate to the plough. Men of that sort had strengthened their village on every side, had extended its victories already over Italians and even over Greeks, when they found themselves confronted with a war that changed the world. I have called it here the war of the gods and demons.

There was established on the opposite coast of the inland sea a city that bore the name of the New Town. It was already much older, more powerful, and more prosperous than the Italian town; but there still remained about it an atmosphere that made the name not inappropriate. It had been called new because it was a colony like New York or New Zealand. It was an outpost or settlement of the energy and expansion of the great commercial cities of Tyre and Sidon. There was a note of the new countries and colonies about it; a confident and commercial outlook. It was fond of saying things that rang with a certain metallic assurance; as that nobody could wash his hands in the sea without the leave of the New Town. For it depended almost entirely on the greatness of its ships, as did the two great ports and markets from which its people came. It brought from Tyre and Sidon a prodigious talent for trade and considerable experience of travel. It brought other things as well.

In a previous chapter I have hinted at something of the psychology that lies behind a certain type of religion. There was a tendency in those hungry for practical results, apart from poetical results, to call upon spirits of terror and compulsion; to move Acheron in despair of bending the gods. There is always a sort of dim idea that these darker powers will really do things, with no nonsense about it. In the interior psychology of the Punic peoples this strange sort of pessimistic practicality had grown to great proportions. In the New Town which the Romans called Carthage, as in the parent cities of Phoenicia, the god who got things done bore the name Moloch, who was perhaps identical with the other deity whom we know as Baal, the Lord. The Romans did not at first quite know what to call him or what to make of him; they had to go back to the grossest myth of Greek or Roman Origins and compare him to Saturn devouring his children. But the worshippers of Moloch were not gross or primitive. They were members of a mature and polished civilisation abounding in refinements and luxuries; they were probably far more civilised than the Romans. And Moloch was not a myth; or at any rate his meal was not a myth. These highly civilised people really met together to invoke the blessing of heaven on their empire by throwing hundreds of their infants into a large furnace. We can only realise the combination by imagining a number of Manchester merchants with chimneypot hats and mutton-chop whiskers, going to church every Sunday at eleven o'clock to see a baby roasted alive.

The first stages of the political or commercial quarrel can be followed in far too much detail, precisely because it is merely political or commercial. The Punic Wars looked at one time as if they would never end; and it is not easy to say when they ever began. The Greeks and the Sicilians had already been fighting vaguely on the European side against the African city. Carthage had defeated Greece and conquered Sicily. Carthage had also planted herself firmly in Spain; and between Spain and Sicily the Latin city was contained and would have been crushed; if the Romans had been of the sort to be easily crushed. Yet the interest of the story really consists in the fact that Rome was crushed. If there had not been certain moral elements as well as the material elements, the story would have ended where Carthage certainly thought it had ended. It is common enough to blame Rome for not making peace. But it was a true popular instinct that there could be no peace with that sort of people. It is common enough to blame the Roman for his *Delenda est Carthago*; Carthage must be destroyed. It is commoner to forget that, to all appearance, Rome itself was destroyed. The sacred savour that hung round Rome forever, it is too often forgotten, clung to her partly because she had risen suddenly from the dead.

Carthage was an aristocracy, as are most of such mercantile states. The pressure of the rich on the poor was impersonal as well as irresistible. For such aristocracies never permit personal government, which is perhaps why this one was jealous of personal talent. But genius can turn up anywhere, even in a governing class. As if to make the world's supreme test as terrible as possible, it was ordained that one of the great houses of Carthage should produce a man who came out of those gilded palaces with all the energy and originality of Napoleon coming from nowhere. At the worst crisis of the war, Rome learned that Italy itself, by a military miracle, was invaded from the north. Hannibal, the Grace of Baal as his name ran in his own tongue, had dragged a ponderous chain of armaments over the starry solitudes of the Alps; and pointed southward to the city which he had been pledged by all his dreadful gods to destroy.

Hannibal marched down the road to Rome, and the Romans who rushed to war with him felt as if they were fighting with a magician. Two great armies sank to right and left of him into the swamps of the Trebia; more and more were sucked into the horrible whirlpool of Cannae; more and more went forth only to fall in ruin at his touch. The supreme sign of all disasters, which is treason, turned tribe after tribe against the falling cause of Rome, and still the unconquerable enemy rolled nearer and nearer to the city; and following their great leader the swelling cosmopolitan army of Carthage passed like a pageant of the whole world: the elephants shaking the earth like marching mountains and the gigantic Gauls with their barbaric panoply and the dark Spaniards girt in gold and the brown Numidians on their unbridled desert horses wheeling and darting like hawks, and whole mobs of deserters and mercenaries and miscellaneous peoples; and the Grace of Baal went before them.

The Roman augurs and scribes who said in that hour that it brought forth unearthly prodigies, that a child was born with the head of an elephant or that stars fell down like hailstones, had a far more philosophical grasp of what had really happened than the modern historian who can see nothing in it but a success of strategy concluding a rivalry in commerce. Something far different was felt at the

time and on the spot as it is always felt by those who experience a foreign atmosphere entering their own like a fog
or a foul savour. It was no mere military defeat, it was certainly no mere mercantile rivalry, that filled the Roman
imagination with such hideous omens of nature herself
becoming unnatural. It was Moloch upon the mountain of
the Latins, looking with his appalling face across the plain;
it was Baal who trampled the vineyards with his feet of
stone; it was the voice of Tanit the invisible, behind her
trailing veils, whispering of the love that is more horrible
than hate. The burning of the Italian cornfields, the ruin of
the Italian vines were something more than actual; they
were allegorical. They were the destruction of domestic
and fruitful things, the withering of what was human before that inhumanity that is far beyond the human thing
called cruelty. The household gods bowed low in darkness
under their lowly roofs; and above them went the demons
upon a wind from beyond all walls, blowing the trumpet of
the Tramontane. The door of the Alps was broken down;
and in no vulgar but a very solemn sense, it was Hell let
loose. The war of the gods and demons seemed already to
have ended; and the gods were dead. The eagles were lost,
the legions were broken; and in Rome nothing remained
but honour and the cold courage of despair.

In the whole world one thing still threatened Carthage,
and that was Carthage. There still remained the inner
working of an element strong in all successful commercial
states, and the presence of a spirit that we know. There
was still the solid sense and shrewdness of the men who
manage big enterprises; there was still the advice of the
best financial experts; there was still business government;
there was still the broad and sane outlook of practical men
of affairs; and in these things could the Romans hope. As
the war trailed on to what seemed its tragic end, there grew
gradually a faint and strange possibility that even now they
might not hope in vain. The plain business men of Carthage, thinking as such men do in terms of living and dying
races, saw clearly that Rome was not only dying but dead.

The war was over; it was obviously hopeless for the Italian city to resist any longer, and inconceivable that anybody should resist when it was hopeless. Under these circumstances, another set of broad, sound business principles remained to be considered. Wars were waged with money, and consequently cost money; perhaps they felt in their hearts, as do so many of their kind, that after all war must be a little wicked because it costs money. The time had now come for peace; and still more for economy. The messages sent by Hannibal from time to time asking for reinforcements were a ridiculous anachronism; there were much more important things to attend to now. It might be true that some consul or other had made a last dash to the Metaurus, had killed Hannibal's brother and flung his head, with Latin fury, into Hannibal's camp; and mad actions of that sort showed bow utterly hopeless the Latins felt about their cause. But even excitable Latins could not be so mad as to cling to a lost cause forever. So argued the best financial experts; and tossed aside more and more letters, full of rather queer alarmist reports. So argued and acted the great Carthaginian Empire. That meaningless prejudice, the curse of commercial states, that stupidity is in some way practical and that genius is in some way futile, led them to starve and abandon that great artist in the school of arms, whom the gods had given them in vain.

Why do men entertain this queer idea that what is sordid must always overthrow what is magnanimous; that there is some dim connection between brains and brutality, or that it does not matter if a man is dull so long as he is also mean? Why do they vaguely think of all chivalry as sentiment and all sentiment as weakness? They do it because they are, like all men, primarily inspired by religion. For them, as for all men the first fact is their notion of the nature of things; their idea about what world they are living in. And it is their faith that the only ultimate thing is fear and therefore that the very heart of the world is evil. They believe that death is stronger than life, and therefore dead things must be stronger than living things; whether those

dead things are gold and iron and machinery or rocks and
rivers and forces of nature. It may sound fanciful to say
that men we meet at tea tables or talk to at garden-parties
are secretly worshippers of Baal or Moloch. But this sort
of commercial mind has its own cosmic vision and it is the
vision of Carthage. It has in it the brutal blunder that was
the ruin of Carthage. The Punic power fell, because there
is in this materialism a mad indifference to real thought. By
disbelieving in the soul, it comes to disbelieving in the
mind. Being too practical to be moral it denies what every
practical soldier calls the moral of an army. It fancies that
money will fight when men will no longer fight. So it was
with the Punic merchant princes. Their religion was a religion of despair, even when their practical fortunes were
hopeful. How could they understand that the Romans
could hope even when their fortunes were hope less? Their
religion was a religion of force and fear; how could they
understand that men can still despise fear even when they
submit to force? Their philosophy of the world had weari-
ness in its very heart; above all they were weary of warfare;
how should they understand those who still wage war even
when they are weary of it? In a word, how should they understand the mind of Man, who had so long bowed down
before mindless things, money and brute force and gods
who had the hearts of beasts? They awoke suddenly to the
news that the embers they had disdained too much even to
tread out were again breaking everywhere into flames; that
Hasdrubal was defeated; that Hannibal was outnumbered,
that Scipio had carried the war into Spain; that he had carried it into Africa. Before the very gates of the golden city
Hannibal fought his last fight for it and lost; and Carthage
fell as nothing has fallen since Satan. The name of the
New City remains only as a name. There is no stone of it
left upon the sand. Another war was indeed waged before
the final destruction: but the destruction was final. Only
men digging in its deep foundations centuries after found a
heap of hundreds of little skeletons, the holy relics of that
religion. For Carthage fell because she was faithful to her

own philosophy and had followed out to its logical conclusion her own vision of the universe. Moloch had eaten his children.

The gods had risen again, and the demons had been defeated after all. But they had been defeated by the defeated, and almost defeated by the dead. Nobody understands the romance of Rome, and why she rose afterwards to a representative leadership that seemed almost fated and fundamentally natural. Who does not keep in mind the agony of horror and humiliation through which she had continued to testify to the sanity that is the soul of Europe? She came to stand alone in the midst of an empire because she had once stood alone in the midst of a ruin and a waste. After that all men knew in their hearts that she had been representative of mankind, even when she was rejected of men. And there fell on her the shadow from a shining and as yet invisible light and the burden of things to be. It is not for us to guess in what manner or moment the mercy of God might in any case have rescued the world; but it is certain that the struggle which established Christendom would have been very different if there had been an empire of Carthage instead of an empire of Rome. We have to thank the patience of the Punic wars if, in after ages, divine things descended at least upon human things and not inhuman. Europe evolved into its own vices and its own impotence, as will be suggested on another page; but the worst into which it evolved was not like what it had escaped. Can any man in his senses compare the great wooden doll, whom the children expected to eat a little bit of the dinner, with the great idol who would have been expected to eat the children? That is the measure of how far the world went astray, compared with how far it might have gone astray. If the Romans were ruthless, it was in a true sense to an enemy, and certainly not merely a rival. They remembered not trade routes and regulations, but the faces of sneering men; and hated the hateful soul of Carthage. And we owe them something if we never needed to cut down the groves of Venus exactly as men cut down the groves of Baal. We owe it partly to their harshness that our thoughts of our human past are not wholly harsh. If the passage from heathenry to Christianity was a bridge as well as a breach we owe it to those who kept that heathenry human. If, after all these ages, we are in some sense at peace with paganism, and can think more kindly of our fathers, it is well to remember the things that were, and the things that might have been. For this reason alone we can take lightly the load of antiquity and need not shudder at a nymph on a fountain or a cupid on a valentine. Laughter and sadness link us with things long passed away and remembered without dishonour; and we can see not altogether without tenderness the twilight sinking around the Sabine farm and hear the household gods rejoice when Catullus comes home to Sirmio. *Deleta est Carthago.*

8

THE END OF THE WORLD

I WAS ONCE SITTING on a summer day in a meadow in Kent under the shadow of a little village church, with a rather curious companion with whom I had just been walking through the woods. He was one of a group of eccentrics I had come across in my wanderings who had a new religion called Higher Thought; in which I had been so far initiated as to realise a general atmosphere of loftiness or height, and was hoping at some later and more esoteric stage to discover the beginnings of thought. My companion was the most amusing of them, for however he may have stood towards thought, he was at least very much their superior in experience, having travelled beyond the tropics while they were meditating in the suburbs; though he had been charged with excess in telling travellers' tales. In spite of anything said against him, I preferred him to his companions and willingly went with him through the wood; where I could not but feel that his sunburned face and fierce, tufted eyebrows and pointed beard gave him something of the look of Pan. Then we sat down in the meadow and gazed idly at the tree-tops and the spire of the village church; while the warm afternoon began to mellow into early evening and the song of a speck of a bird was faint far up in the sky and no more than a whisper of breeze soothed rather than stirred the ancient orchards of the garden of England. Then my companion said to me: 'Do you know why the spire of that church goes up like that?' I expressed a respectable agnosticism, and he answered in an off-hand way, 'Oh, the same as the obelisks; the Phallic Worship of antiquity.' Then I looked across at him suddenly as he lay there leering above his goat-like

beard; and for the moment I thought he was not Pan but
the Devil. No mortal words can express the immense, the
insane incongruity and unnatural perversion of thought
involved in saying such a thing at such a moment and in
such a place. For one moment was in the mood in which
men burned witches; and then a sense of absurdity equally
enormous seemed to open about like a dawn. 'Why, of
course,' I said after a moment's reflection, 'if it hadn't been
for phallic worship, they would have built the spire pointing downwards and standing on its own apex.' I could
have sat in that field and laughed for an hour. My friend
did not seem offended, for indeed he was thin-skinned
about his scientific discoveries. I had only met him by
chance and I never met him again, and I believe he is now
dead; but though it has nothing to do with the argument, it
may be worthwhile to mention the name of this adherent
of Higher Thought and interpreter of primitive religious
origins; or at any rate the name by which he was known. It
was Louis de Rougemont.

That insane image of the Kentish church standing on
the point of its spire, as in some old rustic topsy-turvy tale,
always comes back into my imagination when I hear these
things said about pagan origins; and calls to my aid the
laughter of the giants. Then I feel as genially and charitably
to a11 other scientific investigators, higher critics, and authorities on ancient and modern religion, as I do to poor
Louis de Rougemont. But the memory of that immense
absurdity remains as a sort of measure and check by which
to keep sane, not only on the subject of Christian
churches, but also on the subject of heathen temples. Now
a great many people have talked about heathen origins as
the distinguished traveller talked about Christian origins.
Indeed a great many modern heathens have been very hard
on heathenism. A great many modern humanitarians have
been very hard on the real religion of humanity. They have
represented it as being everywhere and from the first
rooted only in these repulsive arcana; and carrying the
character of something utterly shameless and anarchical.

Now I do not believe this for a moment. I should never dream of thinking about the whole worship of Apollo what De Rougemont could think about the worship of Christ. I would never admit that there was such an atmosphere in a Greek city as that madman was able to smell in a Kentish village. On the contrary, it is the whole point, even of this final chapter upon the final decay of paganism, to insist once more that the worst sort of paganism had already been defeated by the best sort. It was the best sort of paganism that conquered the gold of Carthage. It was the best sort of paganism that wore the laurels of Rome. It was the best thing the world had yet seen, all things considered and on any large scale, that ruled from the wall of the Grampians to the garden of the Euphrates. It was the best that conquered; it was the best that ruled; and it was the best that began to decay.

Unless this broad truth be grasped, the whole story is seen askew. Pessimism is not in being tired of evil but in being tired of good. Despair does not lie in being weary of suffering, but in being weary of joy. It is when for some reason or other the good things in a society no longer work that the society begins to decline; when its food does not feed, when its cures do not cure, when its blessings refuse to bless. We might almost say that in a society without such good things we should hardly have any test by which to register a decline; that is why some of the static commercial oligarchies like Carthage have rather an air in history of standing and staring like mummies, so dried up and swathed and embalmed that no man knows when they are new or old. But Carthage at any rate was dead, and the worst assault ever made by the demons on mortal society had been defeated. But how much would it matter that the worst was dead if the best was dying?

To begin with, it must be noted that the relation of Rome to Carthage was partially repeated and extended in her relation to nations more normal and more nearly akin to her than Carthage. I am not here concerned to controvert the merely political view that Roman statesmen acted unscrupulously towards Corinth or the Greek cities. But I am concerned to contradict the notion that there was nothing but a hypocritical excuse in the ordinary Roman dislike of Greek vices. I am not presenting these pagans as paladins of chivalry, with a sentiment about nationalism never known until Christian times. But I am presenting them as men with the feelings of men; and those feelings were not a pretence. The truth is that one of the weaknesses in nature-worship and mere mythology had already produced a perversion among the Greeks, due to the worst sophistry; the sophistry of simplicity. Just as they became unnatural by worshipping nature, so they actually became unmanly by worshipping man. If Greece led her conqueror, she might have misled her conqueror; but these were things he did originally wish to conquer – even in himself. It is true that in one sense there was less inhumanity even in Sodom and Gomorrah than in Tyre and Sidon. When we consider the war of the demons on the children we cannot compare even Greek decadence to Punic devil worship. But it is not true that the sincere revulsion from either need be merely pharisaical. It is not true to human nature or to common sense. Let any lad who has had the look to grow up sane and simple in his day-dreams of love hear for the first time of the cult of Ganymede; he will not be merely shocked but sickened. And that first impression, as has been said here so often about first impressions, will be right. Our cynical indifference is an illusion; it is the greatest of all illusions; the illusion of familiarity. It is right to conceive the more or less rustic virtues of the ruck of the original Romans as reacting against the very rumour of it with complete spontaneity and sincerity. It is right to regard them as reacting, if in a lesser degree, exactly as they did .against the cruelty of Carthage. Because it was in a less degree they did not destroy Corinth as they destroyed Carthage. But if their attitude and action was rather destructive, in neither case need their indignation have been mere self-righteousness covering mere selfishness. And if anybody insists that nothing could have operated in either case but reasons of state and commercial conspiracies, we can only tell him that there is something which he does not understand; something which possibly he will never understand; something which, until he does understand, he will never understand the Latins. That something is called democracy. He has probably heard the word a good many times and even used it himself; but he has no notion of what it means. All through the revolutionary history of Rome there was an incessant drive towards democracy; the state and the statesman could do nothing without a considerable backing of democracy; the sort of democracy that never has anything to do with diplomacy. It is precisely because of the presence of Roman democracy that we hear so much about Roman oligarchy. For instance, recent historians have tried to explain the valour and victory of Rome in terms of that detestable and detested usury which was practiced by some of the Patricians; as if Curius had conquered the men of the Macedonian phalanx by lending them money; or the Consul Nero had negotiated the victory of Metaurus at five per cent. But we realise the usury of the Patricians because of the perpetual revolt of the Plebeians. The rule of the Punic merchant princes had the very soul of usury. But there was never a Punic mob that dared to call them usurers.

Burdened like all mortal things with all mortal sin and weakness, the rise of Rome had really been the rise of normal and especially of popular things; and in nothing more than in the thoroughly normal and profoundly popular hatred of perversion. Now among the Greeks a perversion had become a convention. It is true that it had become so much of a convention, especially a literary convention, that it was sometimes conventionally copied by Roman literary men. But this is one of those complications that always arise out of conventions. It must not obscure our sense of the difference of tone in the two societies as a whole. It is true that Virgil would once in a way take over a theme of Theocritus; but nobody can get the impression that Virgil was particularly fond of that theme. The themes

of Virgil were specially and notably the normal themes and
nowhere more than in morals; piety and patriotism and the
honour of the countryside. And we may well pause upon
the name of the poet as we pass into the autumn of antiquity, upon his name who was in so supreme a sense the
very voice of autumn, of its maturity and its melancholy; of
its fruits of fulfilment and its prospect of decay. Nobody
who reads even a few lines of Virgil can doubt that he understood what moral sanity means to mankind. Nobody
can doubt his feelings when the demons were driven in
flight before the household gods. But there are two particular points about him and his work which are particularly important to the main thesis here. The first is that the
whole of his great is in a very peculiar sense founded upon
the fall of Troy; that is upon an avowed pride in Troy although she had fallen. In tracing to Trojans the foundation
of his beloved race and republic, he began what may be
called the great Trojan tradition which runs through medieval and modern history. We have already seen the first
hint of it in the pathos of Homer about Hector. But Virgil
turned it not merely into a literature but into a legend. And
it was a legend of the almost divine dignity that belongs to
the defeated. This was one of the traditions that did truly
prepare the world for the coming of Christianity and especially of Christian chivalry. This is what did help to sustain
civilisation through the incessant defeats of the Dark Ages
and the barbarian wars; out of which what we call chivalry
was born. It is the moral attitude of the man with his back
to the wall; and it was the wall of Troy. All through medieval and modern times this version of the virtues in the
Homeric conflict can be traced in a hundred ways co-
operating with all that was akin to it in Christian sentiment.
Our own countrymen, and the men of other countries,
loved to claim like Virgil that their own nation was descended from the heroic Trojans. All sorts of people
thought it the most superb sort of heraldry to claim to be
descended from Hector. Nobody seems to have wanted to
be descended from Achilles. The very fact that the Trojan

name has become a Christian name, and been scattered to
the last limits of Christendom, to Ireland or the Gaelic
Highlands, while the Greek name has remained relatively
rare and pedantic, is a tribute to the same truth. Indeed it
involves a curiosity of language almost in the nature of a
joke. The name has been turned into a verb; and the very
phrase about hectoring, in the sense of swaggering, suggests the myriads of soldiers who have taken the fallen
Trojan for a model. As a matter of fact, nobody in antiquity was less given to hectoring than Hector. But even the
bully pretending to be a conqueror took his title from the
conquered. That is why the popularisation of the Trojan
origin by Virgil has a vital relation to all those elements
that have made men say that Virgil was almost a Christian.
It is almost as if two great tools or toys of the same timber,
the divine and the human, had been in the hands of Providence; and the only thing comparable to the Wooden
Cross of Calvary was the Wooden Horse of Troy. So, in
some wild allegory, pious in purpose if almost profane in
form, the Holy Child might have fought the dragon with a
wooden sword and a wooden horse.

The other element in Virgil which is essential to the argument is the particular nature of his relation to mythology; or what may here in a special sense be called folk-lore,
the faiths and fancies of the populace. Everybody knows
that his poetry at its most perfect is less concerned with
the pomposity of Olympus than with the *numina* of natural
and agricultural life. Everyone knows where Virgil looked
for the causes of things. He speaks of finding them not so
much in cosmic allegories of Uranus and Chronos; but
rather in Pan and the sisterhood of the nymphs and Syl-
vanus the old man of the forest. He is perhaps most himself in some passages of the Eclogues, in which he has
perpetuated forever the great legend of Arcadia and the
shepherds. Here again it is easy enough to miss the point
with petty criticism about all the in things that happen to
separate his literary convention from ours. There is nothing more artificial than the cry of artificiality as directed

against the old pastoral poetry. We have entirely missed all
that our fathers meant by looking at the externals of what
they wrote. People have been so much amused with the
mere fact that the china shepherdess was made of china
that they have not even asked why she was made at all.
They have been so content to consider the Merry Peasant
as a figure in an opera that they have not asked even how
he came to go to the opera, or how he strayed on to the
stage.

In short, we have only to ask why there is a china
shepherdess and not a china shopkeeper. Why were not
mantelpieces adorned with figures of city merchants in
elegant attitudes; of iron masters wrought in iron or gold
speculators in gold? Why, did the opera exhibit a Merry
Peasant and not a Merry Politician? Why was there not a
ballet of bankers, pirouetting upon pointed toes? Because
the ancient instinct and humour of humanity have always
told them, under whatever conventions, that the conventions of complex cities were less really healthy than the
customs of the countryside. So it is with the eternity of the
Eclogues. A modern poet did indeed write things called
Fleet Street Eclogues, in which poets took the place of the
shepherds. But nobody has yet written anything called Wall
Street Eclogues, in which millionaires should take the place
of the poets. And the reason is that there is a real if only a
recurrent yearning for that sort of simplicity; and there is
never that sort of yearning for that sort of complexity. The
key to the mystery of the Merry Peasant is that the peasant
often is merry. Those who do not believe it are simply
those who do not know anything about him and therefore
do not know which are his times for merriment. Those
who do not believe in the shepherd's feast or song are
merely ignorant of the shepherd's calendar. The real shepherd is indeed very different from the ideal shepherd, but
that is no reason for forgetting the reality at the root of the
ideal. It needs a truth to make a tradition. It needs a tradition to make a convention. Pastoral poetry is certainly often a convention, especially in a social decline. It was in a

social decline that Watteau shepherds and shepherdesses lounged about the gardens of Versailles. It was also in a social decline that shepherds and shepherdesses continued to pipe and dance through the most faded imitations of Virgil. But that is no reason for dismissing the dying paganism without ever understanding its life. It is no reason for forgetting that the very word Pagan is the same as the word Peasant. We may say that this art is only artificiality; but it is not a love of the artificial. On the contrary, it is in its very nature only the lure of nature-worship, or the love of the natural.

For the shepherds were dying because their gods were dying. Paganism lived upon poetry; that poetry already considered under the name of mythology. But everywhere, and especially in Italy, it had been a mythology and a poetry rooted in the countryside; and that rustic religion had been largely responsible for the rustic happiness. Only as the whole society grew in age and experience, there began to appear that weakness in all mythology already noted in the chapter under that name. This religion was not quite a religion. In other words, this religion was not quite a reality. It was the young world's riot with images and ideas like a young man's riot with wine or love-making; it was not so much immoral as irresponsible; it had no foresight of the final test of time. Because it was creative to any extent it was credulous to any extent. It belonged to the artistic side of man, yet even considered artistically it had long become overloaded and entangled. The family trees sprung from the seed of Jupiter were a jungle rather than a forest; the claims of the gods and demigods seemed like things to be settled rather by a lawyer or a professional herald than by a poet. But it is needless to say that it was not only in the artistic sense that these things had grown more anarchic. There had appeared in more and more flagrant fashion that flower of evil that is really implicit in the very seed of nature-worship, however natural it may seem. I have said that I do not believe that natural worship necessarily begins with this particular passion; I am not of the De

Rougemont school of scientific folk-lore. I do not believe
that mythology must begin with eroticism. But I do believe
that mythology must end in it. I am quite certain that mythology did end in it. Moreover, not only did the poetry
grow more immoral, but the immorality grew more indefensible. Greek vices, oriental vices, hints of the old horrors of the Semitic demons began to fill the fancies of decaying Rome, swarming like flies on a dung-heap. The psychology of it is really human enough, to anyone who will
try that experiment of seeing history from the inside.
There comes an hour in the afternoon when the child is
tired of 'pretending'; when he is weary of being a robber or
a Red Indian. It is then that he torments the cat. There
comes a time in the routine of an ordered civilisation when
the man is tired at playing at mythology and pretending
that a tree is a maiden or that the moon made love to a
man. The effect of this staleness is the same everywhere; it
is seen in all drug-taking and dram-drinking and every
form of the tendency to increase the dose. Men seek
stranger sins or more startling obscenities as stimulants to
their jaded sense. They seek after mad oriental religions for
the same reason. They try to stab their nerves to life, if it
were with the knives of the priests of Baal. They are walking in their sleep and try to wake themselves up with
nightmares.

At that stage even of paganism therefore the peasant
songs and dances sound fainter and fainter in the forest.
For one thing the peasant civilisation was fading, or had
already faded from the whole countryside. The Empire at
the end was organised more and more on that servile system which generally goes with the boast of organisation;
indeed it was almost as servile as the modern schemes for
the organisations of industry. It is proverbial that what
would once have been a peasantry came a mere populace
of the town dependent for bread and circuses; which may
again suggest to some a mob dependent upon doles and
cinemas. In this as in many other respects, modern return
to heathenism has been a return not even the heathen

youth but rather to the heathen old age. But causes of it were spiritual in both cases; and especially the spirit of paganism had departed with its familiar spirits. The heart had gone out of it with its household gods, who went along with the gods of the garden and the field and the forest. The Old Man of the Forest was too old; he was already dying. It is said truly in a sense that Pan died because Christ was born. It is almost as true in another sense that men knew that Christ was born because Pan was already dead. A void was made by the vanishing of the whole mythology of mankind, which would have asphyxiated like a vacuum if it had not been filled with theology. But the point for the moment is that the mythology could not have lasted like a theology in any case. Theology is thought, whether we agree with it or not. Mythology was never thought, and nobody could really agree with it or disagree with it. It was a mere mood of glamour and when the mood went it could not be recovered. Men not only ceased to believe in the gods, but they realised that they had never believed in them. They had sung their praises; they had danced round their altars. They had played the flute; they had played the fool.

So came the twilight upon Arcady and the last notes of the pipe sound sadly from the beechen grove. In the great Virgilian poems there is already something of the sadness; but the loves and the household gods linger in lovely lines like that which Mr. Belloc took for a test of understanding; *incipe Parve Puer risu cognoscere matrem*. But with them as with us, the human family itself began to break down under servile organisation and the herding of the towns. The urban mob became enlightened; that it lost the mental energy that could create myths. All round the circle of the Mediterranean cities the people mourned for the loss of gods and were consoled with gladiators. And meanwhile something similar was happening to that intellectual aristocracy of antiquity that had been walking about and talking at large ever since Socrates and Pythagoras. They began to betray to the world the fact that they were walking in a circle and saying the same thing over and over again. Philosophy began to be a joke; it also began to be a bore. That unnatural simplification of everything into one system or another, which we have noted as the fault of the philosopher, revealed at once its finality and its futility. Everything was virtue or everything was happiness or everything was fate or everything was good or everything was bad; anyhow, everything was everything and there was no more to be said; so they said it. Everywhere the sages had degenerated into sophists; that is, into hired rhetoricians or askers of riddles. It is one of the symptoms of this that the sage begins to turn not only into a sophist but into a magician. A touch of oriental occultism is very much appreciated in the best houses. As the philosopher is already a society entertainer, he may as well also be a conjurer.

Many moderns have insisted on the smallness of that Mediterranean world; and the wider horizons that might have awaited it with the discovery of the other continents. But this is an illusion; one of the many illusions of materialism. The limits that paganism had reached in Europe were the limits of human existence; at its best it had only reached the same limits anywhere else. The Roman stoics did not need any Chinamen to teach them stoicism. The Pythagoreans did not need any Hindus to teach them about recurrence or the simple life or the beauty of being a vegetarian. In so far as they could get these things from the East, they had already got rather too much of them from the East. The Syncretists were as convinced as Theosophists that all religions are really the same. And how else could they have extended philosophy merely by extending geography? It can hardly be proposed that they should learn a purer religion from the Aztecs or sit the feet of the Incas of Peru. All the rest of the world was a welter of barbarism. It is essential to recognise that the Roman Empire was recognised as the highest achievement of the human race; and also as the broadest. A dreadful secret seemed to be written as in obscure hieroglyphics across those mighty works of marble and stone, those colossal amphitheatres and aqueducts. Man could do no more.

For it was not the message blazed on the Babylonian wall, that one king was found wanting or his one kingdom given to a stranger. It was no such good news as the news of invasion conquest. There was nothing left that could conquer Rome but there was also nothing left that could improve it. It was the strongest thing that was growing weak. It was the thing that was going to the bad. It is necessary to insist again and again that many civilisations had met in one civilisation of the Mediterranean sea; that it was already universal with a stale and sterile universality. The peoples had pooled their resources and still there was not enough. The empires had gone into partnership and they were still bankrupt. No philosopher who was really philosophical could think anything except that, in that central sea, the wave of the world had risen to its highest, seeming to touch the stars. But the wave was already stooping; for it was only the wave of the world.

That mythology and that philosophy into which paganism has already been analyzed had thus both of them been drained most literally to the dregs. If with the multiplication of magic the third department, which we have called the demons, was even increasingly active, it was never anything but destructive. There remains only the fourth element or rather the first; that which had been in a sense forgotten because it was the first. I mean the primary and overpowering yet impalpable impression that the universe after all has one origin and one aim; and because it has an aim must have an author. What became of this great truth in the background of men's minds, at this time, it is perhaps more difficult to determine. Some of the Stoics undoubtedly saw it more and more clearly as the clouds of mythology cleared and thinned away; and great men among them did much even to the last to lay the foundations of a concept of the moral unity of the world. The Jews still held their secret certainty of it jealously behind high fences of exclusiveness; yet it is intensely characteristic of the society and the situation that some fashionable

figures, especially fashionable ladies, actually embraced
Judaism. But in the case of many others I fancy there entered at this point a new negation. Atheism became really
possible in that abnormal time; for atheism is abnormality.
It is not merely the denial of a dogma. It is the reversal of a
subconscious assumption in the soul; the sense that there
is a meaning and a direction in the world it sees. Lucretius,
the first evolutionist who endeavoured to substitute Evolution for God, had already dangled before men's eyes his
dance of glittering atoms, by which he conceived cosmos
as created by chaos. But it was not his strong poetry or his
sad philosophy, as I fancy, that made it possible for men to
entertain such a vision. It was something in the sense of
impotence and despair with which men shook their fists
vainly at the stars, as they saw all the best work of humanity sinking slowly and helplessly into a swamp. They could
easily believe that even creation itself was not a creation
but a perpetual fall, when they saw that the weightiest and
worthiest of all human creations was falling by its own
weight. They could fancy that all the stars were falling
stars; and that the very pillars of their own solemn porticos
were bowed under a sort of gradual Deluge. To men in
that mood there was a reason for atheism that is in some
sense reasonable. Mythology might fade and philosophy
might stiffen; but if behind these things there was a reality,
surely that reality might have sustained things as they sank.
There was no God; if there had been a God, surely this
was the very moment when He would have moved and
saved the world.

The life of the great civilisation went on with dreary industry and even with dreary festivity. It was the end of the
world, and the worst of it was that it need never end. A
convenient compromise had been made between all the
multitudinous myths and religions of the Empire; that each
group should worship freely and merely give a sort of official flourish of thanks to the tolerant Emperor, by tossing
a little incense to him under his official title of Divus.
Naturally there was no difficulty about that; or rather it

was a long time before the world realised that there ever had been even a trivial difficulty anywhere. The members of some Eastern sect or secret society or other seemed to have made a scene somewhere; nobody could imagine why. The incident occurred once or twice again and began to arouse irritation out of proportion to its insignificance. It was not exactly what these provincials said; though of course it sounded queer enough. They seemed to be saying that God was dead and that they themselves had seen him die. This might be one of the many manias produced by the despair of the age; only they did not seem particularly despairing. They seemed quite unnaturally joyful about it, and gave the reason that the death of God had allowed them to cut him and drink his blood. According to other accounts God was not exactly dead after all; there trailed through the bewildered imagination some sort of fantastic procession of the funeral of God, at which the sun turned black, but which ended with the dead omnipotence break-ing out of the tomb and rising again like the sun. But it was not the strange story to which anybody paid any particular attention; people in that world had seen queer religions enough to fill a madhouse. It was something in the tone of the madmen and their type of formation. They were a scratch company of barbarians and slaves and poor and unimportant people; but their formation was military; they moved together and were very absolute about who and what was really a part of their little system; and about what they said, however mildly, there was a ring like iron. Men used to many mythologies and moralities could make no analysis of the mystery, except the curious conjecture that they meant what they said. All attempts to make them see reason in the perfectly simple matter of the Emperor's statue seemed to be spoken to deaf men. It was as if a new meteoric metal had fallen on the earth; it was a difference of substance to the touch. Those who touched their foun-dation fancied they had struck a rock.

With a strange rapidity, like the changes of a dream, the proportions of things seemed to change in their presence.

Before most men knew what had happened, these few men were palpably present. They were important enough to be ignored. People became suddenly silent about them and walked stiffly past them. We see a new scene, in which the world has drawn its skirts away from these men and women and they stand in the centre of a great space like lepers. The scene changes again and the great space where they stand is overhung on every side with a cloud of witnesses, interminable terraces full of faces looking down towards them intently; for strange things are happening to them. New tortures have been invented for the madmen who have brought good news. That sad and weary society seems almost to find a new energy in establishing its first religious persecution. Nobody yet knows very clearly why that level world has thus lost its balance about the people in its midst; but they stand unnaturally still while the arena and the world seem to revolve round then And there shone on them in that dark hour a light that has never been darkened; a white fire clinging to that group like an unearthly phosphorescence, blazing its track through the twilights of history and confounding every effort to confound it with the mists of mythology and theory; that shaft of light or lightening by which the world itself has struck and isolated and crowned it; by which its own enemies have made it more illustrious and its own critics have made it more inexplicable; the halo of hatred around the Church of God.

PART II

ON THE MAN CALLED CHRIST

1
THE GOD IN THE CAVE

THIS SKETCH OF the human story began in a cave; the cave which popular science associates with the cave-man and in which practical discovery has really found archaic drawings of animals. The second half of human history, which was like a new creation of the world, also begins in a cave. There is even a shadow of such a fancy in the fact that animals were again present; for it was a cave used as a stable by the mountaineers of the uplands about Bethlehem; who still drive their cattle into such holes and caverns at night. It was here that a homeless couple had crept underground with the cattle when the doors of the crowded caravanserai had been shut in their faces; and it was here beneath the very feet of the passersby, in a cellar under the very floor of the world, that Jesus Christ was born. But in that second creation there was indeed something symbolical in the roots of the primeval rock or the horns of the prehistoric herd. God also was a Cave-Man, and had also traced strange shapes of creatures, curiously coloured upon the wall of the world; but the pictures that he made had come to life.

A mass of legend and literature, which increases and will never end has repeated and rung the changes on that single paradox; that the hands that had made the sun and stars were too small to reach the huge heads of the cattle. Upon this paradox, we might almost say upon this jest, all the literature of our faith is founded. It is at least like a jest in this; that it is something which the scientific critic cannot see. He laboriously explains the difficulty which we have always defiantly and almost derisively exaggerated; and mildly condemns as improbable something that we

have almost madly exalted as incredible; as something that
would be much too good to be true, except that it is true.
When that contrast between the cosmic creation and the
little local infancy has been repeated, reiterated, underlined,
emphasised, exulted in, sung, shouted, roared, not to say
howled, in a hundred thousand hymns, carols, rhymes,
rituals pictures, poems, and popular sermons, it may be
suggested that we hardly need a higher critic to draw our
attention to something a little odd about it; especially one
of the sort that seems to take a long time to see a joke,
even his own joke. But about this contrast and combination of ideas one thing may be said here, because it is relevant to the whole thesis of this book. The sort of modern
critic of whom I speak is generally much impressed with
the importance of education in life and the importance of
psychology in education. That sort of man is never tired of
telling us that first impressions fix character by the law of
causation; and he will become quite nervous if a child's
visual sense is poisoned by the wrong colours on a golli-
wog or his nervous system prematurely shaken by a cacophonous rattle. Yet he will think us very narrow-minded
if we say that this is exactly why there really is a difference
between being brought up as a Christian and being
brought up as a Jew or a Moslem or an atheist. The difference is that every Catholic child has learned from pictures,
and even every Protestant child from stones, this incredible combination of contrasted ideas as one of the very first
impressions on his mind. It is not merely a theological difference. It is a psychological difference which can outlast
any theologies. It really is, as that sort of scientist loves to
say about anything, incurable. Any agnostic or atheist
whose childhood has known a real Christmas has ever afterwards, whether he likes it or not, an association in his
mind between two ideas that most of mankind must regard
as remote from each other; the idea of a baby and the idea
of unknown strength that sustains the stars. His instincts
and imagination can still connect them, when his reason
can no longer see the need of the connection; for him

there will always be some savour of religion about the
mere picture of a mother and a baby; some hint of mercy
and softening about the mere mention of the dreadful
name of God. But the two ideas are not naturally or necessarily combined. They would not be necessarily combined
for an ancient Greek or a Chinaman, even for Aristotle or
Confucius. It is no more inevitable to connect God with
an infant than to connect gravitation with a kitten. It has
been created in our minds by Christmas because we are
Christians; because we are psychological Christians even
when we are not theological ones. In other words, this
combination of ideas has emphatically, in the much disputed phrase, altered human nature. There is really a difference between the man who knows it and the man who
does not. It may not be a difference of moral worth, for
the Moslem or the Jew might be worthier according to his
lights; but it is a plain fact about the crossing of two particular lights, the conjunction of two stars in our particular
horoscope. Omnipotence and impotence, or divinity and
infancy, do definitely make a sort of epigram which a million repetitions cannot turn into a platitude. It is not unreasonable to call it unique. Bethlehem is emphatically a
place where extremes meet.

Here begins, it is needless to say, another mighty influence for the humanisation of Christendom. If the world
wanted what is called a non-controversial aspect of Christianity, it would probably select Christmas. Yet it is obviously bound up with what is supposed to be a controversial aspect (I could never at any stage of my opinions imagine why); the respect paid to the Blessed Virgin. When I
was a boy a more Puritan generation objected to a statue
upon my parish church representing the Virgin and Child.
After much controversy, they compromised by taking away
the Child. One would think that this was even more cor-
rupted with Mariolatry, unless the mother was counted less
dangerous when deprived of a sort of weapon. But the
practical difficulty is also a parable. You cannot chip away
the statue of a mother from all round that of a newborn

child. You cannot suspend the newborn child in mid-air; indeed you cannot really have a statue of a newborn child at all. Similarly, you cannot suspend the idea of a newborn child in the void or think of him without thinking of his mother. You cannot visit the child without visiting the mother, you cannot in common human life approach the child except through the mother. If we are to think of Christ in this aspect at all, the other idea follows as it is followed in history. We must either leave Christ out of Christmas, or Christmas out of Christ, or we must admit, if only as we admit it in an old picture, that those holy heads are too near together for the haloes not to mingle and cross.

It might be suggested, in a somewhat violent image, that nothing had happened in that fold or crack in the great gray hills except that the whole universe had been turned inside out. I mean that all the eyes of wonder and worship which had been turned outwards to the largest thing were now turned inward to the smallest. The very image will suggest all that multitudinous marvel of converging eyes that makes so much of the coloured Catholic imagery like a peacock's tail. But it is true in a sense that God who had been only a circumference was seen as a centre; and a centre is infinitely small. It is true that the spiritual spiral henceforward works inwards instead of outwards, and in that sense is centripetal and not centrifugal. The faith becomes, in more ways than one, a religion of little things. But its traditions in art and literature and popular fable have quite sufficiently attested, as has been said, this particular paradox of the divine being in the cradle. Perhaps they have not so clearly emphasised the significance of the divine being in the cave. Curiously enough, indeed, tradition has not very clearly emphasised the cave. It is a familiar fact that the Bethlehem scene has been represented in every possible setting of time and country, of landscape and architecture; and it is a wholly happy and admirable fact that men have conceived it as quite different according to their different individual traditions and tastes. But while all have realised that it was a stable, not so many have realised that it was a cave. Some critics have even been so silly as to suppose that there was some contradiction between the stable and the cave; in which case they cannot know much about caves or stables in Palestine. As they see differences that are not there, it is needless to add that they do not see differences that are there. When a well-known critic says, for instance, that Christ being born in a rocky cavern is like Mithras having sprung alive out of a rock, it sounds like a parody upon comparative religion. There is such a thing as the point of a story, even if it is a story in the sense of a lie. And the notion of a hero appearing, like Pallas from the brain of Zeus, mature and without a mother, is obviously the very opposite of the idea of a god being born like an ordinary baby and entirely dependent on a mother. Whichever ideal we might prefer, we should surely see that they are contrary ideals. It is as stupid to connect them because they both contain a substance called stone as to identify the punishment of the Deluge with the baptism in the Jordan because they both contain a substance called water. Whether as a myth or a mystery, Christ was obviously conceived as born in a hole in the rocks primarily because it marked the position of one outcast and homeless. Nevertheless it is true, as I have said, that the cave has not been so commonly or so clearly used as a symbol as the other realities that surrounded the first Christmas.

And the reason for this also refers to the very nature of that new world. It was in a sense the difficulty of a new dimension. Christ was not only born on the level of the world, but even lower than the world. The first act of the divine drama was enacted, not only on a stage set up above the sightseer, but on a dark and curtained stage sunken out of sight; and that is an idea very difficult to express in most modes of artistic expression. It is the idea of simultaneous happenings on different levels of life. Something like it might have been attempted in the more archaic and decorative medieval art. But the more the artists learned of real-

ism and perspective, the less they could depict at once the
angels in the heavens and the shepherds on the hills, and
the glory in the darkness that was under the hills. Perhaps
it could have been best conveyed by the characteristic expedient of some of the medieval guilds, when they wheeled
about the streets a theatre with three stages one above the
other, with heaven above the earth and hell under the
earth. But in the riddle of Bethlehem it was heaven that
was under the earth.

There is in that alone the touch of a revolution, as of
the world turned upside down. It would be vain to attempt
to say anything adequate, or anything new, about the
change which this conception of a deity born like an outcast or even an outlaw had upon the whole conception of
law and its duties to the poor and outcast. It is profoundly
true to say that after that moment there could be no slaves.
There could be and were people bearing that legal title,
until the Church was strong enough to weed them out, but
there could be no more of the pagan repose in the mere
advantage to the state of keeping it a servile state. Individuals became important, in a sense in which no instru-
ments can be important. A man could not be a means to
an end, at any rate to any other man's end. All this popular
and fraternal element in the story has been rightly attached
by tradition to the episode of the Shepherds; the hinds
who found themselves talking face to face with the princes
of heaven. But there is another aspect of the popular element as represented by the shepherds which has not perhaps been so fully developed; and which is more directly
relevant here.

Men of the people, like the shepherds, men of the
popular tradition, had everywhere been the makers of the
mythologies. It was they who had felt most directly, with
least check or chill from philosophy or the corrupt cults of
civilisation, the need we have already considered the images that were adventures of the imagination; the mythology that was a sort of search; the tempting and tantalising
hints of something half human in nature; the dumb signifi-

cance of seasons and special places. They had best understood that the soul of a landscape is a story and the soul of
a story is a personality. But rationalism had already begun
to rot away these really irrational though imaginative treas-
ures of the peasant; even as systematic slavery had eaten
the peasant out of house and home. Upon all such peasantries everywhere there was descending a dusk and twilight
of disappointment, in the hour when these few men discovered what they sought. Everywhere else Arcadia was
fading from the forest. Pan was dead and the shepherds
were scattered like sheep. And though no man knew it, the
hour was near which was to end and to fulfil all things; and
though no man heard it, there was one far-off cry in an
unknown tongue upon the heaving wilderness of the
mountains. The shepherds had found their Shepherd.

And the thing they found was of a kind with the things
they sought. The populace had been wrong in many things;
but they had not been wrong in believing that holy things
could have a habitation and that divinity need not disdain
the limits of time and space. And the barbarian who conceived the crudest fancy about the sun being stolen and
hidden in a box, or the wildest myth about the god being
rescued and his enemy deceived with a stone, was nearer
to the secret of the cave and knew more about the crisis of
the world, than all those in the circle of cities round the
Mediterranean who had become content with cold abstractions or cosmopolitan generalisations; than all those who
were spinning thinner and thinner threads of thought out
of the transcendentalism of Plato or the orientalism of Pythagoras. The place that the shepherds found was not an
academy or an abstract republic; it was not a place of
myths allegorised or dissected or explained or explained
away. It was a place of dreams come true. Since that hour
no mythologies have been made in the world. Mythology is
a search.

We all know that the popular presentation of this
popular story, in so many miracle plays and carols, has
given to the shepherds the costume, the language, and the

landscape of the separate English and European country-side. We all know that one shepherd will talk in a Somerset dialect or another talk of driving his sheep from Conway towards the Clyde. Most of us know by this time how true is that error, how wise, how artistic, how intensely Christian and Catholic is that anachronism. But some who have seen it in these scenes of medieval rusticity have perhaps not seen it in another sort of poetry, which it is sometimes the fashion to call artificial rather than artistic. I fear that many modern critics will see only a faded classicism in the fact that men like Crashaw and Herrick conceived the shepherds of Bethlehem under the form of the shepherds of Virgil. Yet they were profoundly right; and in turning their Bethlehem play into a Latin Eclogue they took up one of the most important links in human history. Virgil, as we have already seen, does stand for all that saner hea-thenism that had overthrown the insane heathenism of human sacrifice; but the very fact that even the Virgilian virtues and the sane heathenism were in incurable decay is the whole problem to which the revelation to the shep-herds is the solution. If the world had ever had the chance to grow weary of being demoniac, it might have been healed merely by becoming sane. But if it had grown weary even of being sane, what was to happen, except what did happen? Nor is it false to conceive the Arcadian shepherd of the Eclogues as rejoicing in what did happen. One of the Eclogues has even been claimed as a prophecy of what did happen. But it is quite as much in the tone and inci-dental diction of the great poet that we feel the potential sympathy with the great event; and even in their own hu-man phrases the voices of the Virgilian shepherds might more than once have broken upon more than the tender-ness of Italy . . . . *Incipe, parve puer, risu cognoscere matrem* . . . . . They might have found in that strange place all that was best in the last traditions of the Latins; and something bet-ter than a wooden idol standing up forever for the pillar of the human family; a household god. But they and all the other mythologists would be justified in rejoicing that the event had fulfilled not merely the mysticism but the materialism of mythology. Mythology had many sins; but it had not been wrong in being as carnal as the Incarnation. With something of the ancient voice that was supposed to have rung through the groves, it could cry again, 'We have seen, he hath seen us, a visible god.' So the ancient shepherds might have danced, and their feet have been beautiful upon the mountains, rejoicing over the philosophers. But the philosophers had also heard.

It is still a strange story, though an old one, how they came out of orient lands, crowned with the majesty of kings and clothed with something of the mystery of magicians. That truth that is tradition has wisely remembered them almost as unknown quantities, as mysterious as their mysterious and melodious names; Melchior, Caspar, Balthazar. But there came with them all that world of wisdom that had watched the stars in Chaldea and the sun in Persia; and we shall not be wrong if we see in them the same curiosity that moves all the sages. They would stand for the same human ideal if their names had really been Confucius or Pythagoras or Plato. They were those who sought not tales but the truth of things; and since their thirst for truth was itself a thirst for God, they also have had their reward. But even in order to understand that reward, we must understand that for philosophy as much as mythology, that reward was the completion of the incomplete.

Such learned men would doubtless have come, as these learned men did come, to find themselves confirmed in much that was true in their own traditions and right in their own reasoning. Confucius would have found a new foundation for the family in the very reversal of the Holy Family; Buddha would have looked upon a new renunciation, of stars rather than jewels and divinity than royalty. These learned men would still have the right to say, or rather a new right to say, that there was truth in their old teaching. But after all these learned men would have come to learn. They would have come to complete their conceptions with something they had not yet conceived; even to balance their imperfect universe with something they might once have contradicted. Buddha would have come from his impersonal paradise to worship a person. Confucius would have come from his temples of ancestor-worship to worship a child.

We must grasp from the first this character in the new cosmos; that it was larger than the old cosmos. In that sense Christendom is larger than creation; as creation had been before Christ. It included things that had not been there; it also included the things that had been there. The point happens to be well illustrated in this example of Chinese piety, but it would be true of other pagan virtues or pagan beliefs. Nobody can doubt that a reasonable respect for parents is part of a gospel in which God himself was subject in childhood to earthly parents. But the other sense in which the parents were subject to him does introduce an idea that is not Confucian. The infant Christ is not like the infant Confucius; our mysticism conceives him in an immortal infancy. I do not know what Confucius would have done with the Bambino, had it come to life in his arms as it did in the arms of St. Francis. But this is true in relation to all the other religions and philosophies; it is the challenge of the Church. The Church contains what the world does not contain. Life itself does not provide as she does for all sides of life. That every other single system is narrow and insufficient compared to this one, that is not a rhetorical boast; it is a real fact and a real dilemma. Where is the Holy Child amid the Stoics and the ancestor-worshippers? Where is Our Lady of the Moslems, a woman made for no man and set above all angels? Where is St. Michael of the monks of Buddha, rider and master of the trumpets, guarding for every soldier the honour of the sword? What could St. Thomas Aquinas do with the mythology of Brahmanism, he who set forth all the science and rationality and even rationalism of Christianity? Yet even if we compare Aquinas with Aristotle, at the other extreme of reason, we shall find the same sense of something added. Aquinas could understand the most logical parts of Aristotle; it is doubtful if Aristotle could have understood the most mystical parts of Aquinas. Even where we can hardly call the Christian greater, we are forced to call him larger. But it is so to whatever philosophy or heresy or modern movement we may turn. How would Francis the Troubadour have fared among the Calvinists, or for that matter among the Utilitarians of the Manchester School? Yet men like Bossuet and Pascal could be as stern and logical as any Calvinist or Utilitarian. How would St. Joan of Arc, a woman waving on men to war with the sword, have fared among the Quakers or the Doukhabors or the Tolstoyan sect of pacifists? Yet any number of Catholic saints have spent their lives in preaching peace and preventing wars. It is the same with all the modern attempts at Syncretism. They are never able to make something larger than the Creed without leaving something out. I do not mean leaving out something divine but something human; the flag or the inn or the boy's tale of battle or the hedge at the end of the field. The Theosophists build a pantheon; but it is only a pantheon for pantheists. They call a Parliament of Religions as a reunion of all the peoples; but it is only a reunion of all the prigs. Yet exactly such a pantheon had been set up two thousand years before by the shores of the Mediterranean; and Christians were invited to set up the image of Jesus side by side with the image of Jupiter, of Mithras, of Osiris, of Atys, or of Ammon. It was the refusal of the Christians that was the turning-point of history. If the Christians had accepted, they and the whole world would have certainly, in a grotesque but exact metaphor, gone to pot. They would all have been boiled down to one lukewarm liquid in that great pot of cosmopolitan corruption in which all the other myths and mysteries were already melting. It was an awful and an appalling escape. Nobody understands the nature of the Church, or the ringing note of the creed descending from antiquity, who does not realise that the whole world once very nearly died of broad-mindedness and the brotherhood of all religions.

Here it is the important point that the Magi, who stand for mysticism and philosophy, are truly conceived as seeking something new and even as finding something unexpected. That tense sense of crisis which still tingles in the Christmas story and even in every Christmas celebration, accentuates the idea of a search and a discovery. The discovery is, in this case, truly a scientific discovery. For the other mystical figures in the miracle play, for the angel and the mother, the shepherds and the soldiers of Herod, there may be aspects both simpler and more supernatural, more elemental or more emotional. But the Wise Men must be seeking wisdom; and for them there must be a light also in the intellect. And this is the light; that the Catholic creed is catholic and that nothing else is catholic. The philosophy of the Church is universal. The philosophy of the philosophers was not universal. Had Plato and Pythagoras and Aristotle stood for an instant in the light that came out of that little cave, they would have known that their own light was not universal. It is far from certain, indeed, that they did not know it already. Philosophy also, like mythology, had very much the air of a search. It is the realisation of this truth that gives its traditional majesty and mystery to the figures of the Three Kings; the discovery that religion is broader than philosophy and that this is the broadest of religions, contained within this narrow space. The Magicians were gazing at the strange pentacle with the human triangle reversed; and they have never come to the end of their calculations about it. For it is the paradox of that group in the cave, that while our emotions about it are of childish simplicity, our thoughts about it can branch with a never-ending complexity. And we can never reach the end even of our own ideas about the child who was a father and the mother who was a child.

We might well be content to say that mythology had come with the shepherds and philosophy with the philosophers; and that it only remained for them to combine in the recognition of religion. But there was a third element that must not be ignored and one which that religion forever refuses to ignore, in any revel or reconciliation. There was present in the primary scenes of the drama that Enemy that had rotted the legends with lust and frozen the theories into atheism, but which answered the direct challenge with something of that more direct method which we have seen in the conscious cult of the demons. In the description of that demon-worship, of the devouring detestation of innocence shown in the works of its witchcraft and the most inhuman of its human sacrifice, I have said less of its indirect and secret penetration of the saner paganism; the soaking of mythological imagination with sex; the rise of imperial pride into insanity. But both the indirect and the direct influence make themselves felt in the drama of Bethlehem. A ruler under the Roman suzerainty, probably equipped and surrounded with the Roman ornament and order though himself of eastern blood, seems in that hour to have felt stirring within him the spirit of strange things. We all know the story of how Herod, alarmed at some rumour of a mysterious rival, remembered the wild gesture of the capricious despots of Asia and ordered a massacre of suspects of the new generation of the populace. Everyone knows the story; but not everyone has perhaps noted its place in the story of the strange religions of men. Not everybody has seen the significance even of its very contrast with the Corinthian columns and Roman pavement of that conquered and superficially civilised world. Only, as the purpose in his dark spirit began to show and shine in the eyes of the Admen, a seer might perhaps have seen something like a great gray ghost that looked over his shoulder; have seen behind him filling the dome of night and hovering for the last time over history that vast and fearful face that was Moloch of the Carthaginians; awaiting his last tribute from a ruler of the races of Shem. The demons also, in that first festival of Christmas, feasted after their own fashion.

Unless we understand the presence of that enemy, we shall not only miss the point of Christianity, but even miss the point of Christmas. Christmas for us in Christendom has become one thing, and in one sense even a simple thing. But like all the truths of that tradition, it is in another sense a very complex thing. Its unique note is the simultaneous striking of many notes; of humility, of gaiety, of gratitude, of mystical fear, but also of vigilance and of drama. It is not only an occasion for the peacemakers any more than for the merry makers; it is not only a Hindu peace conference any more than it is only a Scandinavian winter feast. There is something defiant in it also; something that makes the abrupt bells at midnight sound like the great guns of a battle that has just been won. All this indescribable thing that we call the Christmas atmosphere only bangs in the air as something like a lingering fragrance or fading vapour from the exultant, explosion of that one hour in the Judean hills nearly two thousand years ago. But the savour is still unmistakable, and it is something too subtle or too solitary to be covered by our use of the word peace. By the very nature of the story the rejoicings in the cavern were rejoicings in a fortress or an outlaws den; properly understood it is not unduly flippant to say they were rejoicing in a dug-out. It is not only true that such a subterranean chamber was a hiding-place from enemies; and that the enemies were already scouring the stony plain that lay above it like a sky. It is not only that the very horse-hoofs of Herod might in that sense have passed like thunder over the sunken head of Christ. It is also that there is in that image a true idea of an outpost, of a piercing through the rock and an entrance into an enemy territory. There is in this buried divinity an idea of undermining the world; of shaking the towers and palaces from below; even as Herod the great king felt that earthquake under him and swayed with his swaying palace.

That is perhaps the mightiest of the mysteries of the cave. It is already apparent that though men are said to have looked for hell under the earth, in this case it is rather heaven that is under the earth. And there follows in this strange story the idea of an upheaval of heaven. That is the paradox of the whole position; that henceforth the highest thing can only work from below. Royalty can only return to its own by a sort of rebellion. Indeed the Church from its beginnings, and perhaps especially in its beginnings, was not so much a principality as a revolution against the prince of the world. This sense that the world had been conquered by the great usurper, and was in his possession, has been much deplored or derided by those optimists who identify enlightenment with case. But it was responsible for all that thrill of defiance and a beautiful danger that made the good news seem to be really both good and new. It was in truth against a huge unconscious usurpation that it raised a revolt, and originally so obscure a revolt. Olympus still occupied the sky like a motionless cloud moulded into many mighty forms; philosophy still sat in the high places and even on the thrones of the kings, when Christ was born in the cave and Christianity in the catacombs.

In both cases we may remark the same paradox of revolution; the sense of something despised and of something feared. The cave in one aspect is only a hole or comer into which the outcasts are swept like rubbish; yet in the other aspect it is a hiding-place of something valuable which the tyrants are seeking like treasure. In one sense they are there because the inn-keeper would not even remember them, and in another because the king can never forget them. We have already noted that this paradox appeared also in the treatment of the early Church. It was important while it was still insignificant, and certainly while it was still impotent. It was important solely because it was intolerable; and in that sense it is true to say that it was intolerable because it was intolerant. It was resented, because, in its own still and almost secret way, it had declared war. It had risen out of the ground to wreck the heaven and earth of heathenism. It did not try to destroy all that creation of gold and marble; but it contemplated a world without it. It dared to look right through it as though the gold and marble had been glass. Those who charged the Christians with burning down Rome with fire-

brands were slanderers; but they were at least far nearer to
the nature of Christianity than those among the moderns
who tell us that the Christians were a sort of ethical society, being martyred in a languid fashion for telling men
they had a duty to their neighbours, and only mildly disliked because they were meek and mild.

Herod had his place, therefore, in the miracle play of
Bethlehem because he is the menace to the Church Militant and shows it from the first as under persecution and
fighting for its life. For those who think this a discord, it is
a discord that sounds simultaneously with the Christmas
bells. For those who think the idea of the Crusade is one
that spoils the idea of the Cross, we can only say that for
them the idea of the Cross is spoiled; the idea of the Cross
is spoiled quite literally in the cradle. It is not here to the
purpose to argue with them on the abstract ethics of fighting; the purpose in this place is merely to sum up the combination of ideas that make up the Christian and Catholic
idea, and to note that all of them are already crystallised in
the first Christmas story. They are three distinct and commonly contrasted things which are nevertheless one thing;
but this is the only thing which can make them one. The
first is the human instinct for a heaven that shall be as literal and almost as local as a home. It is the idea pursued by
all poets and pagans making myths; that a particular place
must be the shrine of the god or the abode of the blest;
that fairyland is a land; or that the return of the ghost must
be the resurrection of the body. I do not here reason about
the refusal of rationalism to satisfy this need. I only say
that if the rationalists refuse to satisfy it, the pagans will
not be satisfied. This is present in the story of Bethlehem
and Jerusalem as it is present in the story of Delos and
Delphi, and as it is *not* present in the whole universe of
Lucretius or the whole universe of Herbert Spencer. The
second element is a philosophy *larger* than other philosophies; larger than that of Lucretius and infinitely larger
than that of Herbert Spencer. It looks at the world through
a hundred windows where the ancient stoic or the modern

agnostic only looks through one. It sees life with thousands of eyes belonging to thousands of different sorts of people, where the other is only the individual standpoint of a stoic or an agnostic. It has something for all moods of man, it finds work for all kinds of men, it understands secrets of psychology, it is aware of depths of evil, it is able to distinguish between real and unreal marvels and miraculous exceptions, it trains itself in tact about bard cases, all with a multiplicity and subtlety and imagination about the varieties of life which is far beyond the bald or breezy platitudes of most ancient or modern moral philosophy. In a word, there is more in it; it finds more in existence to think about; it gets more out of life. Masses of this material about our many-sided life have been added since the time of St. Thomas Aquinas. But St. Thomas Aquinas alone would have found himself limited in the world of Confucius or of Comte. And the third point is this; that while it is local enough for poetry and larger than any other philosophy, it is also a challenge and a fight. While it is deliberately broadened to embrace every aspect of truth, it is still stiffly embattled against every mode of error. It gets every kind of man to fight for it, it gets every kind of weapon to fight with, it widens its knowledge of the things that are fought for and against with every art of curiosity or sympathy; but it never forgets that it is fighting. It proclaims peace on earth and never forgets why there was war in heaven.

This is the trinity of truths symbolised here by the three types in the old Christmas story; the shepherds and the kings and that other king who warred upon the children. It is simply not true to say that other religions and philosophies are in this respect its rivals. It is not true to say that any one of them combines these characters; it is not true to say that any one of them pretends to combine them. Buddhism may profess to be equally mystical; it does not even profess to be equally military. Islam may profess to be equally military; it does not even profess to be equally metaphysical and subtle. Confucianism may profess to sat-

isfy the need of the philosophers for order and reason; it
does not even profess to satisfy the need of the mystics for
miracle and sacrament and the consecration of concrete
things. There are many evidences of this presence of a
spirit at once universal and unique. One will serve here
which is the symbol of the subject of this chapter; that no
other story, no pagan legend or philosophical anecdote or
historical event, does in fact affect any of us with that peculiar and even poignant impression produced on us by
the word Bethlehem. No other birth of a god or childhood
of a sage seems to us to be Christmas or anything like
Christmas. It is either too cold or too frivolous, or too
formal and classical, or too simple and savage, or too oc-
cult and complicated. Not one of us, whatever his opinions, would ever go to such a scene with the sense that he
was going home. He might admire it because it was poetical, or because it was philosophical or any number of other
things in separation; but not because it was itself. The truth
is that there is a quite peculiar and individual character
about the hold of this story on human nature; it is not in
its psychological substance at all like a mere legend or the
life of a great man. It does not exactly in the ordinary sense
turn our minds to greatness; to those extensions and exaggerations of humanity which are turned into gods and heroes, even by the healthiest sort of hero worship. It does
not exactly work outwards, adventurously to the wonders
to be found at the ends of the earth. It is rather something
that surprises us from behind, from the hidden and personal part of our being; like that which can sometimes take
us off our guard in the pathos of small objects or the blind
pieties of the poor. It is rather as if a man had found an
inner room in the very heart of his own house, which he
had never suspected; and seen a light from within. It is if
he found something at the back of his own heart that betrayed him into good. It is not made of what the world
would call strong materials; or rather it is made of materials whose strength is in that winged levity with which they
brush and pass. It is all that is in us but a brief tenderness

that there made eternal; all that means no more than a momentary softening that is in some strange fashion become strengthening and a repose; it is the broken speech and the lost word that are made positive and suspended unbroken; as the strange kings fade into a far country and the mountains resound no more with the feet of the shepherds; and only the night and the cavern lie in fold upon fold over something more human than humanity.

2
THE RIDDLES OF THE GOSPEL

TO UNDERSTAND THE nature of this chapter, it is necessary to recur to the nature of this book. The argument which is meant to be the backbone of the book is of the kind called the *reductio ad absurdum*. It suggests that the results of assuming the rationalist thesis are more irrational than ours; but to prove it we must assume that thesis. Thus in the first section I often treated man as merely an animal, to show that the effect was more impossible than if he were treated as an angel. In the sense in which it was necessary to treat man merely as an animal, it is necessary to treat Christ merely as a man. I have to suspend my own beliefs, which are much more positive; and assume this limitation even in order to remove it. I must try to imagine what would happen to a man who did really read the story of Christ as the story of a man; and even of a man of whom he had never heard before. And I wish to point out that a really impartial reading of that kind would lead, if not immediately to belief, at least to a bewilderment of which there is really no solution except in belief. In this chapter, for this reason, I shall bring in nothing of the spirit of my own creed; I shall exclude the very style of diction and even of lettering, which I should think fitting in speaking in my own person. I am speaking as an imaginary heathen human being, honestly staring at the Gospel story for the first time.

Now it is not at all easy to regard the New Testament as a New Testament. It is not at all easy to realise the good news as new. Both for good and evil, familiarity fills us with assumptions and associations; and no man of our civilisation, whatever he thinks of our religion, can really read the thing as if he had never heard of it before. Of course it is in any case utterly unhistorical to talk as if the New Testament were a neatly bound book that had fallen from heaven. It is simply the selection made by the authority of the Church from a mass of early Christian literature. But apart from any such question, there is a psychological difficulty in feeling the New Testament as new. There is a psychological difficulty in seeing those well-known words simply as they stand and without going beyond what they intrinsically stand for. And this difficulty must indeed be very great; for the result of it is very curious. The result of it is that most modern critics and most current criticism, even popular criticism, makes a comment that is the exact reverse of the truth. It is so completely the reverse of the truth that one could almost suspect that they had never read the New Testament at all.

We have all heard people say a hundred times over, for they seem never to tire of saying it, that the Jesus of the New Testament is indeed a most merciful and humane lover of humanity, but that the Church has hidden this human character in repellent dogmas and stiffened it with ecclesiastical terrors till it has taken on an inhuman character. This is, I venture to repeat, very nearly the reverse of the truth. The truth is that it is the image of Christ in the churches that is almost entirely mild and merciful. It is the image of Christ in the Gospels that is a good many other things as well. The figure in the Gospels does indeed utter in words of almost heartbreaking beauty his pity for our broken hearts. But they are very far from being the only sort of words that he utters. Nevertheless they are almost the only kind of words that the Church in its popular imagery ever represents him as uttering. That popular imagery is inspired by a perfectly sound popular instinct. The mass of the poor are broken, and the mass of the people are poor, and for the mass of mankind the main thing is to carry the conviction of the incredible compassion of God. But nobody with his eyes open can doubt that it is chiefly this idea of compassion that the popular machinery of the

Church does seek to carry. The popular imagery carries a
great deal to excess the sentiment of 'Gentle Jesus, meek
and mild.' It is the first thing that the outsider feels and
criticises in a Pieta or a shrine of the Sacred Heart. As I
say, while the art may be insufficient, I am not sure that
the instinct is unsound. In any case there is something appalling, something that makes the blood run cold, in the
idea of having a statue of Christ in wrath. There is something insupportable even to imagination in the idea of
turning the corner of a street coming out into the spaces of
a market-place, to meet petrifying petrifaction of *that* figure
as it turned upon a generation of vipers, or that face as it
looked at the face of a hypocrite. The Church can reasonably be justified therefore if she turns the most merciful face or aspect towards men; it is certainly the most
merciful aspect that she does turn. And the point is here
that it is very much more specially and exclusively merciful
than any impression that could that could be formed by a
man merely reading the New Testament for the first time.
A man simply taking the words of the story as they stand
would form quite another impression; an impression full
of mystery and possibly of inconsistency; but certainly not
merely an impression of mildness. It would be intensely
interesting; but part of the interest would consist in its
leaving a good deal to be guessed at or explained. It is full
of sudden gestures evidently significant except that we
hardly know what they signify; of enigmatic silences; of
ironical replies. The outbreaks of wrath, like storms above
our atmosphere, do not seem to break out exactly where
we should expect them, but to follow some higher
weather-chart of their own. The Peter whom popular
Church teaching presents is very rightly the Peter to whom
Christ said in forgiveness, 'Feed my lambs!' He is not the
Peter upon whom Christ turned as if he were the devil,
crying in that obscure wrath, 'Get thee behind me, Satan!'
Christ lamented with nothing but love and pity over Jerusalem which was to murder him. We do not know what
strange spiritual atmosphere or spiritual insight led him to

sink Bethsaida lower in the pit than Sodom. I am putting
aside for the moment all questions of doctrinal inferences
or expositions, orthodox or otherwise; I am simply imagining the effect on a man's mind if he did do what these critics are always talking about doing; if he did really read the
New Testament without reference to orthodoxy and even
without reference to doctrine. He would find a number of
things which fit in far less with the current unorthodoxy
than they do with the current orthodoxy. He would find,
for instance, that if there are any descriptions that deserved
to be called realistic, they are precisely the descriptions of
the supernatural. If there is one aspect of the New Testament Jesus in which he may be said to present himself
eminently as a practical person, it is in the aspect of an
exorcist. There is nothing meek and mild, there is nothing
even in the ordinary sense mystical, about the tone of the
voice that says 'Hold thy peace and come out of him.' It is
much more like the tone of a very businesslike lion-tamer
or a strong-minded doctor dealing with a homicidal maniac. But this is only a side issue for the sake of illustration;
I am not now raising these controversies; but considering
the case of the imaginary man from the moon to whom
the New Testament is new.

Now the first thing to note is that if we take it merely
as a human story, it is in some ways a very strange story. I
do not refer here to its tremendous and tragic culmination
or to any implications involving triumph in that tragedy. I
do not refer to what is commonly called the miraculous
element; for on that point philosophies vary and modern
philosophies very decidedly waver. Indeed the educated
Englishman of today may be said to have passed from an
old fashion, in which he would not believe in any miracles
unless they were ancient, and adopted a new fashion in
which he will not believe in any miracles unless they are
modern. He used to hold that miraculous cures stopped
with the first Christians and is now inclined to suspect that
they began with the first Christian Scientists. But I refer
here rather specially to unmiraculous, and even to unno-

ticed and inconspicuous parts of the story. There are a great many things about it which nobody would have invented, for they are things that nobody has ever made any particular use of; things which if they were remarked at all have remained rather as puzzles. For instance, there is that long stretch of silence in the life of Christ up to the age of thirty. It is of all silences the most immense and imaginatively impressive. But it is not the sort of thing that anybody is particularly likely to invent in order to prove something; and nobody so far as I know has ever tried to prove anything in particular from it. It is impressive, but it is only impressive as a fact; there is nothing particularly popular or obvious about it as a fable. The ordinary trend of hero-worship and myth-making is much more likely to say the precise opposite. It is much more likely to say (as I believe some of the gospels rejected by the Church do say) that Jesus displayed a divine precocity and began his mission at a miraculously early age. And there is indeed something strange in the thought that he who of all humanity needed least preparation seems to have had most. Whether it was some mode of the divine humility, or some truth of which we see the shadow in the longer domestic tutelage of the higher creatures of the earth, I do not propose to speculate; I mention it simply as an example of the sort of thing that does in any case give rise to speculations, quite apart from recognised religious speculations. Now the whole story is full of these things. It is not by any means as badly presented in print, a story that it is easy to get to the bottom of. It is anything but what these people talk of as a simple Gospel. Relatively speaking, it is the Gospel that has the mysticism and the Church that has the rationalism. As I should put it, of course, it is the Gospel that is the riddle and the Church that is the answer. But whatever be the answer, the Gospel as it stands is almost a book of riddles.

First, a man reading the Gospel sayings would not find platitudes. If he had read even in the most respectful spirit the majority of ancient philosophers and of modern moral-

ists, he would appreciate the unique importance of saying
that he did not find platitudes. It is more than can be said
even of Plato. It is much more than can be said of Epictetus or Seneca or Marcus Aurelius or Apollonius of
Tyana. And it is immeasurably more than can be said of
most of the agnostic moralists and the preachers of the
ethical societies; with their songs of service and their religion of brotherhood. The moral of most moralists, ancient
and modern, has been one solid and polished cataract of
platitudes flowing forever and ever. That would certainly
not be the impression of the imaginary independent outsider studying the New Testament. He would be conscious
of nothing so commonplace and in a sense of nothing so
continuous as that stream. He would find a number of
strange claims that might sound like the claim to be the
brother of the sun and moon; a number of very startling
pieces of advice; a number of stunning rebukes; a number
of strangely beautiful stories. He would see some very gi-
gantesque figures of speech about the impossibility of
threading a needle with a camel or the possibility of throwing a mountain into the sea. He would see a number of
very daring simplifications of the difficulties of life; like the
advice to shine upon everybody indifferently as does the
sunshine or not to worry about the future any more than
the birds. He would find on the other hand some passages
of almost impenetrable darkness, so far as he is concerned,
such as the moral of the parable of the Unjust Steward.
Some of these things might strike him as fables and some
as truths; but none as truisms. For instance, he would not
find the ordinary platitudes in favour of peace. He would
find several paradoxes in favour of peace. He would find
several ideals of non-resistance, which taken as they stand
would be rather too pacific for any pacifist. He would be
told in one passage to treat a robber *not* with passive resis-
tance, but rather with positive and enthusiastic encouragement, if the terms be taken literally; heaping up gifts
upon the man who had stolen goods. But he would not
find a word of all that obvious rhetoric against war which

has filled countless books and odes and orations; not a word about the wickedness of war, the wastefulness of war, the appalling scale of the slaughter in war and all the rest of the familiar frenzy; indeed not a word about war at all. There is nothing that throws any particular light on Christ's attitude towards organised warfare, except that he seems to have been rather fond of Roman soldiers. Indeed it is another perplexity, speaking from the same external and human standpoint, that he seems to have got on much better with Romans than he did with Jews. But the question here is a certain tone to be appreciated by merely reading a certain text; and we might give any number of instances of it.

The statement that the meek shall inherit the earth is very far from being a meek statement. I mean it is not meek in the ordinary sense of mild and moderate and inoffensive. To justify it, it would be necessary to go very deep into history and anticipate things undreamed of then and by many unrealised even now; such as the way in which the Mystical monks reclaimed the lands which the practical kings had lost. If it was a truth at all, it was because it was a prophecy. But certainly it was not a truth in the sense of a truism. The blessing upon the meek would seem to be a very violent statement in the sense of doing violence to reason and probability. And with this we come to another important stage in the speculation. As a prophecy it really was fulfilled; but it was only fulfilled long afterwards. The monasteries were the most practical and prosperous estates and experiments in reconstruction after the barbaric deluge; the meek did really inherit the earth. But nobody could have known anything of the sort at the time – unless indeed there was one who knew. Something of the same thing may be said about the incident of Martha and Mary, which has been interpreted in retrospect and from the inside by the mystics of the Christian contemplative life. But it was not at all an obvious view of it; and most moralists, ancient and modern, could be trusted to make a rush for the obvious. What torrents of effortless eloquence would have flowed from them to swell any slight superiority on the part of Martha; what splendid sermons about the Joy of Service and the Gospel of Work and the World Left Better Than We Found It, and generally all the ten thousand platitudes can be uttered in favour of taking trouble – by people who need take no trouble to utter them. If in Mary the mystic and child of love, Christ was guarding the seed of something more subtle, who was likely to understand it at the time? Nobody else could have seen Clare and Catherine and Teresa shining above the little roof at Bethany. It is so in another way with that magnificent menace about bringing into the world a sword to sunder and divide. Nobody could have guessed then either how it could be fulfilled or how it could be justified. Indeed some freethinkers are still so simple as to fall into the trap and be shocked at a phrase so deliberately defiant. They actually complain of the paradox for not being a platitude.

But the point here is that if we *could* read the Gospel reports as things as new as newspaper reports, they would puzzle us and perhaps terrify us much *more* than the same things as developed by historical Christianity. For instance: Christ, after a clear allusion to the eunuchs of eastern courts, said there would be eunuchs of the kingdom of heaven. If this does not mean the voluntary enthusiasm of virginity, it could only be made to mean something much more unnatural or uncouth. It is the historical religion that humanises it for us by experience of Franciscans or of Sisters of Mercy. The mere statement standing by itself might very well suggest a rather dehumanised atmosphere; the sinister and inhuman silence of the Asiatic harem and divan. This is but one instance out of scores; but the moral is that the Christ of the Gospel might actually seem more strange and terrible than the Christ of the Church.

I am dwelling on the dark or dazzling or defiant or mysterious side of the Gospel words, not because they had not obviously a more obvious and popular side, but because this is the answer to a common criticism on a vital point. The freethinker frequently says that Jesus of Naz-

areth was a man of his time, even if he was in advance of
his time; and that we cannot accept his ethics as final for
humanity. The freethinker then goes on to criticise his ethics, saying plausibly enough that men cannot turn the other
cheek, or that they must take thought for the morrow, or
that the self-denial is too ascetic or the monogamy too
severe. But the Zealots and the Legionaries did not turn
the other cheek any more than we do, if so much. The
Jewish traders and Roman tax-gatherers took thought for
the morrow as much as we, if not more. We cannot pretend to be abandoning the morality of the past for one
more suited to the present. It is certainly not the morality
of another age, but it might be of another world.

In short, we can say that these ideals are impossible in
themselves. Exactly what we cannot say is that they are
impossible for us. They are rather notably marked by a
mysticism which, if it be a sort of madness, would always
have struck the same sort of people as mad. Take, for instance, the case of marriage and the relations of the sexes.
It might very well have been true that a Galilean teacher
taught things natural to a Galilean environment, but it is
not. It might rationally be expected that a man in the time
of Tiberius would have advanced a view conditioned by
the time of Tiberius; but he did not. What he advanced
was something quite different; something very difficult;
but something no more difficult now than it was then.
When, for instance, Mahomet made his polygamous compromise we may reasonably say that it was conditioned by
a polygamous society. When he allowed a man four wives
he was really doing something suited to the circumstances,
which might have been less suited to other circumstances.
Nobody will pretend that the four wives were like the four
winds, something seemingly a part of the order of nature;
nobody will say that the figure four was written forever in
stars, upon the sky. But neither will anyone say that the
figure four is an inconceivable ideal; that it is beyond the
power of the mind of man to count up to four; or to count
the number of his wives and see whether it amounts to

four. It is a practical compromise carrying with it the character of a particular society. If Mahomet had been born in Acton in the nineteenth century, we may well doubt whether he would instantly have filled that suburb with harems of four wives apiece. As he was born in Arabia in the sixth century, he did in his conjugal arrangements suggest the conditions of Arabia in the sixth century. But Christ in his view of marriage does not in the least suggest the conditions of Palestine in the first century. He does not suggest anything at all except the sacramental view of marriage as developed long afterwards by the Catholic Church. It was quite as difficult for people then as for people now. It was much more puzzling to people then than to people now. Jews and Romans and Greeks did not believe and did not even understand enough to disbelieve, the mystical idea that the man and the woman had become one sacramental substance. We may think it an incredible or impossible ideal; but we cannot think it any more incredible or impossible than they would have thought it. In other words, whatever else is true it is not true that the controversy has been altered by time. Whatever else is true, it is emphatically not true that the ideas of Jesus of Nazareth were suitable to his time, but are no longer suitable to our time. Exactly how suitable they were to his time is perhaps suggested in the end of his story.

The same truth might be stated in another way by saying that if the story be regarded as merely human and historical, it is extraordinary how very little there is in the recorded words of Christ that ties him at all to his own time. I do not mean the details of a period, which even a man of the period knows to be passing. I mean the fundamentals which even the wisest man often vaguely assumes to be eternal. For instance, Aristotle was perhaps the wisest and most wide-minded man who ever lived. He founded himself entirely upon fundamentals, which have been generally found to remain rational and solid through all social and historical changes. Still, he lived in a world in which it was thought as natural to have slaves as to have children. And

therefore he did permit himself a serious recognition of a
difference between slaves and free men. Christ as much as
Aristotle lived in a world that took slavery for granted. He
did not particularly denounce slavery. He started a movement that could exist in a world with slavery. But he
started a movement that could exist in a world without
slavery. He never used a phrase that made his philosophy
depend even upon the very existence of the social order in
which he lived. He spoke as one conscious that everything
was ephemeral, including the things that Aristotle thought
eternal. By that time the Roman Empire had come to be
merely the *orbis terrarum*, another name for the world. But
he never made his morality dependent on the existence of
the Roman Empire or even on the existence of the world.
'Heaven and earth shall pass away; but my words shall not
pass away.'

The truth is that, when critics have spoken of the local
limitations of the Galilean, it has always been a case of the
local limitations of the critics. He did undoubtedly believe
in certain things that one particular modern sect of materialists do not believe. But they were not things particularly
peculiar to his time. It would be nearer the truth to say that
the denial of them is quite peculiar to our time. Doubtless
it would be nearer still to the truth to say merely that a certain solemn social importance, in the minority disbelieving
them, is peculiar to our time. He believed, for instance, in
evil spirits or in the psychic healing of bodily ills; but not
because he was a Galilean born under Augustus. It is absurd to say that a man believed things because he was a
Galilean under Augustus when he might have believed the
same things if he had been an Egyptian under Tutankhamen or an Indian under Genghis Khan. But with this
general question of the philosophy of diabolism or of divine miracles I deal elsewhere. It is enough to say that the
materialists have to prove the impossibility of miracles
against the testimony of all mankind, not against the prejudices of provincials in North Palestine under the first Roman Emperors. What they have to prove for the present

argument, is the presence in the Gospels of those particular prejudices of those particular provincials. And, humanly speaking, it is astonishing how little they can produce even to make a beginning of proving it.

So it is in this case of the sacrament of marriage. We may not believe in sacraments, as we may not believe in spirits, but it is quite clear that Christ believed in this sacrament in his own way and not in any current or contemporary way. He certainly did not get his argument against divorce from the Mosaic law or the Roman law or the habits of the Palestinian people. It would appear to his critics then exactly what it appears to his critics now; an arbitrary and transcendental dogma coming from nowhere save in the sense that it came in him. I am not at all concerned here to defend that dogma; the point here is that it is just as easy to defend it as it was to defend it then. It is an ideal altogether outside time; difficult at any period; impossible at no period. In other words, if anyone says it is what might be expected of a man walking about in that place at that period, we can quite fairly answer that it is much *more* like what might be the mysterious utterance of a being beyond man, if he walked live among men.

I maintain therefore that a man reading the New Testament frankly and freshly would *not* get the impression of what is now often meant by a human Christ. The merely human Christ is a made-up figure, a piece of artificial selection, like the merely evolutionary man. Moreover, there have been too many of these human Christs found in the same story, just as there have been too many keys to mythology found in the same stories. Three or four separate schools of rationalism have worked over the ground and produced three or four equally rational explanations of his life. The first rational explanation of his life was that he never lived. And this in turn gave an opportunity for three or four different explanations; as that he was a sun-myth or a corn-myth, or any other kind of myth that is also a monomania. Then the idea that he was a divine being who did not exist gave place to the idea that he was a human

being who did exist. In my youth it was the fashion to say
that he was merely an ethical teacher in the manner of the
Essenes, who had apparently nothing very much to say
that Hillel or a hundred other Jews might not have said; as
that it is a kindly thing to be kind and an assistance to puri-
fication to be pure. Then somebody said he was a madman
with a Messianic delusion. Then others said he was indeed
an original teacher because he cared about nothing but
Socialism; or (as others said) about nothing but Pacifism.
Then a more grimly scientific character appeared who said
that Jesus would never have been heard of at all except for
his prophecies of the end of the world. He was important
merely as a Millenarian like Dr. Cumming; and created a
provincial scare by announcing the exact date of the crack
of doom. Among other variants on the same theme was
the theory that he was a spiritual healer and nothing else; a
view implied by Christian Science, which has really to ex-
pound a Christianity without the Crucifixion in order to
explain the curing of Peter's wife's mother or the daughter
of a centurion. There is another theory that concentrates
entirely on the business of diabolism and what it would call
the contemporary superstition about demoniacs; if Christ,
like a young deacon taking his first orders, had got as far as
exorcism and never got any further. Now each of these
explanations in itself seems to me singularly inadequate;
but taken together they do suggest something of the very
mystery which they miss. There must surely have been
something not only mysterious but many sided about
Christ if so many smaller Christs can be carved out of him.
If the Christian Scientist is satisfied with him as a spiritual
healer and the Christian Socialist is satisfied with him as a
social reformer, so satisfied that they do not even expect
him to be anything else, it looks as if he really covered
rather more than they could be expected to expect. And it
does seem to suggest that there might be more than they
fancy in these other mysterious attributes of casting out
devils or prophesying doom.

Above all, would not such a new reader of the New

Testament stumble over something that would startle him much more than it startles us? I have here more than once attempted the rather impossible task of reversing time and the method; and in fancy looking forward to the facts instead of backward through the memories. So I have imagined the monster that man might have seemed at first to the mere nature around him. We should have a worse shock if we really imagined the nature of Christ named for the first time. What should we feel at the first whisper of a certain suggestion about a certain man? Certainly it is not for us to blame anybody who should find that first wild whisper merely impious and insane. On the contrary, stumbling on that rock of scandal is the first step. Stark staring incredulity is a far more loyal tribute to that truth than a modernist metaphysic would make it out, merely a matter of degree. It were better to rend our robes with a great cry against blasphemy, like Caiaphas in the judgment, or to lay hold of the man as a maniac possessed of devils like the kinsmen and the crowd, than to stand stupidly debating fine shades of pantheism in the presence of so catastrophic a claim. There is more of the wisdom that is one with surprise in any simple person full of the sensitiveness of simplicity, who should expect the grass to wither and the birds to drop dead out of the air when a strolling carpenter's apprentice said calmly and almost carelessly like one looking over his shoulder: 'Before Abraham was, I am.'

3
THE STRANGEST STORY
IN THE WORLD

IN THE LAST chapter I have deliberately stressed what seems to be nowadays a neglected side of the New Testament story, but nobody will suppose, I imagine, that it is meant to obscure that side that may truly be called human. That Christ was and is the most merciful of judges and the most sympathetic of friends, is a fact of considerably more importance in our own private lives than in anybody's historical speculations. But the purpose of this book is to point out that something unique has been swamped in cheap generalisations; and for that purpose it is relevant to insist that even what was most universal was also most original. For instance, we might take a topic which really is sympathetic to the modern mood, as the ascetic vocations recently referred to are not. The exaltation of childhood is something which we do really understand; but it was by no means a thing that was then in that sense understood. If we wanted an example of the originality of the Gospel, we could hardly take a stronger or more startling one. Nearly two thousand years afterwards we happen to find ourselves in a mood that does really feel the mystical charm of the child; we express it in romances and regrets about childhood, in *Peter Pan* or *The Child's Garden of Verses*. And we can say of the words of Christ with so angry an anti-Christian as Swinburne:

> *No sign that ever was given*
> *To faithful or faithless eyes*
> *Showed ever beyond clouds riven*
> *So clear a paradise.*

> *Earth's creeds may be seventy times seven*
> *And blood have defiled each creed*
> *But if such be the kingdom of heaven*
> *It must be heaven indeed.*

But that paradise was not clear until Christianity had gradually cleared it. The pagan world, as such, would not have understood any such thing as a serious suggestion that a child is higher or holier than a man. It would have seemed like the suggestion that a tadpole is higher or holier than a frog. To the merely rationalistic mind, it would sound like saying that a bud must be more beautiful than a flower or that an unripe apple must be better than a ripe one. In other words, this modern feeling is an entirely mystical feeling. It is quite as mystical as the cult of virginity; in fact it is the cult of virginity. But pagan antiquity had much more idea of the holiness of the virgin than of the holiness of the child. For various reasons we have come nowadays to venerate children; perhaps partly because we envy children for still doing what men used to do, such as play simple games and enjoy fairy-tales. Over and above this, however, there is a great deal of real and subtle psychology in our appreciation of childhood; but if we turn it into a modern discovery, we must once more admit that the historical Jesus of Nazareth had already discovered it two thousand years too soon. There was certainly nothing in the world around him to help him to the discovery. Here Christ was indeed human; but more human than a human being was then likely to be. Peter Pan does not belong to the world of Pan but the world of Peter.

Even in the matter of mere literary style, if we suppose ourselves thus sufficiently detached to look at it in that light, there is a curious quality to which no critic seems to have done justice. It had among other things a singular air of piling tower upon tower by the use of the *a fortiori;* making a pagoda of degrees like the seven heavens. I have already noted that almost inverted imaginative vision which pictured the impossible penance of the Cities of the Plain.

There is perhaps nothing so perfect in all language or literature as the use of these three degrees in the parable of the lilies of the field; in which he seems first to take one small flower in his hand and note its simplicity and even its impotence; then suddenly expands it in flamboyant colours into all the palaces and pavilions full of a great name in national legend and national glory; and then, by yet a third overturn, shrivels it to nothing once more with a gesture as if flinging it away. '… and if God so clothes the grass that today is and tomorrow is cast into the oven – how much more ….' It is like the building of a good Babel tower by white magic in a moment and in the movement of a hand; a tower heaved suddenly up to heaven on the top of which can be seen afar off, higher than we had fancied possible, the figure of man; lifted by three infinities above all other things, on a starry ladder of light logic and swift imagination. Merely in a literary sense it would be more of a masterpiece than most of the masterpieces in the libraries; yet it seems to have been uttered almost at random while a man might pull a flower. But merely in a literary sense also, this use of the comparative in several degrees has about it a quality which seems to me to hint of much higher things than the modern suggestion of the simple teaching of pastoral or communal ethics. There is nothing that really indicates a subtle and in the true sense a superior mind so much as this power of comparing a lower thing with a higher and yet that higher with a higher still; of thinking on three planes at once. There is nothing that wants the rarest sort of wisdom so much as to see, let us say, that the citizen is higher than the slave and yet that the soul is infinitely higher than the citizen or the city. It is not by any means a faculty that commonly belongs to these simplifiers of the Gospel; those who insist on what they call a simple morality and others call a sentimental morality. It is not at all covered by those who are content to tell everybody to remain at peace. On the contrary, there is a very striking example of it in the apparent inconsistency between Christ's sayings about peace and about a sword. It is precisely this power which perceives that while a good peace is better than a good war, even a good war is better than a bad peace. These far-flung comparisons are nowhere so common as in the Gospels; and to me they suggest something very vast. So a thing solitary and solid, with the added dimension of depth or height, might tower over the flat creatures living only on a plane.

This quality of something that can only be called subtle and superior, something that is capable of long views and even of double meanings, is not noted here merely as a counter-blast to the commonplace exaggerations of amiability and mild idealism. It is also to be noted in connection with the more tremendous truth touched upon at the end of the last chapter. For this is the very last character that commonly goes with mere megalomania; especially such steep and staggering megalomania as might be involved in that claim. This quality that can only be called intellectual distinction is not, of course, an evidence of divinity. But it is an evidence of a probable distaste for vulgar and vainglorious claims to divinity. A man of that sort, if he were only a man, would be the last man in the world to suffer from that intoxication by one notion from nowhere in particular, which is the mark of the self-deluding sensationalist in religion. Nor is it even avoided by denying that Christ did make this claim. Of no such man as that, of no other prophet or philosopher of the same intellectual order, would it be even possible to pretend that he had made it. Even if the Church had mistaken his meaning it would still be true that no other historical tradition except the Church had ever even made the same mistake. Mahometans did not misunderstand Mahomet and suppose he was Allah. Jews did not misinterpret Moses and identify him with Jehovah. Why was this claim alone exaggerated unless this alone was made? Even if Christianity was one vast universal blunder, it is still a blunder as solitary as the Incarnation.

The purpose of these pages is to fix the falsity of certain vague and vulgar assumptions; and we have here one

of the most false. There is a sort of notion in the air everywhere that all the religions are equal because all the religious founders were rivals; that they are all fighting for the
same starry crown. It is quite false. The claim to that
crown, or anything like that crown, is really so rare as to be
unique. Mahomet did not make it any more than Micah or
Malachi. Confucius did not make it any more than Plato or
Marcus Aurelius. Buddha never said he was Brahma. Zoroaster no more claimed to be Ormuz than to be Ahriman.
The truth is that in the common run of cases, it is just as
we should expect it to be, in common sense and certainly
in Christian philosophy. It is exactly the other way. Normally speaking, the greater a man is, the less likely he is to
make the very greatest claim. Outside the unique case we
are considering, the only kind of man who ever does make
that kind of claim is a very small man; a secretive or self-
centred monomaniac. Nobody can imagine Aristotle claiming to be the father of gods and men, come down from the
sky; though we might imagine some insane Roman Emperor like Caligula claiming it for him, or more probably
for himself. Nobody can imagine Shakespeare talking as if
he were literally divine; though we might imagine some
crazy American crank finding it as a cryptogram in Shakespeare's works, or preferably in his own works. It is possible to find here and there human beings who make this
supremely superhuman claim. It is possible to find them in
lunatic asylums; in padded cells; possibly in strait waist-
coats. But what is much more important than their mere
materialistic fate in our very materialistic society, under
very crude and clumsy laws about lunacy, the type we
know as tinged with this, or tending towards it, is a diseased and disproportionate type; narrow yet swollen and
morbid to monstrosity. It is by rather an unlucky metaphor
that we talk of a madman as cracked; for in a sense he is
not cracked enough. He is cramped rather than cracked;
there are not enough holes in his bead to ventilate it. This
impossibility of letting in daylight on a delusion does
sometimes cover and conceal a delusion of divinity. It can

be found, not among prophets and sages and founders of religions, but only among a low set of lunatics. But this is exactly where the argument becomes in tensely interesting; because the argument proves too much. For nobody supposes that Jesus of Nazareth was *that* sort of person. No modern critic in his five wits thinks that the preacher of the Sermon on the Mount was a horrible half-witted imbecile that might be scrawling stars on the walls of a cell. No atheist or blasphemer believes that the author of the Parable of the Prodigal Son was a monster with one mad idea like a Cyclops with one eye. Upon any possible historical criticism, he must be put higher in the scale of human beings than that. Yet by all analogy we have really to put him there or else in the highest place of all.

In fact, those who can really take it (as I here hypothetically take it) in a quite dry and detached spirit, have here a most curious and interesting human problem. It is so intensely interesting, considered as a human problem, that it is in a spirit quite disinterested so to speak, that I wish some of them had turned that intricate human problem into something like an intelligible human portrait. If Christ was simply a human character, he really was a highly complex and contradictory human character. For the combined exactly the two things that lie at the two extremes of human variation. He was exactly what the man with a delusion never is; he was wise; he was a good judge. What he said was always unexpected; but it was always unexpectedly magnanimous and often unexpectedly moderate. Take a thing like the point of the parable of the tares and the wheat. It has the quality that unites sanity and subtlety. It has not the simplicity of a madman. It has not even the simplicity of a fanatic. It might be uttered by a philosopher a hundred years old, at the end of a century of Utopias. Nothing could be less like this quality of seeing beyond and all round obvious things, than the condition of the egomaniac with the one sensitive spot on his brain. I really do not see how these two characters could be convincingly combined, except in the astonishing way in which the creed combines them. For until we reach the full acceptance of the fact as a fact, however marvellous, all mere approximations to it are actually further and further away from it. Divinity is great enough to be divine; it is great enough to call itself divine. But as humanity grows greater, it grows less and less likely to do so. God is God, as the Moslems say; but a great man knows he is not God, and the greater he is the better he knows it. That is the paradox; everything that is merely approaching to that point is merely receding from it. Socrates, the wisest man, knows that he knows nothing. A lunatic may think he is omniscience, and a fool may talk as if he were omniscient. But Christ is in another sense omniscient if he not only knows, but knows that he knows.

Even on the purely human and sympathetic side, therefore, the Jesus of the New Testament seems to me to have in a great many ways the note of something superhuman; that is of something human and more than human. But there is another quality running through all his teachings which seems to me neglected in most modern talk about them as teachings; and that is the persistent suggestion that he has not really come to teach. If there is one incident in the record which affects me personally as grandly and gloriously human, it is the incident of giving wine for the wedding feast. That is really human in the sense in which a whole crowd of prigs, having the appearance of human beings, can hardly be described as human. It rises superior to all superior persons. It is as human as Herrick and as democratic as Dickens. But even in that story there is something else that has that note of things not fully explained; and in a way here very relevant. I mean the first hesitation, not on any ground touching the nature of the miracle, but on that of the propriety of working any miracles at all, at least at that stage; 'my time is not yet come.' What did that mean? At least it certainly meant a general plan or purpose in the mind, with which certain things did or did not fit in. And if we leave out that solitary strategic plan, we not only leave out the point of the story, but the story.

We often hear of Jesus of Nazareth as a wandering teacher; and there is a vital truth in that view in so far as it emphasises an attitude towards luxury and convention which most respectable people would still regard as that of a vagabond. It is expressed in his own great saying about the holes of the foxes and the nests of the birds, and, like many of his great sayings, it is felt as less powerful than it is, through lack of appreciation of that great paradox by which he spoke of his own humanity as in some way collectively and representatively human; calling himself simply the Son of Man; that is, in effect, calling himself simply Man. It is fitting that the New Man or the Second Adam should repeat in so ringing a voice and with so arresting a gesture the great fact which came first in the original story; that man differs from the brutes by everything, even by deficiency; that he is in a sense less normal and even less native; a stranger upon the earth. It is well to speak of his wanderings in this sense and in the sense that he shared the drifting life of the most homeless and hopeless of the poor. It is assuredly well to remember that he would quite certainly have been moved on by the police and almost certainly arrested by the police, for having no visible means of subsistence. For our law has in it a turn of humour or touch of fancy which Nero and Herod never happened to think of; that of actually punishing homeless people for not sleeping at home.

But in another sense the word 'wandering' as applied to his life is a little misleading. As a matter of fact, a great many of the pagan sages and not a few of the pagan sophists might truly be described as wandering teachers. In some of them their rambling journeys were not altogether without a parallel in their rambling remarks. Apollonius of Tyana, who figured in some fashionable cults as a sort of ideal philosopher, is represented as rambling as far as the Ganges and Ethiopia, more or less talking all the time. There was actually a school of philosophers called the Peripatetics; and most even of the great philosophers give us

a vague impression of having very little to do except to
walk and talk. The great conversations which give us our
glimpses of the great minds of Socrates or Buddha or even
Confucius often seem to be parts of a never ending picnic;
and especially, which is the important point, to have neither beginning nor end. Socrates did indeed find the conversation interrupted by the incident of his execution. But
it is the whole point, and the whole particular merit, of the
position of Socrates that death was only an interruption
and an incident. We miss the real moral importance of the
great philosopher if we miss that point; that he stares at
the executioner with an innocent surprise, and almost an
innocent annoyance, at finding anyone so unreasonable as
to cut short a little conversation for the elucidation of
truth. He is looking for truth and not looking for death.
Death is but a stone in the road which can trip him up. His
work in life is to wander on the roads of the world and talk
about truth forever. Buddha, on the other hand, did arrest
attention by one gesture; it was the gesture of renunciation,
and therefore in a sense of denial. But by one dramatic
negation he passed into a world of negation that was not
dramatic; which he would have been the first to insist was
not dramatic. Here again we miss the particular moral importance of the great mystic if we do not see the distinction; that it was his whole point that he had done with
drama, which consists of desire and struggle and generally
of defeat and disappointment. He passes into peace and
lives to instruct others how to pass into it. Henceforth his
life is that of the ideal philosopher; certainly a far more
really ideal philosopher than Apollonius of Tyana; but still
a philosopher in the sense that it is not his business to do
anything but rather to explain everything; in his case, we
might almost say, mildly and softly to explode everything.
For the messages are basically different. Christ said 'Seek
first the kingdom, and all these things shall be added unto
you.' Buddha said 'Seek first the kingdom, and then you
will need none of these things.'

Now compared to these wanderers the life of Jesus

went as swift and straight as a thunderbolt. It was above all things dramatic; it did above all things consist in doing something that had to be done. It emphatically would not have been done, if Jesus had walked about the world forever doing nothing except tell the truth. And even the external movement of it must not be described as a wandering in the sense of forgetting that it was a journey. This is where it was a fulfilment of the myths rather than of the philosophies; it is a journey with a goal and an object, like Jason going to find the Golden Fleece, or Hercules the golden apples of the Hesperides. The gold that he was seeking was death. The primary thing that he was going to do was to die. He was going to do other things equally definite and objective; we might almost say equally external and material. But from first to last the most definite fact is that he is going to die. No two things could possibly be more different than the death of Socrates and the death of Christ. We are meant to feel that the death of Socrates was, from the point of view of his friends at least, a stupid muddle and miscarriage of justice interfering with the flow of a humane and lucid, I had almost said a light, philosophy. We are meant to feel that Death was the bride of Christ as Poverty was the bride of St. Francis. We are meant to feel that his life was in that sense a sort of love affair with death, a romance of the pursuit of the ultimate sacrifice. From the moment when the star goes up like a birthday rocket, to the moment when the sun is extinguished like a funeral torch, the whole story moves on wings with the speed and direction of a drama, ending in an act beyond words.

Therefore the story of Christ is the story of a journey, almost in the manner of a military march; certainly in the manner of the quest of a hero moving to his achievement or his doom. It is a story that begins in the paradise of Galilee, a pastoral and peaceful land having really some hint of Eden, and gradually climbs the rising country into the mountains that are nearer to the storm-clouds and the stars, as to a Mountain of Purgatory. He may be met as if straying in strange places, or stopped on the way for discussion or dispute; but his face is set towards the mountain city. That is the meaning of that great culmination when he crested the ridge and stood at the turning of the road and suddenly cried aloud, lamenting over Jerusalem. Some light touch of that lament is in every patriotic poem or if it is absent, the patriotism stinks with vulgarity. That is the meaning of the stirring and startling incident at the gates of the Temple, when the tables were hurled like lumber down the steps, and the rich merchants driven forth with bodily blows; the incident that must be at least as much of a puzzle to the pacifists as any paradox about non-resistance can be to any of the militarists. I have compared the quest to the journey of Jason, but we must never forget that in a deeper sense it is rather to be compared to the journey of Ulysses. It was not only a romance of travel but a romance of return; and of the end of a usurpation. No healthy boy reading the story regards the rout of the Ithacan suitors as anything but a happy ending. But there are doubtless some who regard the rout of the Jewish merchants and money-changers with that refined repugnance which never fails to move them in the presence of violence, and especially of violence against the well-to-do. The point here, however, is that all these incidents have in them a character of mounting crisis. In other words, these incidents are not incidental. When Apollonius the ideal philosopher is brought before the judgment seat of Domitian and vanishes by magic, the miracle is entirely incidental. It might have occurred at any time in the wandering life of the Tyanean; indeed, I believe it is doubtful in date as well as in substance. The ideal philosopher merely vanished, and resumed his ideal existence somewhere else for an indefinite period. It is characteristic of the contrast perhaps that Apollonius was supposed to have lived to an almost miraculous old age. Jesus of Nazareth was less prudent in his miracles. When Jesus was brought before the judgment seat of Pontius Pilate, he did not vanish. It was the crisis and the goal; it was the hour and the power of darkness. It was the supremely supernatural act of all his miraculous life, that he did not vanish.

Every attempt to amplify that story has diminished it. The task has been attempted by many men of real genius and eloquence as well as by only too many vulgar sentimentalists and self-conscious rhetoricians. The tale has been retold with patronising pathos by elegant sceptics and with fluent enthusiasm by boisterous best-sellers. It will not be retold here. The grinding power of the plain words of the Gospel story is like the power of millstones; and those who can read them simply enough will feel as if rocks had been rolled upon them. Criticism is only words about words; and of what use are words about such words as these? What is the use of word-painting about the dark garden filled suddenly with torchlight and furious faces? 'Are you come out with swords and staves as against a robber? All day I sat in your temple teaching, and you took me not.' Can anything be added to the massive and gathered restraint of that irony; like a great wave lifted to the sky and refusing to fall? 'Daughters of Jerusalem, weep not for me but weep for yourselves and for your children.' As the High Priest asked what further need he had of witnesses, we might well ask what further need we have of words. Peter in a panic repudiated him: 'and immediately the cock crew; and Jesus looked upon Peter, and Peter went out and wept bitterly.' Has anyone any further remarks to offer? Just before the murder he prayed for all the murderous race of men saying, 'They know not what they do'; is there anything to say to that, except that we know as little what we say? Is there any need to repeat and spin out the story of how the tragedy trailed up the Via Dolorosa and how they threw him in haphazard with two thieves in one of the ordinary batches of execution; and how in all that horror and howling wilderness of desertion one voice spoke in homage, a startling voice from the very last place where it was looked for, the gibbet of the criminal; and he said to that nameless ruffian, 'This night shalt thou be with me in Paradise'? Is there anything to put after that but a full-stop? Or is anyone prepared to answer adequately that farewell gesture to all flesh which created for his Mother a new Son?

It is more within my powers, and here more immediately to my purpose, to point out that in that scene were symbolically gathered all the human forces that have been vaguely sketched in this story. As kings and philosophers and the popular element had been symbolically present at his birth, so they were more practically concerned in his death; and with that we come face to face with the essential fact to be realised. All the great groups that stood about the Cross represent in one way or another the great historical truth of the time; that the world could not save itself. Man could do no more. Rome and Jerusalem and Athens and everything else were going down like a sea turned into a slow cataract. Externally indeed the ancient world was still at its strongest, it is always at that moment that the inmost weakness begins. But in order to understand that weakness we must repeat what has been said more than once; that it was not the weakness of a thing originally weak. It was emphatically the strength of the world that was turned to weakness and the wisdom of the world that was turned to folly.

In this story of Good Friday it is the best things in the world that are at their worst. That is what really shows us the world at its worst. It was, for instance, the priests of a true monotheism and the soldiers of an international civilisation. Rome, the legend, founded upon fallen Troy and triumphant over fallen Carthage, had stood for a heroism which was the nearest that any pagan ever came to chivalry. Rome had defended the household gods and the human decencies against the ogres of Africa and the hermaphrodite monstrosities of Greece. But in the lightning flash of this incident, we see great Rome, the imperial republic, going downward under her Lucretian doom. Scepticism has eaten away even the confident sanity of the conquerors of the world. He who is enthroned to say what is justice can only ask, 'What is truth?' So in that drama which decided the whole fate of antiquity, one of the central figures is fixed in what seems the reverse of his true role. Rome was almost another name for responsibility. Yet he stands forever as a sort of rocking statue of the irresponsible. Man could do no more. Even the practical had become the impracticable. Standing between the pillars of his own judgment seat, a Roman had washed his hands of the world.

There too were the priests of that pure and original truth that was behind all the mythologies like the sky behind the clouds. It was the most important truth in the world; and even that could not save the world. Perhaps there is something overpowering in pure personal theism; like seeing the sun and moon and sky come together to form one staring face. Perhaps the truth is too tremendous when not broken by some intermediaries divine or human; perhaps it is merely too pure and far away. Anyhow, it could not save the world; it could not even convert the world. There were philosophers who held it in its highest and noblest form; but they not only could not convert the world, but they never tried. You could no more fight the jungle of popular mythology with a private opinion than you could clear away a forest with a pocket-knife. The Jewish priests had guarded it jealously in the good and the bad sense. They had kept it as a gigantic secret. As savage heroes might have kept the sun in a box, they kept the Everlasting in the tabernacle. They were proud that they alone could look upon the blinding sun of a single deity; and they did not know that they had themselves gone blind. Since that day their representatives have been like blind men in broad daylight, striking to right and left with their staffs, and cursing the darkness. But there has been that in their monumental monotheism that it has at least remained like a monument, the last thing of its kind, and in a sense motionless in the more restless world which it cannot satisfy. For it is certain that for some reason it cannot satisfy. Since that day it has never been quite enough to say that God is in his heaven and all is right with the world; since the rumour that God had left his heavens to set it right.

And as it was with these powers that were good, or at least had once been good, so it was with the element which was perhaps the best, or which Christ himself seems certainly to have felt as the best. The poor to whom he preached the good news, the common people who heard him gladly, the populace that had made so many popular heroes and demigods in the old pagan world showed also the weaknesses that were dissolving the world. They suffered the evils often seen in the mob of the city, and especially the mob of the capital, during the decline of a society. The same thing that makes the rural population live on tradition makes the urban population live on rumour. Just as its myths at the best had been irrational, so its likes and dislikes are easily changed by baseless assertion that is arbitrary without being authoritative. Some brigand or other was artificially turned into a picturesque and popular figure and run as a kind of candidate against Christ. In all this we recognise the urban population that we know, with its newspaper scares and scoops. But there was present in this ancient population an evil more peculiar to the ancient world. We have noted it already as the neglect of the individual, even of the individual voting the condemnation and still more of the individual condemned. It was the soul of the hive; a heathen thing. The cry of this spirit also was heard in that hour, 'It is well that one man die for the people.' Yet this spirit in antiquity of devotion to the city and to the state had so been in itself and in its time a noble spirit. It had its poets and its martyrs; men still to be honoured forever. It was failing through its weakness in not seeing the separate soul of a man, the shrine of all mysticism; but it was only failing as everything else was failing. The mob went along with the Sadducees and the Pharisees, the philosophers and the moralists. It went along with the imperial magistrates and the sacred priests, the scribes and the soldiers, that the one universal human spirit might suffer a universal condemnation; that there might be one deep, unanimous chorus of approval and harmony when Man was rejected of men.

There were solitudes beyond where none shall follow. There were secrets in the inmost and invisible part of that drama that have no symbol in speech; or in any severance of a man from men. Nor is it easy for any words less stark and single-minded than those of the naked narrative even to hint at the horror of exaltation that lifted itself above the hill. Endless expositions have not come to the end of it, or even to the beginning. And if there be any sound that can produce a silence, we may surely be silent about the end and the extremity; when a cry was driven out of that darkness in words dreadfully distinct and dreadfully unintelligible, which man shall never understand in all the eternity they have purchased for him; and for one annihilating instant an abyss that is not for our thoughts had opened even in the unity of the absolute; and God had been forsaken of God.

They took the body down from the cross and one of the few rich men among the first Christians obtained permission to bury it in a rock tomb in his garden; the Romans setting a military guard lest there should be some riot and attempt to recover the body. There was once more a natural symbolism in these natural proceedings; it was well that the tomb should be sealed with all the secrecy of ancient eastern sepulchre and guarded by the authority of the Caesars. For in that second cavern the whole of that great and glorious humanity which we call antiquity was gathered up and covered over; and in that place it was buried. It was the end of a very great thing called human history; the history that was merely human. The mythologies and the philosophies were buried there, the gods and the heroes and the sages. In the great Roman phrase, they had lived. But as they could only live, so they could only die; and they were dead.

On the third day the friends of Christ coming at daybreak to the place found the grave empty and the stone rolled away. In varying ways they realised the new wonder; but even they hardly realised that the world had died in the night. What they were looking at was the first day of a new creation, with a new heaven and a new earth; and in a semblance of the gardener God walked again in the garden, in the cool not of the evening but the dawn.

4
THE WITNESS OF THE HERETICS

CHRIST FOUNDED THE Church with two great figures of speech; in the final words to the Apostles who received authority to found it. The first was the phrase about founding it on Peter as on a rock; the second was the symbol of the keys. About the meaning of the former there is naturally no doubt in my own case; but it does not directly affect the argument here save in two more secondary aspects. It is yet another example of a thing that could only fully expand and explain itself afterwards, and even long afterwards. And it is yet another example of something the very reverse of simple and self-evident even in the language, in so far as it described a man as a rock when he had much more the appearance of a reed.

But the other image of the keys has an exactitude that has hardly been exactly noticed. The keys have been conspicuous enough in the art and heraldry of Christendom; but not everyone has noted the peculiar aptness of the allegory. We have now reached the point in history where something must be said of the first appearance and activities of the Church in the Roman Empire; and for that brief description nothing could be more perfect than that ancient metaphor. The Early Christian was very precisely a person carrying about a key, or what he said was a key. The whole Christian movement consisted in claiming to possess that key. It was not merely a vague forward movement, which might be better represented by a battering-ram. It was not something that swept along with it similar or dissimilar things, as does a modern social movement. As we shall see in a moment it rather definitely refused to do so. It definitely asserted that there was a key and that it possessed that key and that no other key was like it; in that sense it was as narrow as you please. Only it happened to be the key that could unlock the prison of the whole world; and let in the white daylight of liberty.

The creed was like a key in three respects; which can be most conveniently summed up under this symbol. First, a key is above all things a thing with a shape. It is a thing that depends entirely upon keeping its shape. The Christian creed is above all things the philosophy of shapes and the enemy of shapelessness. That is where it differs from all that formless infinity, Manichean or Buddhist, which makes a sort of pool of night in the dark heart of Asia; the ideal of uncreating all the creatures. That is where it differs also from the analogous vagueness of mere evolutionism; the idea of creatures constantly losing their shape. A man told that his solitary latchkey had been melted down with a million others into a Buddhistic unity would be annoyed. But a man told that his key was gradually growing and sprouting in his pocket, and branching into new wards or complications, would not be more gratified.

Second, the shape of a key is in itself a rather fantastic shape. A savage who did not know it was a key would have the greatest difficulty in guessing what it could possibly be. And it is fantastic because it is in a sense arbitrary. A key is not a matter of abstractions; in that sense a key is not a matter of argument. It either fits the lock or it does not. It is useless for men to stand disputing over it, considered by itself; or reconstructing it on pure principles of geometry or decorative art. It is senseless for a man to say he would like a simpler key; it would be far more sensible to do his best with a crowbar. And thirdly, as the key is necessarily a thing with a pattern, so this was one having in some ways a rather elaborate pattern. When people complain of the religion being so early complicated with theology and things of the kind, they forget that the world had not only got into a hole, but had got into a whole maze of holes and corners. The problem itself was a complicated problem; it did not in the ordinary sense merely involve anything so simple as sin. It was also full of secrets, of unexplored and unfathomable fallacies, of unconscious mental diseases, of dangers in all directions. If the faith had faced the world only with the platitudes about peace and simplicity some moralists would confine it to, it would not have had the faintest effect on that luxurious and labyrinthine lunatic asylum. What it did do we must now roughly describe; it is enough to say here that there was undoubtedly much about the key that seemed complex; indeed there was only one thing about it that was simple. It opened the door.

There are certain recognised and accepted statements in this matter which may for brevity and convenience be described as lies. We have all heard people say that Christianity arose in an age of barbarism. They might just as well say that Christian Science arose in an age of barbarism. They may think Christianity was a symptom of social decay, as I think Christian Science a symptom of mental decay. They may think Christianity a superstition that ultimately destroyed a civilisation, as I think Christian Science a superstition capable (if taken seriously) of destroying any number of civilisations. But to say that a Christian of the fourth or fifth centuries was a barbarian living in a barbarous time is exactly like saying that Mrs. Eddy was a Red Indian. And if I allowed my constitutional impatience with Mrs. Eddy to impel me to call her a Red Indian, I should incidentally be telling a lie. We may like or dislike the imperial civilisation of Rome in the fourth century; we may like or dislike the industrial civilisation of America in the nineteenth century; but that they both were what we commonly mean by a civilisation no person of common sense could deny if he wanted to. This is a very obvious fact but it is also a very fundamental one; and we must make it the foundation of any further description of constructive Christianity in the past. For good or evil, it was pre-eminently the product of a civilised age, perhaps of an over-civilised age. This is the first fact apart from all praise or blame; indeed I am so unfortunate as not to feel that I praise a thing when I compare it to Christian Science. But it is at least desirable to know something of the savour of a society in which we are condemning or praising anything; and the science that connects Mrs. Eddy with tomahawks or the Mater Dolorosa with totems may for our general convenience be eliminated. The dominant fact, not merely about the Christian religion, but about the whole pagan civilisation, was that which has been more than once repeated in these pages. The Mediterranean was a lake in the real sense of a pool; in which a number of different cults or cultures were, as the phrase goes, pooled. Those cities facing each other round the circle of the lake became more and more one cosmopolitan culture. On its legal and military side it was the Roman Empire; but it was very many-sided. It might be called superstitious in the sense that it contained a great number of varied superstitions; but by no possibility can any part of it be called barbarous.

In this level of cosmopolitan culture arose the Christian religion and the Catholic Church; and everything in the story suggests that it was felt to be something new and strange. Those who have tried to suggest that it evolved out of something much milder or more ordinary have found that in this case their evolutionary method is very difficult to apply. They may suggest that Essenes or Ebionites or such things were the seed; but the seed is invisible; the tree appears very rapidly full-grown; and the tree is something totally different. It is certainly a Christmas tree in the sense that it keeps the kindliness and moral beauty of the story of Bethlehem. but it was as ritualistic as the seven branched candlestick, and the candles it carried were considerably more than were probably permitted by the first prayer-book of Edward the Sixth. It might well be asked, indeed, why anyone accepting the Bethlehem tradition should object to golden or gilded ornament since the Magi themselves brought gold, why he should dislike incense in the church since incense was brought even to the stable. But these are controversies that do not concern me here. I am concerned only with the historical fact, more and more admitted by historians, that very early in its history this thing became visible to the civilisation of antiquity; and that already the Church appeared as a Church; with everything that is implied in a Church and much that is disliked in a Church. We will discuss in a moment how far it was like other ritualistic or magical or ascetical mysteries in its own time. It was certainly not in the least like merely ethical and idealistic movements in our time. It had a doctrine; it had a discipline; it had sacraments; it had degrees of initiation; it admitted people and expelled people; it affirmed one dogma with authority and repudiated another with anathemas. If all these things be the marks of Antichrist, the reign of Antichrist followed very rapidly upon Christ.

Those who maintain that Christianity was not a Church but a moral movement of idealists have been forced to push the period of its perversion or disappearance further and further back. A bishop of Rome writes claiming authority in the very lifetime of St. John the Evangelist; and it is described as the first papal aggression. A friend of the Apostles writes of them as men he knew and says they taught him the doctrine of the Sacrament; and Mr. Wells can only murmur that the reaction towards barbaric blood-rites may have happened rather earlier than might be expected. The date of the Fourth Gospel, which at one time was steadily growing later and later, is now steadily growing earlier and earlier; until critics are staggered at the dawning and dreadful possibility that it might be something like what it professes to be. The last limit of an early date for the extinction of true Christianity has probably been found by the latest German professor whose authority is invoked by Dean Inge. This learned scholar says that Pentecost was the occasion for the first founding of an ecclesiastical, dogmatic, and despotic Church utterly alien to the simple ideals of Jesus of Nazareth. This may be called, in a popular as well as a learned sense, the limit. What do professors of this kind imagine that men are made of? Suppose it were a matter of any merely human movement, let us say that of the conscientious objectors.

Some say the early Christians were Pacifists; I do not believe it for a moment, but I am quite ready to accept the
parallel for the sake of the argument. Tolstoy or some
great preacher of peace among peasants has been shot as a
mutineer for defying conscription; and a little while afterwards his few followers meet together in an upper room in
remembrance of him. They never had any reason for coming together except that common memory; they are men of
many kinds with nothing to bind them, except that the
greatest event in all their lives was this tragedy of the
teacher of universal peace. They are always repeating his
words, revolving his problems, trying to imitate his character. The Pacifists meet at their Pentecost and are possessed
of a sudden ecstasy of enthusiasm and wild rush of the
whirlwind of inspiration, in a course of which they proceed
to establish universal Conscription, to increase the Navy
Estimates, to insist on everybody going about armed to the
teeth and on all the frontiers bristling with artillery; the
proceedings concluded with the singing of 'Boys of the
Bulldog Breed' and 'Don't let them scrap the British
Navy'! That is something like a fair parallel to the theory of
these critics; that the transition from their idea of Jesus to
their idea of Catholicism could have been made in the little
upper room at Pentecost. Surely anybody's common sense
would tell him that enthusiasts, who only met through
their common enthusiasm for a leader whom they loved,
would not instantly rush away to establish everything that
he hated. No, if the 'ecclesiastical and dogmatic system' is
as old as Pentecost, it is as old as Christmas. If we trace it
back to such very early Christians we must trace it back to
Christ.

   We may begin then with these two negations. It is nonsense to say that the Christian faith appeared in a simple
age; in the sense of an unlettered and gullible age. It is
equally nonsense to say that the Christian faith was a simple thing; in the sense of a vague or childish or merely in-
stinctive thing. Perhaps the only point in which we could
possibly say that the Church fitted into the pagan world, is

the fact that they were both not only highly civilised but rather complicated. They were both emphatically many-sided; but antiquity was then a many-sided hole, like a hexagonal hole waiting for an equally hexagonal stopper. In that sense only the Church was many-sided enough to fit the world. The six sides of the Mediterranean world faced each other across the sea and waited for something that should look all ways at once. The Church had to be both Roman and Greek and Jewish and African and Asiatic. In the very words of the Apostle of the Gentiles, it was indeed all things to all men. Christianity then was not merely crude and simple and was the very reverse of the growth of a barbaric time. But when we come to the contrary charge, we come to a much more plausible charge. It is very much more tenable that the Faith was but the final phase of the decay of civilisation, in the sense of the excess of civilisation; that this superstition was a sign that Rome was dying, and dying of being much too civilised. That is an argument much better worth considering; and we will proceed to consider it.

At the beginning of this book I ventured on a general summary of it, in a parallel between the rise of humanity out of nature and the rise of Christianity out of history. I pointed out that in both cases what had gone before might imply something coming after; but did not in the least imply what did come after. If a detached mind had seen certain apes it might have deduced more anthropoids; it would not have deduced man or anything within a thousand miles of what man has done. In short, it might have seen Pithecanthropus or the Missing Link looming in the future, if possible almost as dimly and doubtfully as we see him looming in the past. But if it foresaw him appearing it would also foresee him disappearing, and leaving a few faint traces just as he has left a few faint traces; if they are traces. To foresee that Missing Link would not be to foresee Man, or anything like Man. Now this earlier explanation must be kept in mind; because it is an exact parallel to the true view of the Church; and the suggestion of it having evolved naturally out of the Empire in decay.

The truth is that in one sense a man might very well have predicted that the imperial decadence would produce something like Christianity. That is, something a little like and gigantically different. A man might very well have said, for instance, 'Pleasure has been pursued so extravagantly that there will be a reaction into pessimism. Perhaps it will take the form of asceticism; men will mutilate themselves instead of merely hanging themselves.' Or a man might very reasonably have said, 'If we weary of our Greek and Latin gods we shall be hankering after some eastern mystery or other; there will be a fashion in Persians or Hindus.' Or a man of the world might well have been shrewd enough to say, 'Powerful people are picking up these fads; some day the court will adopt one of them and it may become official.' Or yet another and gloomier prophet might be pardoned for saying, 'The world is going down hill; dark and barbarous superstitions will return, it does not matter much which. They will all be formless and fugitive like dreams of the night.'

Now it is the intense interest of the case that all these prophecies were really fulfilled; but it was not the Church that fulfilled them. It was the Church that escaped from them, confounded them, and rose above them in triumph. In so far as it was probable that the mere nature of hedonism would produce a mere reaction of asceticism, it did produce a mere reaction of asceticism. It was the movement called Manichean and the Church was its mortal enemy. In so far as it would have naturally appeared at that point of history, it did appear; it did also disappear, which was equally natural. The mere pessimist reaction did come with the Manichees and did go with the Manichees. But the Church did not come with them or go with them; and she had much more to do with their going than with their coming. Or again, in so far as it was probable that even the growth of scepticism would bring in a fashion of eastern religion, it did bring it in; Mithras came from far beyond Palestine out of the heart of Persia, bringing strange mys-

teries of the blood of bulls. Certainly there was everything
to show that some such fashion would have come in any
case. But certainly there is nothing in the world to show
that it would not have passed away in any case. Certainly
an Oriental fad was something eminently fitted to the
fourth or fifth century; but that hardly explains it having
remained to the twentieth century, and still going strong.
In short, in so far as things of the kind might have been
expected then, things like Mithraism were experienced
then; but it scarcely explains our more recent experiences.
And if we were still Mithraists merely because Mithraic
headdresses and other Persian apparatuses might be expected to be all the rage in the days of Domitian, it would
almost seem by this time that we must be a little dowdy.

It is the same, as will be suggested in a moment, with
the idea of official favouritism. In so far as such favouritism shown towards a fad was something that might have
been looked for during the decline and fall of the Roman
Empire, it was something that did exist in that Empire and
did decline and fall with it. It throws no sort of light on the
thing that resolutely refused to decline and fall; that grew
steadily while the other was declining and falling; and
which even at this moment is going forward with fearless
energy, when another eon has completed its cycle and another civilisation seems almost ready to fall or to decline.

Now the curious fact is this: that the very heresies
which the early Church is blamed for crushing, testify to
the unfairness for which she is blamed. In so far as something deserved the blame, it was precisely the things that
she is blamed for blaming. In so far as something was
merely a superstition, she herself condemned that superstition. In so far as something was a mere reaction into barbarism, she herself resisted it because it was a reaction into
barbarism. In so far as something was a fad of the fading
empire, that died and deserved to die, it was the Church
alone that killed it. The Church is reproached for being
exactly what the heresy was repressed for being. The explanations of the evolutionary historians and higher critics

do really explain why Arianism and Gnosticism and Nestorianism were born – and also why they died. They do not explain why the Church was born or why she has refused to die. Above all, they do not explain why she should have made war on the very evils she is supposed to share.

Let us take a few practical examples of the principle; the principle that if there was anything that was really a superstition of the dying empire, it did really die with the dying empire; and certainly was not the same as the very thing that destroyed it. For this purpose we will take in order two or three of the most ordinary explanations of Christian origins among the modern critics of Christianity. Nothing is more common, for instance, than to find such a modern critic writing something like this: 'Christianity was above all a movement of ascetics, a rush into the desert, a refuge in the cloister, a renunciation of all life and happiness; and this was a part of a gloomy and inhuman reaction against nature itself, a hatred of the body, a horror of the material universe, a sort of universal suicide of the senses and even of the self. It came from an eastern fanaticism like that of the fakirs and was ultimately founded on an eastern pessimism, which seems to feel existence itself as an evil.'

Now the most extraordinary thing about this is that it is all quite true; it is true in every detail except that it happens to be attributed entirely to the wrong person. It is not true of the Church; but it is true of the heretics condemned by the Church. It is as if one were to write a most detailed analysis of the mistakes and misgovernment of the ministers of George the Third, merely with the small inaccuracy that the whole story was told about George Washington; or as if somebody made a list of the crimes of the Bolshevists with no variation except that they were all attributed to the Czar. The early Church was indeed very ascetic, in connection with a totally different philosophy; but the philosophy of a war on life and nature as such really did exist in the world, if the critics only knew where to look for it.

What really happened was this. When the Faith first emerged into the world, the very first thing that happened to it was that it was caught in a sort of swarm of mystical and metaphysical sects, mostly out of the East; like one lonely golden bee caught in a swarm of wasps. To the ordinary onlooker, there did not seem to be much difference, or anything beyond a general buzz; indeed in a sense there was not much difference, so far as stinging and being stung were concerned. The difference was that only one golden dot in all that whirring gold dust had the power of going forth to make hives for all humanity, to give the world honey and wax or (as was so finely said in a context too easily forgotten) 'the two noblest things, which are sweetness and light.' The wasps all died that winter; and half the difficulty is that hardly anyone knows anything about them and most people do not know that they ever existed; so that the whole story of that first phase of our religion is lost. Or, to vary the metaphor, when this movement or some other movement pierced the dyke between the east and west and brought more mystical ideas into Europe, it brought with it a whole flood of other mystical ideas besides its own, most of them ascetic and nearly all of them pessimistic. They very nearly flooded and overwhelmed the purely Christian element. They came mostly from that region that was a sort of dim borderland between the eastern philosophies and the eastern mythologies, and which shared with the wilder philosophers that curious craze for making fantastic patterns of the cosmos in the shape of maps and genealogical trees. Those that are supposed to derive from the mysterious Manes are called Manichean; kindred cults are more generally known as Gnostic; they are mostly of a labyrinthine complexity, but the point to insist on is the pessimism; the fact that nearly all in one form or another regarded the creation of the world as the work of an evil spirit. Some of them had that Asiatic atmosphere that surrounds Buddhism, the suggestion that life is a corruption of the purity of being. Some of them suggested a purely spiritual order which had been betrayed by the coarse and clumsy trick of making such toys as the sun and moon and stars. Anyhow all this dark tide out of the metaphysical sea in the midst of Asia poured through the dykes simultaneously with the creed of Christ; but it is the whole point of the story that the two were not the same; that they flowed like oil and water. That creed remained in the shape of a miracle; a river still flowing through the sea. And the proof of the miracle was practical once more; it was merely that while all that sea was salt and bitter with the savour of death, of this one stream in the midst of it a man could drink.

Now that purity was preserved by dogmatic definitions and exclusions. It could not possibly have been preserved by anything else. If the Church had not renounced the Manicheans it might have become merely Manichean. If it had not renounced the Gnostics it might have become Gnostic. But by the very fact that it did renounce them it proved that it was not either Gnostic or Manichean. At any rate it proved that something was not either Gnostic or Manichean; and what could it be that condemned them, if it was not the original good news of the runners from Bethlehem and the trumpet of the Resurrection? The early Church was ascetic, but she proved that she was not pessimistic, simply by condemning the pessimists. The creed declared that man was sinful, but it did not declare that life was evil, and it proved it by damning those who did. The condemnation of the early heretics is itself condemned as something crabbed and narrow; but it was in truth the very proof that the Church meant to be brotherly and broad. It proved that the primitive Catholics were specially eager to explain that they did *not* think man utterly vile; that they did *not* think life incurably miserable; that they did *not* think marriage a sin or procreation a tragedy. They were ascetic because asceticism was the only possible purge of the sins of the world; but in the very thunder of their anathemas they affirmed forever that their asceticism was not to be anti-human or anti-natural; that they did wish to purge the world and not destroy it. And nothing else except those

anathemas could possibly have made it clear, amid a confusion which still confuses them with their mortal enemies.
Nothing else but dogma could have resisted the riot of
imaginative invention with which the pessimists were wag-
ing their war against nature; with their Aeons and their
Demiurge, their strange Logos and their sinister Sophia. If
the Church had not insisted on theology, it would have
melted into a mad mythology of the mystics, yet further
removed from reason or even from rationalism; and,
above all, yet further removed from life and from the love
of life. Remember that it would have been an inverted mythology, one contradicting everything natural in paganism;
a mythology in which Pluto would be above Jupiter and
Hades hang higher than Olympus; in which Brahma and all
that has the breath of life would be subject to Seeva, shining with the eye of death.

That the early Church was itself full of an ecstatic enthusiasm for renunciation and virginity makes this distinction much more striking and not less so. It makes all the
more important the place where the dogma drew the line.
A man might crawl about on all fours like a beast because
he was an ascetic. He might stand night and day on the top
of a pillar and be adored for being an ascetic. But he could
not say that the world was a mistake or the marriage state a
sin without being a heretic. What was it that thus deliberately disengaged itself from eastern asceticism by sharp
definition and fierce refusal, if it was not something with
an individuality of its own; and one that was quite different? If the Catholics are to be confused with the Gnostics,
we can only say it was not their fault if they are. And it is
rather hard that the Catholics should be blamed by the
same critics for persecuting the heretics and also for sym-
pathising with the heresy.

The Church was not a Manichean movement, if only
because it was not a movement at all. It was not even
merely an ascetic movement, because it was not a movement at all. It would be nearer the truth to call it the tamer
of asceticism than the mere leader or loosener of it. It was

a thing having its own theory of asceticism, its own type of asceticism, but most conspicuous at the moment as the moderator of other theories and types. This is the only sense that can be made, for instance, of the story of St. Augustine. As long as he was a mere man of the world, a mere man drifting with his time, he actually was a Manichean. It really was quite modern and fashionable to be a Manichean. But when he became a Catholic, the people he instantly turned on and rent in pieces were the Manicheans. The Catholic way of putting it is that he left off being a pessimist to become an ascetic. But as the pessimists interpreted asceticism, it might be said that he left off being an ascetic to become a saint. The war upon life, the denial of nature were exactly the things he had already found in the heathen world outside the Church, and had to renounce when he entered the Church. The very fact that St. Augustine remains a somewhat sterner or sadder figure than St. Francis or St. Teresa only accentuates the dilemma. Face to face with the gravest or even grimmest of Catholics, we can still ask, 'Why did Catholicism make war on Manichees, if Catholicism was Manichean?'

Take another rationalistic explanation of the rise of Christendom. It is common enough to find another critic saying, 'Christianity did not really rise at all,' that is, it did not merely rise from below; it was imposed from above. It is an example of the power of the executive, especially in despotic states. The Empire was really an Empire; that is, it was really ruled by the Emperor. One of the Emperors happened to become a Christian. He might just as well have become a Mithraist or a Jew or a Fire-Worshipper; it was common in the decline of the Empire for eminent and educated people to adopt these eccentric eastern cults. But when he adopted it, it became the official religion of the Roman Empire; and when it became the official religion of the Roman Empire, it became as strong, as universal and as invincible as the Roman Empire. It has only remained in the world as a relic of that Empire; or, as many have put it, it is but the ghost of Caesar still hovering over Rome. This

also is a very ordinary line taken in the criticism of orthodoxy, to say that it was only officialdoms that ever made it
orthodoxy. And here again we can call on the heretics to
refute it.

The whole great history of the Arian heresy might have
been invented to explode this idea. It is a very interesting
history often repeated in this connection; and the upshot
of it is, in so far as there ever was a merely official religion,
it actually died because it was merely an official religion;
and what destroyed it was the real religion. Arius advanced
a version of Christianity which moved, more or less
vaguely, in the direction of what we should call Unitarianism; though it was not the same, for it gave to Christ a curious intermediary position between the divine and human.
The point is that it seemed to many more reasonable and
less fanatical; and among these were many of the educated
class in a sort of reaction against the first romance of con-
version. Arians were a sort of moderates and a sort of
modernists. And it was felt that after the first squabbles
this was the final form of rationalised, religion into which
civilisation might well settle down. It was accepted by Divus Caesar himself and became the official orthodoxy; the
generals and military princes drawn from the new barbarian powers of the north, full of the future, supported it
strongly. But the sequel is still more important. Exactly as
a modern man might pass through Unitarianism to complete agnosticism, so the greatest of the Arian emperors
ultimately shed the last and thinnest pretence of Christianity; he abandoned even Arius and returned to Apollo. He
was a Caesar of the Caesars; a soldier, a scholar, a man of
large ambitions and ideals; another of the philosopher
kings. It seemed to him as if at his signal the sun rose
again. The oracles began to speak like birds beginning to
sing at dawn; paganism was itself again; the gods returned.
It seemed the end of that strange interlude of an alien superstition. And indeed it was the end of it, so far as there
was a mere interlude of mere superstition. It was the end
of it, in so far as it was the fad of an emperor or the fash-

ion of a generation. If there really was something that began with Constantine, then it ended with Julian.

But there was something that did not end. There had
arisen in that hour of history, defiant above the democratic
tumult of the Councils of the Church, Athanasius against
the world. We may pause upon the point at issue; because
it is relevant to the whole of this religious history, and the
modern world seems to miss the whole point of it. We
might put it this way. If there is one question which the
enlightened and liberal have the habit of deriding and
holding up as a dreadful example of barren dogma and
senseless sectarian strife, it is this Athanasian question of
the co-Eternity of the Divine Son. On the other hand, if
there is one thing that the same liberals always offer us as a
piece of pure and simple Christianity, untroubled by doctrinal disputes, it is the single sentence, 'God is Love.' Yet
the two statements are almost identical; at least one is very
nearly nonsense without the other. The barren dogma is
only the logical way of stating the beautiful sentiment. For
if there be a being without beginning, existing before all
things, was He loving when there was nothing to be loved?
If through that unthinkable eternity He is lonely, what is
the meaning of saying He is love? The only justification of
such a mystery is the mystical conception that in His own
nature there was something analogous to self-expression;
something of what begets and beholds what it has begot-
ten. Without some such idea, it is really illogical to complicate the ultimate essence of deity with an idea like love. If
the moderns really want a simple religion of love, they
must look for it in the Athanasian Creed. The truth is that
the trumpet of true Christianity, the challenge of the chari-
ties and simplicities of Bethlehem or Christmas Day, never
rang out more arrestingly and unmistakably than in the
defiance of Athanasius to the cold compromise of the
Arians. It was emphatically he who really was fighting for a
God of Love against a God of colourless and remote cosmic control; the God of the stoics and the agnostics. It was
emphatically he who was fighting for the Holy Child

against the grey deity of the Pharisees and the Sadducees. He was fighting for that very balance of beautiful interdependence and intimacy, in the very Trinity of the Divine Nature, that draws our hearts to the Trinity of the Holy Family. His dogma, if the phrase be not misunderstood, turns even God into a Holy Family.

That this purely Christian dogma actually for a second time rebelled against the Empire, and actually for a second time re-founded the Church in spite of the Empire, is itself a proof that there was something positive and personal working in the world, other than whatever official faith the Empire chose to adopt. This power utterly destroyed the official faith that the Empire did adopt. It went on its own way as it is going on its own way still. There are any number of other examples in which is repeated precisely the same process we have reviewed in the case of the Manichean and the Arian. A few centuries afterwards, for instance, the Church had to maintain the same Trinity, which is simply the logical side of love, against another appearance of the isolated and simplified deity in the religion of Islam. Yet there are some who cannot see what the Crusaders were fighting for; and some even who talk as if Christianity had never been anything but a form of what they called Hebraism coming in with the decay of Hellenism. Those people must certainly be very much puzzled by the war between the Crescent and the Cross. If Christianity had never been anything but a simpler morality sweeping away polytheism, there is no reason why Christendom should not have been swept into Islam. The truth is that Islam itself was a barbaric reaction against that very humane complexity that is really a Christian character; that idea of balance in the deity, as of balance in the family, that makes that creed a sort of sanity, and that sanity the soul of civilisation. And that is why the Church is from the first a thing holding its own position and point of view, quite apart from the accidents and anarchies of its age. That is why it deals blows impartially right and left, at the pessimism of the Manichean or the optimism of the Pelagian. It was not a Manichean movement because it was not a movement at all. It was not an official fashion because it was not a fashion at all. It was something that could coincide with movements and fashions, could control them and could survive them.

So might rise from their graves the great heresiarchs to confound their comrades of today. There is nothing that the critics now affirm that we cannot call on these great witnesses to deny. The modern critic will say lightly enough that Christianity was but a reaction into asceticism and anti-natural spirituality, a dance of fakirs furious against life and love. But Manes the great mystic will answer them from his secret throne and cry, 'These Christians have no right to be, called spiritual; these Christians have no title to be called ascetics; they who compromised with the curse of life and all the filth of the family. Through them the earth is still foul with fruit and harvest and polluted with population. Theirs was no movement against nature, or my children would have carried it to triumph; but these fools renewed the world when I would have ended it with a gesture.' And another critic will write that the Church was but the shadow of the Empire, the fad of a chance Emperor, and that it remains in Europe only as the ghost of the power of Rome. And Arius the deacon will answer out of the darkness of oblivion: 'No, indeed, or the world would have followed my more reasonable religion. For mine went down before demagogues and men defying Caesar and around my champion was the purple cloak and mine was the glory of the eagles. It was not for lack of these things that I failed.' And yet a third modern will maintain that the creed spread only as a sort of panic of hell-fire; men everywhere attempting impossible things in fleeing from incredible vengeance; a nightmare of imaginary remorse; and such an explanation will satisfy many who see something dreadful in the doctrine of orthodoxy. And then there will go up against it the terrible voice of Tertullian, saying, 'And why then was I cast out; and why did soft hearts and heads decide against me when

I proclaimed the perdition of all sinners; and what was this power that thwarted me when I threatened all backsliders with hell? For none ever went up that hard road so far as I; and mine was the *Credo Quia Impossible*.' Then there is the fourth suggestion that there was something of the Semitic secret society in the whole matter; that it was a new invasion of the nomad's spirit shaking a kindlier and more comfortable paganism, its cities and its household gods; whereby the jealous monotheistic races could after all establish their jealous God. And Mahomet shall answer out of the whirlwind, the red whirlwind of the desert, 'Who ever served the jealousy of God as I did or left him more lonely in the sky? Who ever paid more honour to Moses and Abraham or won more victories over idols and the images of paganism? And what was this thing that thrust me back with the energy of a thing alive, whose fanaticism could drive me from Sicily and tear up my deep roots out of the rock of Spain? What faith was theirs who thronged in thousands of every class and country crying out that my ruin was the will of God; and what hurled great Godfrey as from a catapult over the wall of Jerusalem; and what brought great Sobieski like a thunderbolt to the gates of Vienna? I think there was more than you fancy in the religion that has so matched itself with mine.'

Those who would suggest that the faith was a fanaticism are doomed to an eternal perplexity. In their account it is bound to appear as fanatical for nothing, and fanatical against everything. It is ascetic and at war with ascetics, Roman and in revolt against Rome, monotheistic and fighting furiously against monotheism; harsh in its condemnation of harshness; a riddle not to be explained even as unreason. And what sort of unreason is it that seems reasonable to millions of educated Europeans through all the revolutions of some sixteen hundred years? People are not amused with a puzzle or a paradox or a mere muddle in the mind for all that time. I know of no explanation except that such a thing is not unreason but reason; that if it is fanatical it is fanatical for reason and fanatical against all the unreasonable things. That is the only explanation I can find of a thing from the first so detached and so confident condemning things that looked so like itself, refusing help from powers that seemed so essential to its existence, sharing on its human side all the passions of the age, yet always at the supreme moment suddenly rising superior to them, never saying exactly what it was expected to say and never needing to unsay what it had said; I can find no explanation except that, like Pallas from the brain of Jove, it had indeed come forth out of the mind of God, mature and mighty and armed for judgment and for war.

5
THE ESCAPE FROM PAGANISM

THE MODERN MISSIONARY, with his palm-leaf hat and his umbrella has become rather a figure of fun. He is chaffed among men of the world for the ease with which he can be eaten by cannibals and the narrow bigotry which makes him regard the cannibal culture as lower than his own. Perhaps the best part of the joke is that the men of the world do not see that the joke is against themselves. It is rather ridiculous to ask a man just about to be boiled in a pot and eaten, at a purely religious feast, why be does not regard all religions as equally friendly and fraternal. But there is a more subtle criticism uttered against the more old-fashioned missionary; to the effect that he generalises too broadly about the heathen and pays too little attention to the difference between Mahomet and Mumbo-Jumbo. There was probably truth in this complaint, especially in the past; but it is my main contention here that the exaggeration is all the other way at present. It is the temptation of the professors to treat mythologies too much as theologies; as things thoroughly thought out and seriously held. It is the temptation of the intellectuals to take much too seriously the fine shades of various schools in the rather irresponsible metaphysics of Asia. Above all it is their temptation to miss the real truth implied in the idea of Aquinas contra Gentiles or Athanasius contra mundum.

If the missionary says, in fact, that he is exceptional in being a Christian, and that the rest of the races and religions can be collectively classified as heathen, he is perfectly right. He may say it in quite the wrong spirit, in which case he is spiritually wrong. But in the cold light of philosophy and history, he is intellectually right. He may not be right-minded, but he is right. He may not even have a right to be right, but he is right. The outer world to which he brings his creed really is something subject to certain generalisations covering all its varieties, and is not merely a variety of similar creeds. Perhaps it is in any case too much of a temptation to pride or hypocrisy to call it heathenry Perhaps it would be better simply to call it humanity. But there are certain broad characteristics of what we call humanity while it remains in what we call heathenry. They are not necessarily had characteristics; some of them are worthy of the respect of Christendom; some of them have been absorbed and transfigured in the substance of Christendom. But they existed before Christendom and they still exist outside Christendom, as certainly as the sea existed before a boat and all round a boat; and they have as strong and as universal and as unmistakable a savour as the sea.

For instance, all real scholars who have studied the Greek and Roman culture say one thing about it. They agree that in the ancient world religion was one thing and philosophy quite another. There was very little effort to rationalise and at the same time to realise a real belief in the gods. There was very little pretence of any such real belief among the philosophers. But neither had the passion or perhaps the power to persecute the other, save in particular and peculiar cases; and neither the philosopher in his school nor the priest in his temple seems ever to have seriously contemplated his own concept as covering the world. A priest sacrificing to Atrius in Caledonia did not seem to think that people would someday sacrifice to her instead of to Isis beyond the sea; a sage following the vegetarian rule of the Neo-Pythagoreans did not seem to think it would universally prevail and exclude the methods of Epictetus or Epicures. We may call this liberality if we like; I am not dealing with an argument but describing an atmosphere. All this, I say, is admitted by all scholars; but what neither the learned nor the unlearned have fully realised, perhaps, is that this description is really an exact description of all non-Christian civilisation today; and espe-

cially of the great civilisations of the East. Eastern paganism really is much more all of a piece, just as ancient paganism was much more all of a piece, than the modern
critics admit. It is a many-coloured Persian carpet as the
other was a varied and tessellated Roman pavement; but
the one real crack right across that pavement came from
the earthquake of the Crucifixion.

   The modern European seeking his religion in Asia is
reading his religion into Asia. Religion there is something
different; it is both more and less. He is like a man map-
ping out the sea as land; marking waves as mountains; not
understanding the nature of its peculiar permanence. It is
perfectly true that Asia has its own dignity and poetry and
high civilisation. But it is not in the least true that Asia has
its own definite dominions of moral government, where all
loyalty is conceived in terms of morality; as when we say
that Ireland is Catholic or that New England was Puritan.
The map is not marked out in religions, in our sense of
churches. The state of mind is far more subtle, more relative, more secretive, more varied and changing, like the
colours of the snake. The Moslem is the nearest approach
to a militant Christian; and that is precisely because he is a
much nearer approach to an envoy from western civilisation. The Moslem in the heart of Asia almost stands for
the soul of Europe. And as he stands between them and
Europe in the matter of space, so he stands between them
and Christianity in the matter of time. In that sense the
Moslems in Asia are merely like the Nestorians in Asia.
Islam, historically speaking, is the greatest of the Eastern
heresies. It owed something to the quite isolated and
unique individuality of Israel; but it owed more to Byzan-
tium and the theological enthusiasm of Christendom. It
owed something even to the Crusades. It owed nothing
whatever to Asia. It owed nothing to the atmosphere of
the ancient and traditional world of Asia, with its immemorial etiquette and its bottomless or bewildering philosophies. All that ancient and actual Asia felt the entrance of
Islam as something foreign and western and warlike, pierc-

ing it like a spear.

Even where we might trace in dotted lines the domains
of Asiatic religions, we should probably be reading into
them something dogmatic and ethical belonging to our
own religion. It is as if a European ignorant of the American atmosphere were to suppose that each 'state' was a
separate sovereign state as patriotic as France or Poland; or
that when a Yankee referred fondly to his 'home town' he
meant he had no other nation, like a citizen of ancient
Athens or Rome. As he would be reading a particular sort
of loyalty into America, so we are reading a particular sort
of loyalty into Asia. There are loyalties of other kinds; but
not what men in the west mean by being a believer, by
trying to be a Christian, by being a good Protestant or a
practicing Catholic. In the intellectual world it means
something far more vague and varied by doubts and
speculations. In the moral world it means something far
more loose and drifting. A professor of Persian at one of
our great universities, so passionate a partisan of the East
as practically to profess a contempt for the West, said to a
friend of mine: 'You will never understand oriental religions, because you always conceive religion as connected
with ethics. This kind has really nothing to do with ethics.'
We have most of us known some Masters of the Higher
Wisdom, some Pilgrims upon the Path to Power, some
eastern esoteric saints and seers, who had really nothing to
do with ethics. Something different, something detached
and irresponsible, tinges the moral atmosphere of Asia and
touches even that of Islam. It was very realistically caught
in the atmosphere of *Hassan*; and a very horrible atmosphere too. It is even more vivid in such glimpses as we get
of the genuine and ancient cults of Asia. Deeper than the
depths of metaphysics, far down in the abysses of mystical
meditations, under all that solemn universe of spiritual
things, is a secret, an intangible and a terrible levity. It does
not really very much matter what one does. Either because
they do not believe in a devil, or because they do believe in
a destiny, or because experience here is everything and

eternal life something totally different, but for some reason they are totally different. I have read somewhere that there were three great friends famous in medieval Persia for their unity of mind. One became the responsible and re-spected Vizier of the Great King; the second was the poet Omar, pessimist and epicurean, drinking wine in mockery of Mahomet; the third was the Old Man of the Mountain who maddened his people with hashish that they might murder other people with daggers. It does not really much matter what one does.

The Sultan in *Hassan* would have understood all those three men; indeed he was all those three men. But this sort of universalist cannot have what we call a character; it is what we call a character. He cannot choose; he cannot fight; he cannot repent; he cannot hope. He is not in the same sense creating something; for creation means rejec-tion. He is not, in our religious phrase, making his soul. For our doctrine of salvation does really mean a labour like that of a man trying to make a statue beautiful; a victory with wings. For that there must be a final choice; for a man cannot make statues without rejecting stone. And there really is this ultimate immorality behind the meta-physics of Asia. And the reason is that there has been nothing through all those unthinkable ages to bring the human mind sharply to the point; to tell it that the time has come to choose. The mind has lived too much in eter-nity. The soul has been too immortal; in the special sense that it ignores the idea of mortal sin. It has had too much of eternity, in the sense that it has not had enough of the hour of death and the day of judgment. It is not crucial enough; in the liberal sense that it has not had enough of the cross. That is what we mean when we say that Asia is very old. But strictly speaking Europe is quite as old as Asia; indeed in a sense any place is as old as any other place. What we mean is that Europe has not merely gone on growing older. It has been born again.

Asia is all humanity; as it has worked out its human doom. Asia, in its vast territory, in its varied populations,

in its heights of past achievement and its depths of dark
speculation, is itself a world; and represents something of
what we mean when we speak of the world. It is a cosmos
rather than a continent. It is the world as man has made it;
and contains many of the most wonderful things that man
has made. Therefore Asia stands as the one representative
of paganism and the one rival to Christendom. But everywhere else where we get glimpses of that mortal destiny,
they suggest stages in the same story. Where Asia trails
away into the southern archipelagos of the savages, or
where a darkness full of nameless shapes dwells in the
heart of Africa, or where the last survivors of lost races
linger in the cold volcano of prehistoric America, it is all
the same story; sometimes perhaps later chapters of the
same story. It is men entangled in the forest of their own
mythology; it is men drowned in the sea of their own
metaphysics. Polytheists have grown weary of the wildest
of fictions. Monotheists have grown weary of the most
wonderful of truths. Diabolists here and there have such a
hatred of heaven and earth that they have tried to take refuge in hell. It is the Fall of Man; and it is exactly that fall
that was being felt by our own fathers at the first moment
of the Roman decline. We also were going down that wide
road; down that easy slope; following the magnificent procession of the high civilisations of the world.

If the Church had not entered the world then, it seems
probable that Europe would be now very much what Asia
is now. Something may be allowed for a real difference of
race and environment, visible in the ancient as in the modern world. But after all we talk about the changeless East
very largely because it has not suffered the great change.
Paganism in its last phase showed considerable signs of
becoming equally changeless. This would not mean that
new schools or sects of philosophy would not arise; as new
schools did arise in Antiquity and do arise in Asia. It does
not mean that there would be no real mystics or visionar-
ies; as there were mystics in Antiquity and are mystics in
Asia. It does not mean that there would be no social codes,

as there were codes in Antiquity and are codes in Asia. It does not mean that there could not be good men or happy lives, for God has given all men a conscience and conscience can give all men a kind of peace. But it does mean that the tone and proportion of all these things, and especially the proportion of good and evil things, would be in the unchanged West what they are in the changeless East. And nobody who looks at that changeless East honestly, and with a real sympathy, can believe that there is anything there remotely resembling the challenge and revolution of the Faith.

In short, if classic paganism had lingered until now, a number of things might well have lingered with it; and they would look very like what we call the religions of the East. There would still be Pythagoreans teaching reincarnation, as there are still Hindus teaching reincarnation. There would still be Stoics making a religion out of reason and virtue, as there are still Confucians making a religion out of reason and virtue. There would still be Neo-Platonists studying transcendental truths, the meaning of which was mysterious to other people and disputed even amongst themselves; as the Buddhists still study a transcendentalism mysterious to others and disputed among themselves. There would still be Apollonians apparently worshipping the sun-god but explaining that they were worshipping the divine principle; just as there are still intelligent Parsees apparently worshipping the sun but explaining that they are worshipping the deity. There would still be wild Dionysians dancing on the mountain as there are still wild Dervishes dancing in the desert. There would still be crowds of people attending the feasts of the gods, in pagan Europe as in pagan Asia. There would still be crowds of gods, local and other, for them to worship. And there would still be a great many more people who worshipped them than people who believed in them. Finally, there would still be a very large number of people who did worship gods and did believe in gods; and who believed in gods and worshipped gods simply because they were demons. There would still be Levantines secretly sacrificing to Moloch as there are still Thugs secretly sacrificing to Kalee. There would still be a great deal of magic; and a great deal of it would be black magic. There would still be a considerable admiration of Seneca and a considerable imitation of Nero; just as the exalted epigrams of Confucius could coexist with tortures of China. And over all that tangled forest of traditions growing wild or withering would brood the broad silence of a singular and even nameless mood; but the nearest name of it is nothing. All these things, good and bad, would have an indescribable air of being too old to die.

None of these things occupying Europe in the absence of Christendom would bear the least likeness to Christendom. Since the Pythagorean Metempsychosis would still be there, we might call it the Pythagorean religion as we talk about the Buddhist religion. As the noble maxims of Socrates would still be there, we might call it the Socratic religion as we talk about the Confucian religion. As the popular holiday was still marked by a mythological hymn to Adonis, we might call it the religion of Adonis as we talk about the religion of juggernaut. As literature would still be based on the Greek mythology, we might call that mythology a religion, as we call the Hindu mythology a religion. We might say that there were so many thousands or millions of people belonging to that religion, in the sense of frequenting such temples or merely living in a land full of such temples. But if we called the last tradition of Pythagoras or the lingering legend of Adonis by the name of a religion, then we must find some other name for the Church of Christ.

If anybody says that philosophic maxims preserved through many ages, or mythological temples frequented by many people are things of the same class and category as the Church, it is enough to answer quite simply that they are not. Nobody thinks they are the same when he sees them in the old civilisation of Greece and Rome; nobody would think they were the same if that civilisation had lasted two thousand years longer and existed at the present day; nobody can in reason think they are the same in the parallel pagan civilisation in the East, as it is at the present day. None of these philosophies or mythologies are anything like a Church; certainly nothing like a Church Militant. And, as I have shown elsewhere, even if this rule were not already proved, the exception would prove the rule. The rule is that pre-Christian or pagan history does not produce a Church Militant; and the exception, or what some would call the exception, is that Islam is at least militant if it is not Church. And that is precisely because Islam is the one religious rival that is *not* pre-Christian and therefore not in that sense pagan. Islam was a product of Christianity; even if it was a by-product; even if it was a bad product. It was a heresy or a parody emulating and therefore imitating the Church. It is no more surprising that Mahometanism had something of her fighting spirit than that Quakerism had something of her peaceful spirit. After Christianity there are any number of such emulations or extensions. Before it there are none.

The Church Militant is thus unique because it is an army marching to effect a universal deliverance. The bondage from which the world is thus to be delivered is something that is very well symbolised by the state of Asia as by the state of pagan Europe. I do not mean merely their moral or immoral state. The missionary, as a matter of fact, has much more to say for himself than the enlightened imagine, even when he says that the heathen are idolatrous and immoral. A touch or two of realistic experience about Eastern religion, even about Moslem religion, will reveal some startling insensibilities in ethics, such as the practical indifference to the line between passion and perversion. It is not prejudice but practical experience which says that Asia is full of demons as well as gods. But the evil I mean is in the mind. And it is in the mind wherever the mind has worked for a long time alone. It is what happens when all dreaming and thinking have come to an end in an emptiness that is at once negation and necessity.

It sounds like an anarchy, but it is also a slavery. It is what
has been called already the wheel of Asia; all those recurrent arguments about cause and effect or things beginning
and ending in the mind, which make it impossible for the
soul really to strike out and go anywhere or do anything.
And the point is that it is not necessarily peculiar to Asiatics; it would have been true in the end of Europeans – if
something had not happened. If the Church Militant had
not been a thing marching, all men would have been marking time. If the Church Militant had not endured a discipline, all men would have endured a slavery.

What that universal yet fighting faith brought into the
world was hope. Perhaps the one thing common to mythology and philosophy was that both were really sad; in
the sense that they had not this hope even if they had
touches of faith or charity. We may call Buddhism a faith;
though to us it seems more like a doubt. We may call the
Lord of Compassion a Lord of Charity, though it seems to
us a very pessimistic sort of pity. But those who insist
most on the antiquity and size of such cults must agree
that in all their ages they have not covered all their areas
with that sort of practical and pugnacious hope. In Christendom hope has never been absent; rather it has been
errant, extravagant, excessively fixed upon fugitive
chances. Its perpetual revolution and reconstruction has at
least been an evidence of people being in better spirits.
Europe did very truly renew its youth like the eagles; just
as the eagles of Rome rose again over the legions of Napoleon, or we have seen soaring but yesterday the silver eagle
of Poland. But in the Polish case even revolution always
went with religion. Napoleon himself sought a reconciliation with religion. Religion could never be finally separated
even from the most hostile of the hopes; simply because it
was the real source of the hopefulness. And the cause of
this is to be found simply in the religion itself. Those who
quarrel about it seldom even consider it in itself. There is
neither space nor place for such a full consideration here;
but a word may be said to explain a reconciliation that al-

ways recurs and still seems to require explanation.

There will be no end to the weary debates about liberalising theology, until people face the fact that the only liberal part of it is really the dogmatic part. If dogma is incredible, it is because it is incredibly liberal. If it is irrational, it can only be in giving us more assurance of freedom than is justified by reason. The obvious example is that essential form of freedom which we call free will. It is absurd to say that a man shows his liberality in denying his liberty. But it is tenable that he has to affirm a transcendental doctrine in order to affirm his liberty. There is a sense in which we might reasonably say that if man has a primary power of choice, he has in that fact a supernatural power of creation, as if he could raise the dead or give birth to the unbegotten. Possibly in that case a man must be a miracle; and certainly in that case he must be a miracle in order to be a man; and most certainly in order to be a free man. But it is absurd to forbid him to be a free man and do it in the name of a more free religion.

But it is true in twenty other matters. Anybody who believes at all in God must believe in the absolute supremacy of God. But in so far as that supremacy does allow of any degrees that can be called liberal or illiberal, it is self-evident that the illiberal power is the deity of the rationalists and the liberal power is the deity of the dogmatists. Exactly in proportion as you turn monotheism into monism you turn it into despotism. It is precisely the unknown God of the scientist, with his impenetrable purpose and his inevitable and unalterable law, that reminds us of a Prussian autocrat making rigid plans in a remote tent and moving mankind like machinery. It is precisely the God of miracles and of answered prayers who reminds us of a liberal and popular prince, receiving petitions, listening to parliaments and considering the cases of a whole people. I am not now arguing the rationality of this conception in other respects; as a matter of fact it is not, as some suppose, irrational; for there is nothing irrational in a wisest and most well-informed king acting differently according to the action of those he wishes to save. But I am here only noting the general nature of liberality, or of free or enlarged atmosphere of action. And in this respect it is certain that the king can only be what we call magnanimous if he is what some call capricious. It is the Catholic, who has the feeling that his prayers do make a difference, when offered for the living and the dead, who also has the feeling of living like a free citizen in something almost like a constitutional commonwealth. It is the monist who lives under a single iron law who must have the feeling of living like a slave under a sultan. Indeed I believe that the original use of the word *suffragium*, which we now use in politics for a vote, was that employed in theology about a prayer. The dead in Purgatory were said to have the suffrages of the living. And in this sense, of a sort of right of petition to the supreme ruler, we may truly say that the whole of the Communion of Saints, as well as the whole of the Church Militant, is founded on universal suffrage.

But above all, it is true of the most tremendous issue; of that tragedy which has created the divine comedy of our creed. Nothing short of the extreme and strong and startling doctrine of the divinity of Christ will give that particular effect that can truly stir the popular sense like a trumpet; the idea, of the king himself serving in the ranks like a common soldier. By making that figure merely human we make that story much less human. We take away the point of the story which actually pierces humanity; the point of the story which is quite literally the point of a spear. It does not especially humanise the universe to say that good and wise men can die for their opinions; any more than it would be any sort of uproariously popular news in an army that good soldiers may easily get killed. It is no news that King Leonidas is dead any more than that Queen Anne is dead; and men did not wait for Christianity to be men, in the full sense of being heroes. But if we are describing, for the moment, the atmosphere of what is generous and popular and even picturesque, any knowledge of human nature will tell us that no sufferings of the sons of men, or even of the servants of God, strike the same note as the notion of the master suffering instead of his servants. And this is given by the theological and emphatically not by the scientific deity. No mysterious monarch, hidden in his starry pavilion at the base of the cosmic campaign, is in the least like that celestial chivalry of the Captain who carries his five wounds in the front of battle.

What the denouncer of dogma really means is not that dogma is bad; rather that dogma is too good to be true. That is, he means that dogma is too liberal to be likely. Dogma gives man too much freedom when it permits him to fall. Dogma gives even God too much freedom when it permits him to die. That is what the intelligent sceptics ought to say; and it is not in the least my intention to deny that there is something to be said for it. They mean that the universe is itself a universal prison; that existence itself is a limitation and a control; and it is not for nothing that they call causation a chain. In a word, they mean quite simply that they cannot believe these things; not in the least that they are unworthy of belief. We say, not lightly but very literally, that the truth has made us free. They say that it makes us so free that it cannot be the truth. To them it is like believing in fairyland to believe in such freedom as we enjoy. It is like believing in men with wings to entertain the fancy of men with wills. It is like accepting a fable about a squirrel in conversation with a mountain to believe in a man who is free to ask or a God who is free to answer. This is a manly and a rational negation for which I for one shall always show respect. But I decline to show any respect for those who first of all clip the wings and cage the squirrel, rivet the chains and refuse the freedom, close all the doors of the cosmic prison on us with a clang of eternal iron, tell us that our emancipation is a dream and our dungeon a necessity; and then calmly turn round and tell us they have a freer thought and a more liberal theology.

The moral of all this is an old one; that religion is revelation. In other words, it is a vision, and a vision received by faith but it is a vision of reality. The faith consists in a conviction of its reality. That, for example, is the difference between a vision and a day-dream. And that is the difference between religion and mythology. That is the difference between faith and all that fancywork, quite human and more or less healthy, which we considered under the head of mythology. There is something in the reasonable use of the very word vision that implies two things about it; first that it comes very rarely, possibly that it comes only once; and secondly that it probably comes once and for all. A day-dream may come every day. A day-dream may be different every day. It is something more than the difference between telling ghost stories and meeting a ghost.

But if it is not a mythology, neither is it a philosophy. It is not a philosophy because, being a vision, it is not a pattern but a picture. It is not one of those simplifications which resolve everything into an abstract explanation; as that everything is recurrent; or everything is relative; or everything is inevitable; or everything is illusive. It is not a process but a story. It has proportions, of the sort seen in a picture or a story; it has not the regular repetitions of a pattern or a process; but it replaces them by being convincing as a picture or a story is convincing. In other words, it is exactly, as the phrase goes, like life. For indeed it is life. An example of what is meant here might well be found in the treatment of the problem of evil. It is easy enough to make a plan of life of which the background is black, as the pessimists do; and then admit a speck or two of star-dust more or less accidental, or in the literal sense insignificant. And it is easy enough to make another plan on white paper, as the Christian Scientists do, and explain or explain away somehow such dots or smudges as may be difficult to deny. Lastly it is easiest of all, perhaps, to say as the dualists do, that life is like a chessboard in which the two are equal; and can as truly be said to consist of white squares on a black board or of black squares on a white board. But every man feels in his heart that none of these three paper plans is like life; that none of these worlds is one in which he can live. Something tells him that the ultimate idea of a world is not bad or even neutral; staring at the sky or the grass or the truths of mathematics or even a new-laid egg, he has a vague feeling like the shadow of that saying of the great Christian philosopher, St. Thomas Aquinas, 'Every existence, as such, is good.' On the other hand, something else tells him that it is unmanly and debased and even diseased to minimise evil to a dot or even a blot. He realises that optimism is morbid. It is if possible even more morbid than pessimism. These vague but healthy feelings, if he followed them out, would result in the idea that evil is in some way an exception but an enormous exception; and ultimately that evil is an invasion or yet more truly a rebellion. He does not think that everything is right or that everything is wrong, or that everything is equally right and wrong. But he does think that right has a right to be right and therefore a right to be there; and wrong has no right to be wrong and therefore no right to be there. It is the prince of the world; but it is also a usurper. So he will apprehend vaguely what the vision will give to him vividly; no less than all that strange story of treason in heaven and the great desertion by which evil damaged and tried to destroy a cosmos that it could not create. It is a very strange story and its proportions and its lines and colours are as arbitrary and absolute as the artistic composition of a picture. It is a vision which we do in fact symbolise in pictures by titanic limbs and passionate tints of plumage; all that abysmal vision of falling stars and the peacock panoplies of the night. But that strange story has one small, advantage over the diagrams. It is like life.

Another example might be found, not in the problem of evil, but in what is called the problem of progress. One of the ablest agnostics of the age once asked me whether I thought mankind grew better or grew worse or remained the same. He was confident that the alternative covered all possibilities. He did not see that it only covered patterns and not pictures; processes and not stories. I asked him

whether he thought that Mr. Smith of Golfer's Green got
better or worse or remained exactly the same between the
age of thirty and forty. It then seemed to dawn on him that
it would rather depend on Mr. Smith; and how he chose to
go on. It had never occurred to him that it might depend
on how mankind chose to go on; and that its course was
not a straight line or upward or downward curve, but a
track like that of a man across a valley, going where he
liked and stopping where he chose, going into a church or
falling drunk in a ditch. The life of man is a story; an adventure story; and in our vision same is true even of the
story of God.

The Catholic faith is the reconciliation because it is the
realisation both of mythology and philosophy. It is a story
and in that sense one of a hundred stories; only it is a true
story. It is a philosophy and in that sense one of a hundred
philosophies; only it is a philosophy that is like life. But
above all, it is a reconciliation because it is something that
can only be called the philosophy of stories. That normal
narrative which produced all the fairy-tales is something
that is neglected by all the philosophies – except one. The
Faith is the justification of that popular instinct; the finding of a philosophy for it or the analysis of the philosophy
in it. Exactly as a man in an adventure story has to pass
various tests to save his life, so the man in this philosophy
has to pass several tests and save his soul. In both there is
an idea of free will operating under conditions of design; in
other words, there is an aim and it is the business of a man
to aim at it; we therefore watch to see whether he will hit
it. Now this deep and democratic and dramatic instinct is
derided and dismissed in all the other philosophies. For all
the other philosophies avowedly end where they begin;
and it is the definition of a story that it ends differently;
that it begins in one place and ends in another. From Buddha and his wheel to Ashen Ten and his disc, from Pythagoras with his abstraction of number to Confucius with
his religion of routine, there is not one of them that does
not in some way sin against the soul of a story. There is

none of them that really grasps this human notion of the
tale, the test, the adventure; the ordeal of the free man.
Each of them starves the story-telling instinct, so to speak,
and does something to spoil human life considered as a
romance; either by fatalism (pessimist or optimist) and that
destiny that is the death of adventure; or by indifference
and that detachment that is the death of drama; or by a
fundamental scepticism that dissolves the actors into atoms; or by a materialistic limitation blocking the vista of
moral consequences; or a mechanical recurrence making
even moral tests monotonous; or a bottomless relativity
making even practical tests insecure. There is such a thing
as a human story; and there is such a thing as the divine
story which is also a human story; but there is no such
thing as a Hegelian story or a Monist story or a relativist
story or a determinist story; for every story, yes, even a
penny dreadful or a cheap novelette, has something in it
that belongs to our universe and not theirs. Every short
story does truly begin with creation and end with a last
judgment.

And *that* is the reason why the myths and the philosophers were at war until Christ came. That is why the Athenian democracy killed Socrates out of respect for the gods;
and why every strolling sophist gave himself the airs of a
Socrates whenever he could talk in a superior fashion of
the gods; and why the heretic Pharaoh wrecked his huge
idols and temples for an abstraction and why the priests
could return in triumph and trample his dynasty under
foot; and why Buddhism had to divide itself from Brahmanism, and why in every age and country outside Christendom there has been a feud forever between the philosopher and the priest. It is easy enough to say that the
philosopher is generally the more rational; it is easier still
to forget that the priest is always the more popular. For the
priest told the people stories; and the philosopher did not
understand the philosophy of stories. It came into the
world with the story of Christ.

And this is why it had to be a revelation or vision given

from above. Anyone who will think of the theory of stories or pictures will easily see the point. The true story of
the world must be told by somebody to somebody else. By
the very nature of a story it cannot be left to occur to anybody. A story has proportions, variations, surprises, particular dispositions, which cannot be worked out by rule in
the abstract like a sum. We could not deduce whether or
no Achilles would give back the body of Hector from a
Pythagorean theory of number or recurrence; and we
could not infer for elves in what way the world would get
back the body of Christ merely from being told that all
things go round and round upon the wheel of Buddha. A
man might perhaps work a proposition of Euclid without
having heard of Euclid; he would not work out the precise
legend of Eurydice out having heard of Eurydice. At any
rate he would not entertain how the story would end and
whether Orpheus was rising, not defeated. Still less could
he guess the end of our story or the legend of our Orpheus
rising, not defeated, from the dead.

To sum up: the sanity of the world was restored and
the soul of man offered salvation by something which did
indeed satisfy the two warring tendencies of the past;
which had never been satisfied in full and most certainly
never satisfied together. It met the mythological search for
romance by being a story and the philosophical search for
truth by being a true story. That is why the ideal figure had
to be a historical character as nobody had ever felt Adonis
or Pan to be a historical character. But that is also why the
historical character had to be the ideal figure; and even
fulfil many of the functions given to these other ideal figures; why he was at once the sacrifice and the feast, why he
could be shown under the emblems of the growing vine or
the rising sun. The more deeply we think of the matter the
more we shall conclude that, if there be indeed a God, his
creation could hardly have reached any other culmination
than this granting of a real romance to the world. Otherwise the two sides of the human mind could never have
touched at all; and the brain of man would have remained

cloven and double; one lobe of it dreaming impossible dreams and the other repeating invariable calculations. The picture-makers would have remained forever painting the portrait of nobody. The sages would have remained forever adding up numerals that came to nothing. It was that abyss that nothing but an incarnation could cover; a divine embodiment of our dreams; and he stands above that chasm whose name is more than priest and older even than Christendom; Pontifex: Maximus, the mightiest maker of a bridge.

But even with that we return to the more specially Christian symbol in the same tradition; the perfect pattern of the keys. This is a historical and not a theological outline, and it is not my duty here to defend in detail that theology, but merely to point out that it could not even be justified in design without being justified in detail – like a key. Beyond the broad suggestion of this chapter I attempt no apologetic about why the creed should be accepted. But in answer to the historical query of why it was accepted, and is accepted, I answer for millions of others in my reply: because it fits the lock; because it is like life. It is one among many stories; only it happens to be a true story. It is one among many philosophies; only it happens to be the truth. We accept it; and the ground is solid under our feet and the road is open before us. It does not imprison us in a dream of destiny or a consciousness of the universal delusion. It opens to us not only incredible heavens, but what seems to some an equally incredible earth, and makes it credible. This is the sort of truth that is hard to explain because it is a fact; but it is a fact to which we can call witnesses. We are Christians and Catholics not because we worship a key, but because we have passed a door; and felt the wind that is the trumpet of liberty blow over the land of the living.

6
THE FIVE DEATHS OF THE FAITH

IT IS NOT the purpose of this book to trace the subsequent history of Christianity, especially the later history of Christianity; which involves controversies of which I hope to write more fully elsewhere. It is devoted only to the suggestion that Christianity, appearing amid heathen humanity, had all the character of a unique thing and even of a supernatural thing. It was not like any of the other things; and the more we study it the less it looks like any of them. But there is a certain rather peculiar character which marked it henceforward even down to the present moment, with a note on which this book may well conclude.

I have said that Asia and the ancient world had an air of being too old to die. Christendom has had the very opposite fate. Christendom has had a series of revolutions and in each one of them Christianity has died. Christianity has died many times and risen again; for it had a God who knew the way out of the grave. But the first extraordinary fact which marks this history is this: that Europe has been turned upside down over and over again; and that at the end of each of these revolutions the same religion has again been found on top. The Faith is always converting the age, not as an old religion but as a new religion. This truth is hidden from many by a convention that is too little noticed. Curiously enough, it is a convention of the sort which those who ignore it claim especially to detect and denounce. They are always telling us that priests and ceremonies are not religion and that religious organisation can be a hollow sham; but they hardly realise how true it is. It is so true that three or four times at least in the history of Christendom the whole soul seemed to have gone out of

Christianity; and almost every man in his heart expected its end. This fact is only masked in medieval and other times by that very official religion which such critics pride themselves on seeing through. Christianity remained the official religion of a Renaissance prince or the official religion of an eighteenth century bishop, just as an ancient mythology remained the official religion of Julius Caesar or the Arian creed long remained the official religion of Julian the Apostate. But there was a difference between the cases of Julius and of Julian; because the Church had begun its strange career. There was no reason why men like Julius should not worship gods like Jupiter forever in public and laugh at them forever in private. But when Julian treated Christianity as dead, he found it had come to life again. He also found, incidentally, that there was not the faintest sign of Jupiter ever coming to life again. This case of Julian and the episode of Arianism is but the first of a series of examples that can only be roughly indicated here. Arianism, as has been said, had every human appearance of being the natural way in which that particular superstition of Constantine might be expected to peter out. All the ordinary stages had been passed through; the creed had become a respectable thing, had become a ritual thing, had then been modified into a rational thing; and the rationalists were ready to dissipate the last remains of it, just as they do today. When Christianity rose again suddenly and threw them, it was almost as unexpected as Christ rising from the dead. But there are many other examples of the same thing, even about the same time. The rush of missionaries from Ireland, for instance, has all the air of an unexpected onslaught of young men on an old world, and even on a Church that showed signs of growing old. Some of them were martyred on the coast of Cornwall; and the chief authority on Cornish antiquities told me that he did not believe for a moment that they were martyred by heathens but (as he expressed it with some humour) 'by rather slack Christians.'

Now if we were to dip below the surface of history, as

it is not in the scope of this argument to do, I suspect that we should find several occasions when Christendom was thus to all appearance hollowed out from within by doubt and indifference, so that only the old Christian shell stood as the pagan shell had stood so long. But the difference is that in every such case, the sons were fanatical for the faith where the fathers had been slack about it. This is obvious in the case of the transition from the Renaissance to the Counter Reformation. It is obvious in the case of a transition from the eighteenth century to the many Catholic revivals of our own time. But I suspect many other examples which would be worthy of separate studies.

The Faith is not a survival. It is not as if the Druids had managed somehow to survive somewhere for two thousand years. That is what might have happened in Asia or ancient Europe, in that indifference or tolerance in which mythologies and philosophies could live forever side by side. It has not survived; it has returned again and again in this western world of rapid change and institutions perpetually perishing. Europe, in the tradition of Rome, was always trying revolution and reconstruction; rebuilding a universal republic. And it always began by rejecting this old stone and ended by making it the head of the corner; by bringing it back from the rubbish-heap to make it the crown of the capitol. Some stones of Stonehenge are standing and some are fallen; and as the stone falleth so shall it lie. There has not been a Druidic renaissance every century or two, with the young Druids crowned with fresh mistletoe, dancing in the sun on Salisbury Plain. Stonehenge has not been rebuilt in every style of architecture from the rude round Norman to the last rococo of the Baroque. The sacred place of the Druids is safe from the vandalism of restoration.

But the Church in the West was not in a world where things were too old to die; but in one in which they were always young enough to get killed. The consequence was that superficially and externally it often did get killed; nay, it sometimes wore out even without getting killed. And there follows a fact I find it somewhat difficult to describe, yet which I believe to be very real and rather important. As a ghost is the shadow of a man, and in that sense the shadow of life, so at intervals there passed across this endless life a sort of shadow of death. It came at the moment when it would have perished had it been perishable. It withered away everything that was perishable. If such animal parallels were worthy of the occasion, we might say that the snake shuddered and shed a skin and went on, or even that the cat went into convulsions as it lost only one of its nine-hundred-and-ninety-nine lives. It is truer to say, in a more dignified image, that a clock struck and nothing happened; or that a bell tolled for an execution that was everlastingly postponed.

What was the meaning of all that dim but vast unrest of the twelfth century; when, as it has been so finely said, Julian stirred in his sleep? Why did there appear so strangely early, in the twilight of dawn after the Dark Ages, so deep a scepticism as that involved in urging nominalism against realism? For realism against nominalism was really realism against rationalism, or something more destructive than what we call rationalism. The answer is that just as some might have thought the Church simply a part of the Roman Empire, so others later might have thought the Church only a part of the Dark Ages. The Dark Ages ended as the Empire had ended; and the Church should have departed with them, if she had been also one of the shades of night. It was another of those spectral deaths or simulations of death. I mean that if nominalism had succeeded, it would have been as if Arianism had succeeded, it would have been the beginning of a confession that Christianity had failed. For nominalism is a far more fundamental scepticism than mere atheism. Such was the question that was openly asked as the Dark Ages broadened into that daylight that we call the modern world. But what was the answer? The answer was Aquinas in the chair of Aristotle, taking all knowledge for his province; and tens of thousands of lads down to the lowest ranks of peasant and serf, living in rags and on crusts about the great colleges, to listen to the scholastic philosophy.

What was the meaning of all that whisper of fear that ran round the west under the shadow of Islam, and fills every old romance with incongruous images of Saracen knights swaggering in Norway or the Hebrides? Why were men in the extreme west, such as King John if I remember rightly, accused of being secretly Moslems, as men are accused of being secretly atheists? Why was there that fierce alarm among some of the authorities about the rationalistic Arab version of Aristotle? Authorities are seldom alarmed like that except when it is too late. The answer is that hundreds of people probably believed in their hearts that Islam would conquer Christendom; that Averroes was more rational than Anselm; that the Saracen culture was really, as it was superficially, a superior culture. Here again we should probably find a whole generation, the older generation, very doubtful and depressed and weary. The coming of Islam would only have been the coming of Unitarianism a thousand years before its time. To many it may have seemed quite reasonable and quite probable and quite likely to happen. If so, they would have been surprised at what did happen. What did happen was a roar like thunder from thousands and thousands of young men, throwing all their youth into one exultant counter-charge; the Crusades. It was the sons of St. Francis, the Jugglers of God, wandering singing over all the roads of the world; it was the Gothic going up like a flight of arrows; it was the waking of the world. In considering the war of the Albigensians, we come to the breach in the heart of Europe and the landslide of a new philosophy that nearly ended Christendom forever. In that case the new philosophy was also a very new philosophy; it was pessimism. It was none the less like modern ideas because it was as old as Asia; most modern ideas are. It was the Gnostics returning; but why did the Gnostics return? Because it was the end of an epoch, like the end of the Empire; and should have been the end of the Church. It was Schopenhauer hovering over the future; but it was also Manichaeus rising from the dead; that men might have death and that they might have it more abundantly.

It is rather more obvious in the case of the Renaissance, simply because the period is so much nearer to us and people know so much more about it. But there is more even in that example than most people know. Apart from the particular controversies which I wish to reserve for a separate study, the period was far more chaotic than those controversies commonly imply. When Protestants call Latimer a martyr to Protestantism, and Catholics reply that Campion was a martyr to Catholicism, it is often forgotten that many who perished in such persecutions could only be described as martyrs to atheism or anarchism or even diabolism. That world was almost as wild as our own; the men wandering about in it included the sort of man who says there is no God, the sort of man who says he is himself God, the sort of man who says something that nobody can make head or tail of. If we could have the *conversation* of the age following the Renaissance, we should probably be shocked by its shameless negations. The remarks attributed to Marlowe are probably pretty typical of the talk in many intellectual taverns. The transition from Pre-Reformation to Post-Reformation Europe was through a void of very yawning questions; yet again in the long run the answer was the same. It was one of those moments when, as Christ walked on the water, so was Christianity walking in the air.

But all these cases are remote in date and could only be proved in detail. We can see the fact much more clearly in the case when the paganism of the Renaissance ended Christianity and Christianity unaccountably began all over again. But we can see it most clearly of all in the case which is close to us and full of manifest and minute evidence; the case of the great decline of religion that began about the time of Voltaire. For indeed it is our own case; and we ourselves have seen the decline of that decline. The two hundred years since Voltaire do not flash past us at a glance like the fourth and fifth centuries or the twelfth and thirteenth centuries. In our own case we can see this oft-repeated process close at hand; we know how completely a society can lose its fundamental religion without abolishing its official religion; we know how men can all become agnostics long before they abolish bishops. And we know that also in this last ending, which really did look to us like the final ending, the incredible thing has happened again; the Faith has a better following among the young men than among the old. When Ibsen spoke of the new generation knocking at the door, he certainly never expected that it would be the church-door.

At least five times, therefore, with the Arian and the Albigensian, with the Humanist sceptic, after Voltaire and after Darwin, the Faith has to all appearance gone to the dogs. In each of these five cases it was the dog that died. How complete was the collapse and how strange the reversal, we can only see in detail in the case nearest to our own time.

A thousand things have been said about the Oxford Movement and the parallel French Catholic revival; but few have made us feel the simplest fact about it; that it was a surprise. It was a puzzle as well as a surprise; because it seemed to most people like a river turning backwards from the sea and trying to climb back into the mountains. To have read the literature of the eighteenth and nineteenth centuries is to know that nearly everybody had come to take it for granted that religion was a thing that would continually broaden like a river, till it reached an infinite sea. Some of them expected it to go down in a cataract of catastrophe, most of them expected it to widen into an estuary of equality and moderation; but all of them thought its returning on itself a prodigy as incredible as witchcraft. In other words, most moderate people thought that faith like freedom would be slowly broadened down; and some advanced people thought that it would be very rapidly broadened down, not to say flattened out. All that world of Guizot and Macaulay and the commercial and scientific liberality was perhaps more certain than any men before or since about the direction in which the world is going. People were so certain about the direction that they only differed about the pace. Many anticipated with alarm, and a few with sympathy, a Jacobin revolt that should guillotine the Archbishop of Canterbury or a Chartist riot that should hang the parsons on the lampposts. But it seemed like a convulsion in nature that the Archbishop instead of losing his head should be looking for his mitre; and that instead of diminishing the respect due to parsons we should strengthen it to the respect due to priests. It revolutionised their very vision of revolution; and turned their very topsy-turvydom topsy-turvy.

In short, the whole world being divided about whether the stream was going slower or faster, became conscious of something vague but vast that was going against the stream. Both in fact and figure there is something deeply disturbing about this, and that for an essential reason. A dead thing can go with the stream, but only a living thing can go against it. A dead dog can be lifted on the leaping water with all the swiftness of a leaping hound; but only a live dog can swim backwards. A paper boat can ride the rising deluge with all the airy arrogance of a fairy ship; but if the fairy ship sails upstream it is really rowed by the fairies. And among the things that merely went with the tide of apparent progress and enlargement, there was many a demagogue or sophist whose wild gestures were in truth as lifeless as the movement of a dead dog's limbs wavering in the eddying water; and many a philosophy uncommonly like a paper boat, of the sort that it is not difficult to knock into a cocked hat. But even the truly living and even life-giving things that went with that stream did not thereby prove that they were living or life-giving. It was this other force that was unquestionably and unaccountably alive; the mysterious and unmeasured energy that was thrusting back the river. That was felt to be like the movement of some great monster; and it was none the less clearly a living monster because most people thought it a prehistoric

monster. It was none the less an unnatural, an incongruous, and to some a comic upheaval; as if the Great Sea
Serpent had suddenly risen out of the Round Pond –
unless we consider the Sea Serpent as more likely to live in
the Serpentine. This flippant element in the fantasy must
not be missed, for it was one of the clearest testimonies to
the unexpected nature of the reversal. That age did really
feel that a preposterous quality in prehistoric animals belonged also to historic rituals; that mitres and tiaras were
like the horns or crests of antediluvian creatures; and that
appealing to a Primitive Church was like dressing up as a
Primitive Man.

The world is still puzzled by that movement; but most
of all because it still moves. I have said something elsewhere of the rather random sort of reproaches that are still
directed against it and its much greater consequences; it is
enough to say here that the more such critics reproach it
the less they explain it. In a sense it is my concern here, if
not to explain it, at least to suggest the direction of the
explanation; but above all, it is my concern to point out
one particular thing about it. And that is that it had all
happened before; and even many times before.

To sum up, in so far as it is true that recent centuries
have seen an attenuation of Christian doctrine, recent centuries have only seen what the most remote centuries have
seen. And even the modern example has only ended as the
medieval and pre-medieval examples ended. It is already
clear, and grows clearer every day, that it is not going to
end in the disappearance of the diminished creed; but
rather in the return of those parts of it that had really disappeared. It is going to end as the Arian compromise
ended, as the attempts at a compromise with Nominalism
and even with Albigensianism ended. But the point to
seize in the modern case, as in all the other cases, is that
what returns is not in that sense a simplified theology; not
according to that view a purified theology; it is simply theology. It is that enthusiasm for theological studies that
marked the most doctrinal ages; it is the divine science. An

old Don with D.D. after his name may have become the
typical figure of a bore; but that was because he was himself bored with his theology, not because he was excited
about it. It was precisely because he was admittedly more
interested in the Latin of Plautus than in the Latin of
Augustine, in the Greek of Xenophon than in the Greek
of Chrysostom. It was precisely because he was more interested in a dead tradition than in a decidedly living tradition. In short, it was precisely because he was himself a
type of the time in which Christian faith was weak. It was
not because men would not hail, if they could, the wonderful and almost wild vision of a Doctor of Divinity.

There are people who say they wish Christianity to remain as a spirit. They mean, very literally, that they wish it
to remain as a ghost. But it is not going to remain as a
ghost. What follows this process of apparent death is not
the lingering of the shade; it is the resurrection of the
body. These people are quite prepared to shed pious and
reverential tears over the Sepulchre of the Son of Man;
what they are not prepared for is the Son of God walking
once more upon the hills of morning. These people, and
indeed most people, were indeed by this time quite accustomed to the idea that the old Christian candle-light would
fade into the light of common day. To many of them it did
quite honestly appear like that pale yellow flame of a candle when it is left burning in daylight. It was all the more
unexpected, and therefore all the more unmistakable, that
the seven-branched candle-stick suddenly towered to
heaven like a miraculous tree and flamed until the sun
turned pale. But other ages have seen the day conquer the
candle-light and then the candle-light conquer the day.
Again and again, before our time, men have grown content
with a diluted doctrine. And again and again there has followed on that dilution, coming as out of the darkness in a
crimson cataract, the strength of the red original wine. And
we only say once more today as has been said many times
by our fathers: 'Long years and centuries ago our fathers or
the founders of our people drank, as they dreamed, of the

blood of God. Long years and centuries have passed since the strength of that giant vintage has been anything but a legend of the age of giants. Centuries ago already is the dark time of the second fermentation, when the wine of Catholicism turned into the vinegar of Calvinism. Long since that bitter drink has been itself diluted; rinsed out and washed away by the waters of oblivion and the wave of the world. Never did we think to taste again even that bitter tang of sincerity and the spirit, still less the richer and the sweeter strength of the purple vineyards in our dreams of the age of gold. Day by day and year by year we have lowered our hopes and lessened our convictions; we have grown more and more used to seeing those vats and vineyards overwhelmed in the flood-waters and the last savour and suggestion of that special element fading like a stain of purple upon a sea of grey. We have grown used to dilution, to dissolution, to a watering down and went on forever. But Thou hast kept the good wine until now.'

This is the final fact, and it is the most extraordinary of all. The faith has not only often died but it has often died of old age. It has not only been often killed but it has often died a natural death; in the sense of coming to a natural and necessary end. It is obvious that it has survived the most savage and the most universal persecutions from the shock of the Diocletian fury to the shock of the French Revolution. But it has a more strange and even a more weird tenacity; it has survived not only war but peace. It has not only died often but degenerated often and decayed often; it has survived its own weakness and even its own surrender. We need not repeat what is so obvious about the beauty of the end of Christ in its wedding of youth and death. But this is almost as if Christ had lived to the last possible span, had been a white-haired sage of a hundred and died of natural decay, and then had risen again rejuvenated, with trumpets and the rending of the sky. It was said truly enough that human Christianity in its recurrent weakness was sometimes too much wedded to the powers of the world; but if it was wedded it has very often been widowed. It is a strangely immortal sort of widow. An enemy may have said at one moment that it was but an aspect of the power of the Caesars; and it sounds as strange today as to call it an aspect of the Pharaohs. An enemy might say that it was the official faith of feudalism; and it sounds as convincing now as to say that it was bound to perish with the ancient Roman villa. All these things did indeed run their course to its normal end; and there seemed no course for the religion but to end with them. It ended and it began again.

'Heaven and earth shall pass away, but my words shall not pass away.' The civilisation of antiquity was the whole world: and men no more dreamed of its ending than of the ending of daylight. They could not imagine another order unless it were in another world. The civilisation of the world has passed away and those words have not passed away. In the long night of the Dark Ages feudalism was so familiar a thing that no man could imagine himself without a lord: and religion was so woven into that network that no man would have believed they could be torn asunder. Feudalism itself was torn to rags and rotted away in the popular life of the true Middle Ages; and the first and freshest power in that new freedom was the old religion. Feudalism had passed away, and the words did not pass away. The whole medieval order, in many ways so complete and almost cosmic a home for man, wore out gradually in its turn: and here at least it was thought that the words would die. They went forth across the radiant abyss of the Renaissance and in fifty years were using all its light and learning for new religious foundations, new apologetics, new saints. It was supposed to have been withered up at last in the dry light of the Age of Reason; it was supposed to have disappeared ultimately in the earthquake of the Age of Revolution. Science explained it away; and it was still there. History disinterred it in the past; and it appeared suddenly in the future. Today it stands once more in our path; and even as we watch it, it grows.

If our social relations and records retain their continuity, if men really learn to apply reason to the accumulating facts of so crushing a story, it would seem that sooner or later even its enemies will learn from their incessant and interminable disappointments not to look for anything so simple as its death. They may continue to war with it, but it will be as they war with nature; as they war with the land-scape, as they war with the skies. 'Heaven and earth shall pass away, but my words shall not pass away.' They will watch for it to stumble; they will watch for it to err; they will no longer watch for it to end. Insensibly, even uncon-sciously, they will in their own silent anticipations fulfil the relative terms of that astounding prophecy; they will forget to watch for the mere extinction of what has so often been vainly extinguished; and will learn instinctively to look first for the coming of the comet or the freezing of the star.

CONCLUSION:
THE SUMMARY OF THIS BOOK

I HAVE TAKEN THE liberty once or twice of borrowing the excellent phrase about an Outline of History; though this study of a special truth and a special error can of course claim no sort of comparison with the rich and many-sided encyclopaedia of history, for which that name was chosen. And yet there is a certain reason in the reference; and a sense in which the one thing touches and even cuts across the other. For the story of the world as told by Mr. Wells could here only be criticised as an outline. And, strangely enough, it seems to me that it is only wrong as an outline. It is admirable as an accumulation of history; it is splendid as a storehouse or treasury of history, it is a fascinating disquisition on history, it is most attractive as an amplification of history; but it is quite false as an Outline of history. The one thing that seems to me quite wrong about it is the outline; the sort of outline that can really be a single line, like that which makes all the difference between a caricature of the profile of Mr. Winston Churchill and of Sir Alfred Mond. In simple and homely language, I mean the things that stick out; the things that make the simplicity of a silhouette. I think the proportions are wrong; the proportions of what is certain as compared with what is uncertain, of what played a great part as compared with what played a smaller part, of what is ordinary and what is extraordinary, of what really lies level with an average and what stands out as an exception.

I do not say it as a small criticism of a great writer, and I have no reason to do so; for in my own much smaller task I feel I have failed in very much the same way. I am very doubtful whether I have conveyed to the reader the main point I meant about the proportions of history, and why I have dwelt so much more on some things than others. I doubt whether I have clearly fulfilled the plan that I set out in the introductory chapter; and for that reason I add these lines as a sort of summary in a concluding chapter. I do believe that the things on which I have insisted are more essential to an outline of history than the things which I have subordinated or dismissed. I do not believe that the past is most truly pictured as a thing in which humanity merely fades away into nature, or civilisation merely fades away into barbarism, or religion fades away into mythology, or our own religion fades away into the religions of the world. In short I do not believe that the best way to produce an outline of history is to rub out the lines. I believe that, of the two, it would be far nearer the truth to tell the tale very simply, like a primitive myth about a man who made the sun and stars or a god who entered the body of a sacred monkey. I will therefore sum up all that has gone before in what seems to me a realistic and reasonably proportioned statement; the short story of mankind.

In the land lit by that neighbouring star, whose blaze is the broad daylight, there are many and very various things, motionless and moving. There moves among them a race that is in its relation to others a race of gods. The fact is not lessened but emphasised because it can behave like a race of demons. Its distinction is not an individual illusion, like one bird pluming itself on its own plumes; it is a solid and a many-sided thing. It is demonstrated in the very speculations that have led to its being denied. That men, the gods of this lower world, are linked with it in various ways is true; but it is another aspect of the same truth. That they grow as the grass grows and walk as the beasts walk is a secondary necessity that sharpens the primary distinction. It is like saying that a magician must after all have the appearance of a man; or that even the fairies could not dance without feet. It has lately been the fashion to focus the mind entirely on these mild and subordinate resemblances and to forget the main fact altogether. It is customary to insist that man resembles the other creatures. Yes; and that very resemblance he alone can see. The fish does not trace the fishbone pattern in the fowls of the air, or the elephant and the emu compare skeletons. Even in the sense in which man is at one with the universe it is an utterly lonely universality. The very sense that he is united with all things is enough to sunder him from all.

Looking around him by this unique light, as lonely as the literal flame that he alone has kindled, this demigod or demon of the visible world makes that world visible. He sees around him a world of a certain style or type. It seems to proceed by certain rules or at least repetitions. He sees a green architecture that builds itself without visible hands; but which builds itself into a very exact plan or pattern, like a design already drawn in the air by an invisible finger. It is not, as is now vaguely suggested, a vague thing. It is not a growth or a groping of blind life. Each seeks an end; a glorious and radiant end, even for every daisy or dandelion we see in looking across the level of a common field. In the very shape of things there is more than green growth; there is the finality of the flower. It is a world of crowns. This impression, whether or no it be an illusion, has so profoundly influenced this race of thinkers and masters of the material world, that the vast majority have been moved to take a certain view of that world. They have concluded, rightly or wrongly, that the world had a plan as the tree seemed to have a plan; and an end and crown like the flower. But so long as the race of thinkers was able to think, it was obvious that the admission of this idea of a plan brought with it another thought more thrilling and even terrible. There was someone else, some strange and unseen being, who had designed these things, if indeed they were designed. There was a stranger who was also a friend; a mysterious benefactor who had been before them and built up the woods and hills for their coming, and had kindled the sunrise against their rising, as a servant kindles a fire. Now this idea of a mind that gives a meaning to the universe has received more and more confirmation within the minds of men, by meditations and experiences much more subtle and searching than any such argument about the external plan of the world. But I am concerned here with keeping the story in its most simple and even concrete terms; and it is enough to say here that most men, including the wisest men, have come to the conclusion that the world has such a final purpose and therefore such a first cause. But most men in some sense separated themselves from the wisest men, when it came to the treatment of that idea. There came into existence two ways of treating that idea; which between them make up most of the religious history of the world.

The majority, like the minority, had this strong sense of a second meaning in things; of a strange master who knew the secret of the world. But the majority, the mob or mass of men, naturally tended to treat it rather in the spirit of gossip. The gossip, like all gossip, contained a great deal of truth and falsehood. The world began to tell itself tales about the unknown being or his sons or servants or messengers. Some of the tales may truly be called old wives' tales; as professing only to be very remote memories of the morning of the world; myths about the baby moon or the half-baked mountains. Some of them might more truly be called travellers' tales; as being curious but contemporary, tales brought from certain borderlands of experience; such as miraculous cures or those that bring whispers of what has happened to the dead. Many of them are probably true tales; enough of them are probably true to keep a person of real common sense more or less conscious that there really is something rather marvellous behind the cosmic curtain. But in a sense it is only going by appearances; even if the appearances are called apparitions. It is a matter of appearances – and disappearances. At the most these gods are ghosts; that is, they are glimpses. For most of us they are rather gossip about glimpses. And for the rest, the whole world is full of rumours most of which are almost avowedly romances. The great majority of the tales about gods and ghosts and the invisible king are told, if not for the sake of the tale, at least for the sake of the topic. They are evidence of the eternal interest of the theme; they are not evidence of anything else, and they are not meant to be. They are mythology or the poetry that is not bound in books – or bound in any other way.

Meanwhile the minority, the sages or thinkers, had withdrawn apart and had taken up an equally congenial trade. They were drawing up plans of the world; of the world which all believed to have a plan. They were trying to set forth the plan seriously and to scale. They were setting their minds directly to the mind that had made the mysterious world; considering what sort of a mind it might be and what its ultimate purpose might be. Some of them made that mind much more impersonal than mankind has generally made it; some simplified it almost to a blank; a few, a very few, doubted it altogether. One or two of the more morbid fancied that it might be evil and an enemy; just one or two of the more degraded in the other class worshipped demons instead of gods. But most of these theorists were theists: and they not only saw a moral plan in nature, but they generally laid down a moral plan for humanity. Most of them were good men who did good work: and they were remembered and reverenced in various ways. They were scribes; and their scriptures became more or less holy scriptures. They were law-givers; and their tradition became not only legal but ceremonial. We may say that they received divine honours, in the sense in which kings and great captains in certain countries often received divine honours. In a word, wherever the other popular spirit, the spirit of legend and gossip, could come into play, it surrounded them with the more mystical atmosphere of the myths. Popular poetry turned the sages into saints. But that was all it did. They remained themselves; men never really forgot that they were men, only made into gods in the sense that they were made into heroes. Divine Plato, like Divus Caesar, was a title and not a dogma. In Asia, where the atmosphere was more mythological, the man was made to look more like a myth, but be remained a man. He remained a man of a certain special class or school of men, receiving and deserving great honour from mankind. It is the order or school of the philosophers; the men who have set themselves seriously to trace the order across any apparent chaos in the vision of life. Instead of living on imaginative rumours and remote traditions and the tail-end of exceptional experiences about the mind and meaning behind the world, they have tried in a sense to project the primary purpose of that mind *a priori*. They have tried to put on paper a possible plan of the world; almost as if the world were not yet made.

Right in the middle of all these things stands up an enormous exception. It is quite unlike anything else. It is a thing final like the trump of doom, though it is also a piece of good news; or news that seems too good to be true. It is nothing less than the loud assertion that this mysterious maker of the world has visited his world in person. It declares that really and even recently, or right in the middle of historic times, there did walk into the world this original invisible being; about whom the thinkers make theories and the mythologists hand down myths; the Man Who Made the World. That such a higher personality exists behind all things had indeed always been implied by all the best thinkers, as well as by all the most beautiful legends. But nothing of this sort had ever been implied in any of them. It is simply false to say that the other sages and heroes had claimed to be that mysterious master and maker, of whom the world had dreamed and disputed. Not one of them had ever claimed to be anything of the sort. Not one of their sects or schools had ever claimed that they had claimed to be anything of the sort. The most that any religious prophet had said was that he was the true servant of such a being. The most that any visionary had ever said was that men might catch glimpses of the glory of that spiritual being; or much more often of lesser spiritual beings. The most that any primitive myth had ever suggested was that the Creator was present at the Creation. But that the Creator was present at scenes a little subsequent to the supper-parties of Horace, and talked with tax-collectors and government officials in the detailed daily life of the Roman Empire, and that this fact continued to be firmly asserted by the whole of that great civilisation for more than a thousand years – that is something utterly unlike anything else in nature. It is the one great startling statement that man has made since he spoke his first articulate word, instead of barking like a dog. Its unique character can be used as an argument against it as well as for it. It would be easy to concentrate on it as a case of isolated insanity; but it makes nothing but dust and nonsense of comparative religion.

It came on the world with a wind and rush of running messengers proclaiming that apocalyptic portent; and it is not unduly fanciful to say that they are running still. What puzzles the world, and its wise philosophers and fanciful pagan poets, about the priests and people of the Catholic Church is that they still behave as if they were messengers. A messenger does not dream about what his message might be, or argue about what it probably would be; he delivers it as it is. It is not a theory or a fancy but a fact. It is not relevant to this intentionally rudimentary outline to prove in detail that it is a fact; but merely to point out that these messengers do deal with it as men deal with a fact. All that is condemned in Catholic tradition, authority, and dogmatism and the refusal to retract and modify, are but the natural human attributes of a man with a message relating to a fact. I desire to avoid in this last summary all the controversial complexities that may once more cloud the simple lines of that strange story, which I have already called, in words that are much too weak, the strangest story in the world. I desire merely to mark those main lines and specially to mark where the great line is really to be drawn. The religion of the world, in its right proportions, is not divided into fine shades of mysticism or more or less rational forms of mythology. It is divided by the line between the men who are bringing that message and the men who have not yet heard it, or cannot yet believe it.

But when we translate the terms of that strange tale back into the more concrete and complicated terminology of our time, we find it covered by names and memories of which the very familiarity is a falsification. For instance, when we say that a country contains so many Moslems, we really mean that it contains so many monotheists; and we really mean, by that, that it contains so many men; men with the old average assumption of men – that the invisible ruler remains invisible. They hold it along with the customs of a certain culture and under the simpler laws of a certain law-giver, but so they would if their law-giver were Lycurgus or Solon. They testify to something which is a necessary and noble truth; but was never a new truth. Their creed is not a new colour, it is the neutral and normal tint that is the background of the many-coloured life of man. Mahomet did not, like the Magi, find a new star; he saw through his own particular window a glimpse of the great grey field of the ancient star light. So when we say that the country contains so many Confucians or Buddhists, we mean it contains so many pagans whose prophets have given them another and rather vaguer version of the invisible power; making it not only invisible but almost impersonal. When we say that they also have temples and idols and priests and periodical festivals, we simply mean that this sort of heathen is enough of a human being to admit the popular element of pomp and pictures and feasts and fairytales. We only mean that Pagans have more sense than Puritans. But what the gods are supposed to be, what the priests are commissioned to *say*, is not a sensational secret like what those running messengers of the Gospel had to say. Nobody else except those messengers has any Gospel; nobody else has any good news; for the simple reason that nobody else has any news.

Those runners gather impetus as they run. Ages afterwards they still speak as if something had just happened. They have not lost the speed and momentum of messengers; they have hardly lost, as it were, the wild eyes of witnesses. In the Catholic Church, which is the cohort of the message, there are still those headlong acts of holiness that speak of something rapid and recent; a self-sacrifice that startles the world like a suicide. But it is not a suicide; it is not pessimistic; it is still as optimistic as St. Francis of the flowers and birds. It is newer in spirit than the newest schools of thought; and it is almost certainly on the eve of new triumphs. For these men serve a mother who seems to grow more beautiful as new generations rise up and call her blessed. We might sometimes fancy that the Church grows younger as the world grows old.

For this is the last proof of the miracle; that something so supernatural should have become so natural. I mean that anything so unique when seen from the outside should only seem universal when seen from the inside. I have not minimised the scale of the miracle, as some of our milder theologians think it wise to do. Rather have I deliberately dwelt on that incredible interruption, as a blow that broke the very backbone of history. I have great sympathy with the monotheists, the Moslems, or the Jews, to whom it seems a blasphemy; a blasphemy that might shake the world. But it did not shake the world; it steadied the world. That fact, the more we consider it, will seem more solid and more strange. I think it a piece of plain justice to all the unbelievers to insist upon the audacity of the act of faith that is demanded of them. I willingly and warmly agree that it is, in itself, a suggestion at which we might expect even the brain of the believer to reel, when he realised his own belief. But the brain of the believer does not reel; it is the brains of the unbelievers that reel. We can see their brains reeling on every side and into every extravagance of ethics and psychology; into pessimism and the denial of life; into pragmatism and the denial of logic; seeking their omens in nightmares and their canons in contradictions; shrieking for fear at the far-off sight of things beyond good and evil, or whispering of strange stars where two and two make five. Meanwhile this solitary thing that seems at first so outrageous in outline remains solid and sane in substance. It remains the moderator of all these

manias; rescuing reason from the Pragmatists exactly as it
rescued laughter from the Puritans. I repeat that I have
deliberately emphasised its intrinsically defiant and dogmatic character. The mystery is how anything so startling
should have remained defiant and dogmatic and yet become perfectly normal and natural. I have admitted freely
that, considering the incident in itself, a man who says he
is God may be classed with a man who says he is glass. But
the man who says he is glass is not a glazier making windows for all the world. He does not remain for after ages
as a shining and crystalline figure, in whose light everything
is as clear as crystal.

But this madness has remained sane. The madness has
remained sane when everything else went mad. The madhouse has been a house to which, age after age, men are
continually coming back as to a home. That is the riddle
that remains; that anything so abrupt and abnormal should
still be found a habitable and hospitable thing. I care not if
the sceptic says it is a tall story; I cannot see how so top-
pling a tower could stand so long without foundation. Still
less can I see how it could become, as it has become, the
home of man. Had it merely appeared and disappeared, it
might possibly have been remembered or explained as the
last leap of the rage of illusion the ultimate myth of the
ultimate mood, in which the mind struck the sky and
broke. But the mind did not break. It is the one mind that
remains unbroken in the break-up of the world. If it were
an error, it seems as if the error could hardly have lasted a
day. If it were a mere ecstasy, it would seem that such an
ecstasy could not endure for an hour. It has endured for
nearly two thousand years; and the world within it has
been more lucid, more level-headed, more reasonable in its
hopes, more healthy in it instincts, more humorous and
cheerful in the face of fate and death, than all the world
outside. For it was the soul of Christendom that came
forth from the incredible Christ, and the soul of it was
common sense. Though we dared not look on His face, we
could look on His fruits; and by His fruits we should know

Him. The fruits are solid; the fruitfulness is much more than a metaphor, and nowhere in this sad world are boys happier in apple trees or men in more equal chorus singing as they tread the vine, than under the fixed flash of this instant and intolerant enlightenment, the lightning made eternal as the light.

APPENDIX I:
ON PREHISTORIC MAN

ON REREADING THESE pages I feel that I have tried in many places and with many words, to say something that might be said in one word. In a sense this study is meant to be superficial; that is, it is not meant as a study of the things that need to be studied. It is rather a reminder of the things that are seen so quickly that they are forgotten almost as quickly. Its moral, in a manner of speaking, is that first thoughts are best; so a flash might reveal a landscape, with the Eiffel Tower or the Matterhorn standing up in it as they would never stand up again in the light of common day. I ended the book with an image of everlasting lightning; in a very different sense, alas, this little flash has lasted only too long. But the method has also certain practical disadvantages upon which I think it well to add these two notes. It may seem to simplify too much and to ignore out of ignorance. I feel this especially in the passage about the prehistoric pictures; which is not concerned with all that the learned may learn from prehistoric pictures, but with the single point of what anybody could learn from there being any prehistoric pictures at all. I am conscious that this attempt to express it in terms of innocence may exaggerate even my own ignorance. Without any pretence of scientific research or information, I should be sorry to have it thought that I knew no more than what was needed, in that passage, of the stages into which primitive humanity has been divided. I am aware, of course, that the story is elaborately stratified; and that there were many such stages before the Cro-Magnon or any peoples with whom we associate such pictures. Indeed recent studies about the Neanderthal and other races rather tend to repeat the moral that is here most relevant. The notion noted in these pages of something necessarily slow or late in the development of religion, will gain little indeed from these later revelations about the precursors of the reindeer picture-maker. The learned appear to hold that, whether reindeer picture could be religious or not, the people lived before it were religious already, burying their dead with the significant signs of mystery and hope. This obviously brings us back to the same argument, an argument that is not approached by any measurement of the earlier man's skull. It is little use here to compare the head of the man with head of the monkey, if it certainly never came into the head of the monkey to bury another monkey with nuts in his grave to help him towards a heavenly monkey-house. Talking of skulls, I am also aware of the story of the Cro-Magnon skull that was much larger and finer than a modern skull. It is a very funny story; because an eminent evolutionist, awakening to a somewhat belated caution, protested against anything being inferred from one specimen. It is the duty of a solitary skull to prove that our fathers were our inferiors. Any solitary skull presuming to prove that they were superior is felt to be suffering from swelled head.

APPENDIX II:
ON AUTHORITY AND ACCURACY

IN THIS BOOK which is merely meant as a popular criticism of popular fallacies, often indeed of very vulgar errors, I feel that I have sometimes given an impression of scoffing at serious scientific work. It was however the very reverse of my intentions. I am not arguing with the scientist who explains the elephant, but only with the sophist who explains it away. And as a matter of fact the sophist plays to the gallery, as he did in ancient Greece. He appeals to the ignorant, especially when he appeals to the learned. But I never meant my own criticism to be an impertinence to the truly learned. We all owe an infinite debt to the researches, especially the recent researches, of single-minded students in these matters; and I have only professed to pick up things here and there from them. I have not loaded my abstract argument with quotations and references, which only make a man look more learned than he is; but in some cases I find that my own loose fashion of allusion is rather misleading about my own meaning. The passage about Chaucer and the Child Martyr is badly expressed; I only mean that the English poet probably had in mind the English saint; of whose story he gives a sort of foreign version. In the same way two statements in the chapter on Mythology follow each other in such a way that it may seem to be suggested that the second story about Monotheism refers to the Southern Seas. I may explain that Atahocan belongs not to Australasian but to American savages. So in the chapter called 'The Antiquity of Civilisation', which I feel to be the most unsatisfactory, I have given my own impression of the meaning of the development of Egyptian monarchy too much, perhaps, as if it were identical with the facts on which it was formed as given in works like those of Professor J. L. Myres. But the confusion was not intentional; still less was there any intention to imply, in the remainder of the chapter, that the anthropological speculations about races are less valuable than they undoubtedly are. My criticism is strictly relative; I may say that the Pyramids are plainer than the tracks of the desert; without denying that wiser men than I may see tracks in what is to me the trackless sand.

GRATITUDE

THANK YOU FOR taking time to read this selection of works of a hero of mine. I hope it enlightened and inspired you as they did me; for the prime purpose of this book, as Frédéric Bastiat reportedly declared on his death bed, is 'the truth.'

If it profited you, please consider reviewing and sharing it with others – and please visit Mansion Voice's website, www.mansionvoice.com, to see other titles available as more are added regularly, including my first novel, *The Secret Pastor*.

Thank you, again.

S. R.

Printed in Great Britain
by Amazon

45402517R00172